Perspectives in U.S.
Marxist Anthropology

About the Book and Editors

An assessment of current trends in Marxist anthropology, this collection of essays reflects both the unifying force of Marxist thought and the diversity of contemporary anthropology. Linked by a common approach—a shared commitment to Marxist analysis—the contributors look at a variety of phenomena, including the problems of labor and work, in terms of a coherent theory of Marxism. Examining political, economic, and ethnic situations, the authors discuss social structures, ideology, and class formation. This unique volume warrants the attention of both Marxists and non-Marxists in anthropology and of scholars in other fields.

David Hakken is chair of the Council for Marxist Anthropology and associate professor of anthropology, SUNY–College of Technology. **Hanna Lessinger** is a member of the Council for Marxist Anthropology and research associate at the Southern Asian Institute, Columbia University.

Perspectives in U.S. Marxist Anthropology

edited by
David Hakken and
Hanna Lessinger

Published in cooperation with
the Council for Marxist Anthropology

Westview Press / Boulder and London

This Westview softcover edition is printed on acid-free paper and bound in softcovers that carry the highest rating of the National Association of State Textbook Administrators, in consultation with the Association of American Publishers and the Book Manufacturers' Institute.

Published in 1987 in the United States of America by Westview Press, Inc.; Frederick A. Praeger, Publisher; 5500 Central Avenue, Boulder, Colorado 80301

Library of Congress Catalog Card Number: 87-50604
ISBN: 0-8133-7384-0

Composition for this book was provided by the editors.
This book was produced without formal editing by the publisher.

Printed and bound in the United States of America

The paper used in this publication meets the requirements of the American National Standard for Permanence of Paper for Printed Library Materials Z39.48-1984.

6   5   4   3   2

In Loving Memory
of
Eleanor Leacock
1922-1987

For Happy

CONTENTS

Perspectives in U.S.
Marxist Anthropology

INTRODUCTION

Hanna Lessinger and David Hakken

The Present Moment in Marxist Anthropology

The volume which lies before you presents current work from within a trend of Marxist anthropology now maturing in the United States. In this introduction the editors present their assessment of this important work and what we see as its origins. While placing the selections in historical and organizational context, we point out impediments which still limit the contributions of Marxist anthropology. We conclude by identifying what we think are the distinctive characteristics of this trend and by pointing to its unfinished tasks.

Such an assessment is desirable at this time for a number of reasons. First, we feel that the quality of U.S. Marxist anthropology, manifest in the articles included here as well as evident in much other work, has reached such a level that it warrants the serious attention of both Marxists in other fields and of non-Marxists in anthropology. Secondly, we feel it is imperative right now to encourage development of a common language and a shared sense of problem among our Marxist anthropological colleagues. In order to understand why we feel this way, we need to consider the various contexts within which this volume has developed.

This current Marxist tendency in U.S. anthropology springs from a combination of intellectual, political and disciplinary developments, a confluence of events which has touched most academic fields over the past two decades. The present shift to the right in U.S. cultural and political life has coincided with organizational and intellectual crises within anthropology.

The root of these crises is the present marginalization of the field of anthropology during a period of global capitalist expansion. Anthropology, once deeply involved in the imperial enterprise, is now increasingly marginal or irrelevant to it--largely because of the discipline's liberal (and at times leftist) traditions. This apparent paradox exists because, alongside the field's sporadic involvement in both the ideology and practice of imperialism, working anthropologists have also had the bad habit of sympathizing with those they study. This identification with one's informants, who are often the powerless of the world, has made anthropology as a whole slightly more liberal than many other social sciences. Thus the general narrowing of both economic and ideological possibilities since the mid-1970s has meant that, alone of the social sciences, anthropology has failed to expand or to find non-academic jobs for its practitioners. People who seek to "reform" or "save" the discipline usually advocate the neutralization of anthropology's liberal thrust, and particularly the eradication of the leftist presence within the field. From this viewpoint (shared by the right and also by some liberals), Marxists are, and deserve to be, peripheral to anthropology. We, on the other hand, see Marxism as central to the rejuvenation of the discipline. We feel that dialectical materialism, an understanding of the labor theory of value and a vision of intellectuals' proper role in class struggle allow us to understand what is happening in the world around us. Marxism also gives us the hope that we can change that world.

One of the manifestations of crisis in anthropology has been the struggle over the proper object of anthropological study. For example, the writers in this volume, while often dealing with familiar ethnographic material, direct as much of their attention toward the state and the world capitalist system as they do to internal cultural dynamics. The question of broader analytical foci and wider economic and political contexts takes on particular urgency for U.S. anthropologists whose "own" state is bent on imposing an iniquitous system on the rest of the globe. Unlike many non-Marxist anthropologists, these writers find it impossible to ignore such relationships, and feel impelled to make them a major part of their analyses.

A further aspect of the crisis is the organizational struggle which has taken the form of debate within the discipline over the ethics of anthropological research. The debate flows, of course, from the crisis over what anthropology is, or should be. Many of the authors in this book have been part of a movement to defend the code of anthropological ethics adopted during the Vietnam war. In that code we are defending the discipline's humanistic tradition against those who would domesticate its critical thrust, who would like to de-politicize (or in the words of one hostile observer, "de-Vietnam-ize") anthropology, making it more acceptable to government and business. All of these debates are simply manifestations of a general underlying tension within U.S. higher education--a tension about the purposes of education and the class alliances of intellectuals. Is the purpose of higher education to serve capitalist accumulation or to expand the potential of the human race? If social science cannot be neutral, where do anthropologists align themselves? One of our aims in presenting this collection is to bring these debates, which have raged in an often subterranean fashion, into the open. In doing so we hope to sharpen them, to stake out identifiable Marxist positions in the debate, and in doing so to evaluate and advance these positions.

Yet the articles in this volume, taken as a whole, reflect a dialectic internal to Marxist anthropology as well as the broader processes referred to above. On the one hand these papers reflect a strong, highly-informed interest in and identification with a wide tradition of Marxist discourse extending beyond the confines of anthropology. The papers by Schiller, Hakken and Nash are particularly good examples of this pattern. To the writers in this book, the problematics of Marxism provide more useful analytical frameworks than those of the anthropological mainstream in which we were trained. The processes and relations of production, the importance of class, the force of ideology, as well as questions of definition and conceptualization, provide the themes for many of these articles.

These authors do not by any means represent the whole spectrum of Marxist anthropological thought in this country. Nevertheless their pieces reveal considerable diversity; they do not all appropriate the Marxist tradition in the same way. Indeed, for many of these authors the initial points of departure for their investigations are the formulations of mainstream anthropology. For example, in the essays which follow, Ruyle and Hakken start their arguments from within ecological or economic anthropology, although both ultimately move beyond such categorizations. Babb, Schroder and Keren begin by examining topics currently under debate in their respective geographic areas. Interestingly, while many of the writers aim their critiques primarily at the mainstream, many are equally critical of Marxist colleagues. This, along with the general diversity of outlook represented here, suggests that the current Marxist trend in anthropology is both broad and nonsectarian.

One can argue that this twofold orientation toward both mainstream and Marxist discourse is a symbol of maturity. Marxist anthropology, once banished to the non-professional periphery (or so deeply submerged as to be accessible only to a few), now contends with the mainstream and is becoming part of general scholarly discourse. Yet this diversity and this dual orientation also threaten further development. Without wishing to impose rigid political orthodoxy, the editors of this volume feel that appropriations of the Marxist framework which are too divergent can impede the identification of central questions and the recognition of common approaches. We need to clarify analytic and descriptive terminology, to identify more sharply crucial points of contention, if Marxist anthropology is to develop its full potential.

The Peculiar History of Marxism in U.S. Anthropology

To make sense of the internal intellectual dialectics referred to above, one needs to examine the history of Marxism within anthropology, especially within U.S. anthropology. It is only fair to warn the reader that some of this history is presented very much from the viewpoint of those of us who came into anthropology in the 1960s and early 1970s. There are few systematic accounts of leftist thought and activity among anthropologists in the earlier parts of this century, although Leacock (1982) does provide one. Here we present what is surely a partial account--the way it looked to us.

To begin with, we should recognize that Marx and Engels were among those 19th century social theorists who recognized the importance of the anthropological materials becoming available to them and their contemporaries. For Marx and Engels, interest in these materials was shaped primarily by a desire to critique capitalist social formations, although the available data base was severely limited by the undeveloped state of anthropological research. Given the impressive scope of Marx's and Engels' analytic framework and their ongoing political influence, one might have expected their work to have provided anthropologists with continued stimulation as the field developed. However, in the United States the interplay between a narrowly liberal political and intellectual tradition and a deeply ingrained anticommunism largely prevented this from happening. Instead, interest in the comparative ethnology of Marx and Engels remained concentrated in left political groups. With a few isolated exceptions, an explicitly Marxist approach to the study of other societies moved outside of academia. This was not unique to anthropology--the same process occurred in other social sciences as well. However the virtual absence of an overt, self-conscious Marxist position within anthropology has distinguished the U.S. intellectual scene from that of Europe or the third world.

If anthropology in this country remained largely ignorant of Marxism, Marxist intellectuals were relatively uninterested in the developing science of anthropology. Left political groups did sometimes still refer to 19th century work on society and social evolution. For instance, Socialist Labor Party activists organizing in Chicago in the 1960s stressed the importance of cultural evolution in their educational work. During the same period the Communist Party U.S.A. continued to cite a unilinear form of Morganism, with a heavy stress on the determining role of forces of production. By the 1960s the new left, stimulated by the emerging feminist and third world liberation movements, had also developed an interest in other cultures and in social evolution. However most of this attention was channeled toward study of Marxist classics such as Engels' *The Origin of the Family, Private Property and the State*. We who were studying anthropology during that brief flowering of the new left often found it necessary to convince members of left groups that additional data and new theoretical insights accumulated since the composition of *Origin* might require some re-evaluation of Engels' contentions.

At the time, those of us struggling to create intellectual "fit" between our anthropology, our increasing grasp of Marxism and our involvement in political action were forced to contend with an anti-Marxist legacy within the discipline. Some of this simply reflected this society's general fetishization of "neutral" or "non-political" intellectual endeavor, as it is mythically conceived. Some of the hostility was overtly political. Anthropologists, who have long had to confront the implications of observer bias in their central research method, nevertheless blandly accepted an analytic prejudice against Marxism. They remained convinced that it was--intellectually--much worse to be a Marxist than to be a symbolic anthropologist or a cultural ecologist, since Marxism, it was thought, made one unfit to do "unbiased" scholarship.

The deep antipathy to Marxism goes back to the beginnings of the discipline. Marvin Harris, whose *The Rise of Anthropological Theory* (1968) was one of the first works in mainstream anthropology to locate Marx within the intellectual landscape, argues that identification of Morgan's evolutionary schema with Marxism contributed to the strong anti-evolutionism of the Boasians. Some have viewed Leslie White's materialism as a significant exception to this hostility. However Carolyn Fluehr-Lobban, while arguing the importance of the White legacy to Marxist anthropologists, has cautioned against minimizing the differences between White and Marx (1986).

Although the generation of the 1960s did not understand it at the time, a number of anthropologists had tried to connect Marxism and anthropology, particularly during the 1930s and 1940s when leftist currents were more widespread in U.S. intellectual circles. In the 1940s anthropology graduate students at Columbia organized the Mundial Upheaval Society. Elman Service, Eric Wolf, Sidney Mintz, Stanley Diamond, Morton Fried, Daniel McCall, Rufus Mathewson, Robert Manners and John Murra at various times belonged to this informal group. Participants discussed their own work and formulated their research problems against a background of implicit and tacitly understood Marxism. As Sydel Silverman has noted, the intellectual orientation of the Mundial group reflected the lingering post-World War II impetus of the progressive ideology of the 1930s, and the dislocations experienced by those who had lived through the war (1981:xii). Both Murra and Service had fought in Spain with the International Brigades. The general progressive orientation of such informal groups of graduate students, (which may have existed outside of New York as well) also reflected the impact of British archeologist V. Gordon Childe's work. In New York the presence of such figures as Paul Kirchhoff, Karl Wittfogel, and linguist Morris Swadesh was important. Clearly, at the period the Mundial group and probably many other graduate students elsewhere were grappling intellectually with field experiences in the third world in which they were obliged to confront the phenomenon of colonialism and anticolonial resistance.

Elsewhere in this period Melville Jacobs and Bernhard Stern produced a 1947 textbook, *Outlines of Anthropology*, with strong Marxist overtones. Stern, a sociologist with affinities for anthropology, was also editor of *Science and Society*. Eleanor Leacock organized an important symposium on social stratification and evolutionary theory at the 1957 American Anthropological Association meetings, which presented papers by herself, John Murra, Preston Holder, Robert Armstrong and Joyce Wike (Leacock, 1958).

The intellectual current such informal groups represented was profoundly dampened by the rise of McCarthyism in the U.S. Among the many academics who suffered at the time was Gene Weltfish, fired by Columbia. Jacobs, a student of Boas who had worked in the Northwest Coast, ran afoul of investigating committees at the University of Washington. Swadesh, dismissed from City College, went on to a second career in Mexico. The repressive atmosphere was apparently instrumental in leading many, including the Mundial group, to develop a coded method of referring to essentially Marxist concepts (Lauria 1987). In their work there emerged a use of language more acceptable to non-Marxist colleagues but quite different from standard Marxist rhetoric.

The retreat into an essentially coded form of discourse left those of us in following generations with odd, if not distorted, perceptions of our "elders." Perhaps mistakenly we saw the work of the Mundial group, for instance, not as Marxist but as a kind of left-wing materialism and evolutionism. We were not always able to differentiate the work of the Mundial group from that of the Michigan group around Julian Steward, particularly the work of Service and Sahlins. Many a graduate student has pondered Steward's "levels of sociocultural integration," for instance, or Marvin Harris' "cultural materialism" (Vincent 1985:141) and has wondered just how closely these constructs were supposed to parallel Marxist models. The difficulties succeeding generations of anthropology students experienced in decoding this work was exacerbated by our generation's typical pattern of intellectual development, which started from political activism and the study of anthropology and only later moved into the discovery of Marxist theory. It is not surprising that we were initially unable to grasp the Marxism which was present, in partial disguise, in some of the mainstream anthropology we read. Nevertheless, the re-emergence of an *explicitly* Marxist strain in U.S. anthropology was an eventual product of the social ferment of the 1960s and 1970s. This new strain in anthropology combined a commitment to political activism, the study of Marxist classics and a mandate to integrate these into our scholarship.

As in other disciplines, the initial manifestations of this emerging Marxist current were often negative. To be a Marxist was to oppose the established social sciences. There is a great deal of similarity in tone between Martin Nicolaus' debunking of sociology as "a branch of the tree of political power" (1969:387) and Kathleen Gough's discussion of "Anthropology: Child of Imperialism" (1968). For some of the generation of the 1960s, such critiques led them to abandon anthropology intellectually if not formally. Others of us, believing in the revolutionary potential of a transformed anthropology, still found it difficult to make a connection between our academic enterprises and the social upheaval in which we were participants.

In the 1970s Dell Hymes called for *Reinventing Anthropology* along Marxist lines (1972) and Stanley Diamond founded the journal *Dialectical Anthropology*. These and similar efforts marked for many of us the beginning of an attempt to use Marxism systematically and explicitly as a basis for rethinking the discipline. Among the Mundial group, Wolf and Mintz were active in this endeavor, as was Leacock in a slightly different sphere. It is important to note, however, that these efforts were largely individual, somewhat diluting their effect on an already-disparate field. For most younger scholars just coming to think of themselves as Marxist anthropologists, self-identity grew out of political experiences in the anti-war, working-class, civil rights, Black, Chicano, women's, gay or ecology movements, rather than out of the influence of particular teachers. The essentially coded nature of the debate was heightened by an absence of continuity which might have been produced by institutionalized theoretical "schools," around particular graduate departments or research institutes devoted to leftist anthropology.

Thus in an important sense younger anthropologists felt they had to invent themselves, and to create a Marxist anthropology on their own, often in great isolation. However there was external stimulus for such efforts, from events like the publication of Emmanuel Terray's (1972) *Marxism and 'Primitive' Societies* and the translations of French Marxist anthropological work appearing in the British journal *Critique of Anthropology*. Important homegrown points of identification were Leacock's introductions to Lewis Henry Morgan's *Ancient Society* (1963) and to Engels' *Origin of the Family* (1972). Rayna Reiter [Rapp] established an important Marxist position within the newly emerging feminist anthropology with her *Toward an Anthropology of Women* (1974).

In the 1970s, as the crisis in anthropology began to emerge, the language of Marxism became more acceptable in the discourse of the discipline. Some of this was a response to the work of European and Latin American scholars; some was a response to the pressure of radical political movements of the 1960s. As this growing acceptance of Marxist language continues today, its limitations become clearer. We find ourselves having to distinguish between the sometimes eclectic or haphazard use of analytical tools like "political economy" and the use of a developed Marxist analytical framework. As a consequence, scholars genuinely committed to fostering a Marxist trend within the discipline frequently found it necessary to sort out those with a substantive commitment to Marxist anthropology from those who simply desired to appropriate its symbolism. Vincent (1985), Bloch (1983) and Wessman (1981) all confront this problem to one degree or another.

The question of who is or is not a "real" Marxist anthropologist is further complicated by the coexisting debate over various kinds of materialism and evolutionism, which skirt but do not coincide with some of the concerns of Marxism. For instance, in the long absence of an overtly Marxist position within the discipline, the materialists and cultural ecologists have often been the most visible opposition to the Geertzians and other schools of idealist symbolic analysis, and sometimes the materialists have defined their positions using quasi-Marxist language. The symbolists' real opponent in some of these debates--Marxism--has been absent or operating from deep cover.

In such situations Marxists attempting to define their own positions often find themselves attacking some of the colleagues most sympathetic and most open to Marxist thinking. The sorting process is fraught with additional danger because those spotting "fake" Marxists can easily be accused of trying to stuff rivals into ideological straightjackets. (In popular demonology straightjackets, along with jackboots and horns, are standard-issue Marxist garb.) Yet we feel some such distinction is necessary since Marxist anthropology is something more than another useful paradigm to be grafted onto the body of anthropology-as-usual.

Perhaps we should, following Mao Tse-tung, distinguish dialectical materialists working within the Marxist tradition from two other groups: metaphysical materialists like Harris and dialectical idealists like Marshall Sahlins and Edmund Leach. We feel the metaphysical materialists tend to undervalue the importance of human cultural agency in accounting for the dynamics of social transformation, while the dialectical idealists tend to ignore the ways in which human culture is constrained by material forces. The approaches of Harris and Sahlins are simply examples of a more general trend: the piecemeal appropriation of parts of the Marxist conceptual apparatus into anthropology. This often has negative analytic and political consequences and, as noted above, has sometimes driven those in the Marxist mainstream to apply preemptive political tests in an effort to separate the sheep from the goats among those who have at one time or another called themselves Marxist. It is important for Marxist anthropology to strike a balance, maintaining tolerance for those who are politically sympathetic, while insisting on clarity in the actual debate. Given this history, it is no wonder that current Marxist anthropology in this country is diverse and somewhat fragmented.

The Organizational Context of the Current Volume

As we suggested earlier, organizations and institutions shape the nature of intellectual development. It is not accidental that the current volume originates within an organization, the U.S.-based Council for Marxist Anthropology (CMA). In Britain much of the recent development in Marxist anthropology took place around a journal, *Critique of Anthropology.* In France the center was a research *problematique* spelling out the relationship between the dynamics of precapitalist societies and economic anthropology. In Latin America it was the close association between intellectuals and political liberation movements. CMA, not the first such left caucus within U.S. anthropology, is the descendant of a "radical caucus" which emerged within the American Anthropological Association (AAA) in the 1960s and 1970s. That was succeeded by Anthropologists for Radical Political Action (ARPA) in the mid-1970s. The CMA was founded in 1978.

These organizations are an outgrowth of "the movement" of the 1960s, in which Students for a Democratic Society (SDS) was the major mass organization for whites. Contemporary Marxist anthropology in this country reflects some of the characteristics of these SDS-style organizational forms. The early radical caucus, for instance, served as an outpost of "the movement" within the discipline. It devoted itself to exposing the meretricious character of certain anthropologies and to emphasizing the importance of various liberation struggles against imperialism. ARPA was typical of groups which emerged in other U.S. academic disciplines in the early 1970s, the most vigorous of which was Science for the People

(SftP), still alive and well in Boston. A similar development occurred somewhat later in Britain. Organizationally these groups were radically decentralized and preoccupied with "political," rather than "theoretical," development. Reflected in these groups was that dominant belief of the 1960s--that the only true struggle was a direct one.

The CMA emerged as ARPA faded. The new organization saw its role as the stimulation of theoretical development. At its founding meeting CMA members decided to include "Marxist," rather than "socialist" or "progressive," within the title of their organization. This decision underlined the group's commitment to the development of Marxist theory, a task as important as the political tasks of CMA's predecessors. We understand, as we did not 20 years ago, that theoretical struggle is also a form of class struggle, though it can never stand alone as the only form of resistance.

In practice much CMA theoretical work in the early 1980s has been oriented toward the legitimation of Marxism within the discipline, rather than the cumulative clarification of Marxist anthropology. To do this, we have organized scholarly sessions at meetings of the AAA and of regional anthropology groups. In our efforts to give the Marxist position greater visibility within the discipline, we have had some success. CMA deserves some of the credit for the widening number of sessions at AAA meetings in which Marxist perspectives are evident. The format of these sessions, however, has not always led to sustained or substantive intellectual exchange.

Simultaneously, the CMA has been forced to respond to various AAA organizational maneuvers aimed at eliminating political content from a more "professionalized" anthropology. The profound employment crisis which has already damaged the discipline has given those to the right of the political spectrum new ammunition, since the drive to make anthropologists "marketable" may sometimes disguise a drive to eradicate liberal and leftist thinking within the discipline. At the same time the label "Marxist anthropologist" has rarely improved anyone's chances of employment. Thus CMA's existence has not, in itself, created the conditions or structures necessary for clarifying the meaning of Marxist anthropology or wholly legitimating its presence within the discipline.

Nevertheless, the cautiously positive reception Marxism is beginning to receive in anthropology grows from a recognition that the discipline is in theoretical crisis and that Marxism may offer some vision of why. To many the technicist, metaphysical materialist or semioticist options once so fashionable no longer seem viable as the world itself changes. Conversely, Marxism offers much of the humanistic, holistic appeal of traditional U.S. anthropology.

The larger context of CMA work is, of course, the growth of the political right wing in the United States. Conservatives have chosen to mount ideological battles around evolution and around the study of alternate lifestyles and non-Western cultures. There have been strenuous right-wing efforts to replace the teaching of evolution with "scientific creationism" and to limit cultural studies to the study of the Western tradition (or a middle-class white, male version thereof). John Cole and Gerald Reed have demonstrated how these ideological battles have come together in an assault on the very notion of independent institutions of higher learning, as well as in a particular assault on anthropology (1985, 1986). Institutionally we must recognize the danger of such conservative crusades and must prevent our associations or work places from accommodating or capitulating.

In a larger sense anthropology has a great deal to contribute in combating such rightist world views. For instance anthropology can contribute to the analysis of various world conflicts in which the rightward rush of U.S. policy has embroiled us. Marxist anthropology has an important role to play in ensuring that such analyses are: 1) connected directly to the broader global situation, acknowledging forces of capitalism and imperialism; 2) built upon a progressive vision of future social formations, and 3) grow out of an accurate understanding of the particular peoples involved. One of the most positive elements of the Mundial heritage has been its focus on "applied" problems like that of the anticolonial struggles which we now call struggles for national liberation. We thus see such activities as a continuation of a progressive tradition in anthropology, to be defended through both political action and the development of a vibrant, nonsectarian Marxist intellectual tradition.

The Papers and Perspectives of This Volume

The papers in this book represent, as we noted earlier, a distinct trend in U.S. Marxist anthropology. Eugene Ruyle makes a strong case for an "anthropological Marxism." His "Rethinking

Marxist Anthropology" develops a general anthropology based on Marx's labor theory of value (Ruyle labels this "social thermodynamics"). He contrasts his own approach with that of European structuralist Marxism. Ruyle illustrates the value of his approach in reference to three topics: the emergence of human society; the rise of class society and the analysis of contemporary societies--divided into overdeveloping capitalist, underdeveloping capitalist, and socialist nations. Ruyle's approach is informed by the concerns, if not the total approach, of cultural materialist and ecological trends in U.S. anthropology. This is a reminder of the close, if uneasy, relationship between Marxism and other materialist viewpoints. Ruyle uses the model of human extraction of energy from the physical environment to discuss the exploitation of one class by another. He sees his method as central to the criticism and evaluation of contemporary society, and he places emphasis on the re-allocation of social energy away from elites to other classes. He argues that Marxist anthropologists have an important duty to apply anthropology to the theoretical debates of current political movements.

David Hakken's "Studying Work: Anthropological and Marxist Perspectives" makes a general argument about anthropological theory and the need to integrate dialectics and materialism. He illustrates his perspective with a critical discussion of work, a concept central to much non-Marxist anthropology as well as to Marxism. Not surprisingly, aspects of work are also investigated in many of the other papers included in this volume. Drawing widely upon Marx, Marxist philosophy, the relatively new subfield called the anthropology of work, primate studies and feminist theory, Hakken develops an approach to work which aims to avoid a number of philosophical problems inherent in much previous scholarship. His major emphasis is on the embeddedness of work in collective social relations of reciprocity. Like Ruyle, Hakken identifies with an activist tradition which insists that anthropologists have a responsibility to develop analytic categories which at once satisfy theoretically and illuminate contemporary political problems. Hakken sees his own concern with the definition of work as directly relevant to the plight of unemployed workers in situations of deindustrialization.

Philip Kohl's "Sumer and the Indus Valley Compared: Towards an Historical Understanding of the Evolution of Early States" aims both to revise our understanding of the Indus Valley civilizations and to inject more appropriate theories of cultural evolution into the archeology of early states. Through a comparison of data on urban sites in the two geographic areas, Kohl criticizes neo-evolutionary theory as both inaccurate and as ideologically laden with anti-evolutionism. Kohl believes such perspectives, which he labels "evolutionistic," tend to deny important differences between social formations and to eliminate the concept of class struggle in history. Instead, Kohl uses the Sumerian and Indus Valley cases to develop a perspective integrating specific local history with general evolution. He goes on to make a strong case for the relevance of archeological data to both the analysis of class society and the political issue of self-determination.

Hans Baer argues for the continued relevance of categories such as "Asiatic mode of production" in analyzing the dynamics of recent social formations. His "Nineteenth Century Mormonism as a Partial Asiatic Mode of Production" focuses on changing relations among various modes of production--quasi-communal, Asiatic and capitalist--in 19th and 20th century Utah. Baer places particular analytic importance on the rise and fall of the Asiatic mode, while arguing that analysis of the changing relations among modes is important in understanding contemporary Mormonism, whose present operation he likens to that of a multinational corporation. In addition to upholding the validity of such categories, Baer is also proposing that several diametrically different modes of production can coexist to give distinctive shape to a particular society at any one time. Baer's work raises the question of whether a "partial Asiatic mode of production" is a social reality or simply a useful abstraction.

Barbara Schroder's "Ethnic Identity and Economic Change: Non-Wage Labor Relations in Highland Ecuadorian Haciendas" takes up both the question of local history and the question of how economic development should be analyzed. She is critical of dependency, world systems and "multiple modes of production" theories, as well as of mainstream anthropology. All, she feels, are overly deterministic. Schroder shows, for example, that in Ecuador the same economic forces produce hacienda labor systems and hacienda work forces ranging from the "modern" to the "traditional," with many mixed forms. Like other leftist Latin Americanists, Schroder emphasizes the role of local history--regional ethnic relations, historical patterns of land use and remuneration, and indigenous resistance to Spanish and mestizo dominance--in shaping the area's mixed development. The implication of her argument is that causality and outcome of economic change are more diverse than either Marxist or non-Marxist theory has generally shown.

Donna Keren, in "The Waiting Proletariat: Creating a New Industrial Labor Force in Rural Maquilas," addresses the experiences of women employed by the new wave of small "cooperative" factories in Querétaro, Mexico. Whatever the formal organization of these garment factories, Keren argues that their female employees are being proletarianized. Rather than simply obtaining cheap labor, however, this maquila system is, with the support of the Mexican government, also designed to control labor. In the process what Keren calls a "waiting proletariat" is created. Supporting Marx's emphasis on the importance of labor process control in capitalism, the author shows how a progressive ideology, in this case that of Mexico's cooperative movement, has been harnessed to the process of labor control and capital accumulation.

Florence Babb returns to Marx's definition of petty commodity production in her "Marketers as Producers: The Labor Process and Proletarianization of Peruvian Marketwomen." The paper asks how petty traders, and the work they do, are to be conceptualized. Traders are, she argues, petty commodity producers adding value to what they sell by virtue of the labor they expend on processing goods for resale. Babb suggests that much "informal sector" labor needs to be analyzed in this fashion to make clear both its structural position in the economy and its workers' range of possible class alliances. She points out that Peruvian traders are becoming progressively proletarianized by a variety of events, among them Peru's debt crisis. Babb conceptualizes this transition theoretically as a movement from multiple modes of production to a more unitary social formation. She goes on to discuss the relationship between marketers' economic exploitation, their gender and their impetus toward political action.

Faye Harrison's "Gangs, Grassroots Politics and the Crisis of Dependent Capitalism in Jamaica" grows from field work among the urban poor in Kingston. She shows how neighborhood gangs--partially created by state and international policies--become a crucial part of Jamaica's political structure. Thus gang rivalries and warfare become directly linked to national political party conflict, economic crisis and imperialist intervention. Harrison shows, however, that Kingston slum dwellers are not content to remain the mere victims of such processes but attempt to reassert control over their neighborhoods. She goes on to question how far such grassroots activity can create, or lay the groundwork for, larger progressive social changes. Harrison's work, like Schroder's, lays emphasis on local history as it shapes the working-out of global processes.

Nina Schiller draws not only on anthropology but on management studies and on Marxist theories of the labor process to assess a system of "workers' control" in a U.S. firm. Her "Management By Participation: The Division of Labor, Ideology and Contradiction in a U.S. Firm" uses field work among telephone market researchers in a multinational company to trace the way in which "management by participation" affected and ultimately failed one group of workers. The company-sponsored ideologies of worker control and self-improvement led these employees to try to redefine their jobs and to make the work process less alienating. The attempt, which seems initially to fulfill leftist expectations about the revolutionary potential of such systems, ultimately crumples when management, worried about profit rates, reasserts its power over the work process. Schiller concludes that the workers do not actually develop a revolutionary understanding from the experience. In her paper Schiller is using social science methodology to answer questions which are simultaneously political and scholarly.

June Nash's richly detailed study of culture, consciousness and economic decline appears in "Corporate Hegemony and Industrial Restructuring in a New England Industrial City." Using a long-term study of a single-industry western Massachusetts industrial center to analyze cultural practice in the formation of consciousness, Nash criticizes both economic determinism and approaches which invoke simple "false consciousness." Her analysis starts from the Gramscian concept of hegemony. In fact, as she shows, Pittsfield workers as well as the General Electric Company actively participated in the process of creating hegemony during the 40-year period covered in the study. Now, however, under the impact of a worldwide capitalist crisis, the "social contract" which characterized the area since the 1930s has broken down in Pittsfield's current period of de-industrialization. Nash's methodology, involving a use of participant observation and local history (including oral history), is designed to show how cultural hegemony works within the context of global economic and political forces.

We suggested above that the papers in this volume are diverse, yet share common characteristics, indicating the emergence of a distinct U.S. style of Marxist anthropology. Reading these papers together, one can see certain major elements of that style.

First, these papers manifest a strong reaction against what are perceived as the overly structural analyses of European Marxist anthropology. While Ruyle makes this case most explicitly, it is also stated strongly elsewhere. If one considers "world systems" theory as a structuralist transplant which skims over both class struggle and dialectics, the critique of structuralism seems to underlie virtually all the pieces in the volume. Put positively, there is a strong desire among these writers to let theory flow from the field work experience. This is perhaps a consequence of the historical particularism and the empiricism instilled in U.S. anthropology by scholars like Boas and Mead. Other anti-structural influences include the perspectives of social historians (both British and North American) and of ethnohistory. Our writers share the growing tendency within U.S. anthropology to accept historical materials, including oral history, as legitimate sources of anthropological data. Wolf's 1982 book *Europe and the People Without History* gave enormous impetus to the use of history among U.S. leftist anthropologists. The tendency is most visible in the work of Schroder, Harrison, Nash and Kohl, whose papers in particular emphasize history as an important shaper of social formation dynamics.

At the same time, the writers here make it their overriding concern to locate particular ethnographic situations, however small, within broader political economic contexts. Despite the salutary corrective which world systems approaches initially offered anthropology, these writers criticize such approaches for being too reductionist to account for important ethnographic data and important local differences. Nevertheless, the dynamics of international capital accumulation in shaping local events engage Babb, Keren, Harrison and Schroder, for instance, as they examine societies under U.S. neocolonial influence. Schiller and Nash pinpoint the process in the U.S.--itself an interesting choice of field site given the predilection of U.S. anthropology for the study other cultures. This emphasis on the interaction between global and local (and the careful choice of field sites to emphasize that dynamic) is, of course, very different from that of traditional U.S. particularism, with its presumption of the "primitive isolate." It is interesting that Kohl identifies and attacks an archeological version of the primitive isolate: the "pristine state."

These writers share an appreciation for the continued fruit-fulness of Marx's and Engels' initial analytic categories. Several, for instance, heed Marx's dictum about the role of science in changing the world, and make explicit connections between their academic analyses and contemporary political issues. Perhaps the key concept of the book is the notion of class, or more precisely, the extent to which mode of production/social formation analysis must be built upon an understanding of class dynamics. While none of these writers appropriate Marx uncritically, their major critique is usually directed at later Marxist theories. For instance, Nash rejects the one-sided Gramscian emphasis on bourgeois hegemony but not the idea of working-class pro-action. In short, the authors accept the continuing validity of the initial Marxist problematic, including its emphasis on the role of the state, the nature of ideology as both a class-based phenomenon and and a material force, and perhaps most importantly, the role of op-pressed groups and particular peoples in shaping the history they experience.

The influence of socialist feminism is also felt in this work. This current has entered anthropology by way of considerable work since the mid-1970s. (An excellent recent example is Karen Sacks' and Dorothy Remy's 1984 *My Troubles Are Going to Have Trouble With Me.)* For instance in this volume Keren, Babb and Schiller study work forces which are entirely or largely female. Ruyle and Hakken develop important parts of their analyses with regard to feminist theory. Nash devotes considerable space to the activities of women and even children in the creation of a com-munity. Of particular interest in these papers is the way in which feminist constructs are linked to class analysis in various eth-nographic contexts.

Finally, the authors are interested in theory. It is important for our non-anthropological colleagues to recognize how unusual an interest in theory is among anthropologists. Empiricism, the historical particularists' celebration of the culturally unique, and the field's tendency to structure itself around either geographical or abstract topics (for instance economic anthropology or South Asia) conspire to swamp rigorous treatment of analytic constructs. These writers try to counter that trend in order to create a higher level of theoretical discourse than that promoted by many mainstream journals. And, as one after another indicates, theoreti-cal sophistication does not preclude an engaged, activist stance in anthropology.

Part of the task of this book, however, is to point out what remains to be accomplished in Marxist anthropology--a task made easier by the range of issues and approaches offered here. In reading this collection of papers we have been left with a series of questions.

1) What is the appropriate way to define "mode of production"? Ruyle, for instance, sees it as consisting of both a base and a superstructure. In contrast, Hakken and Babb use mode of production more narrowly to indicate a combination of forces and relations of production. These different conceptions lead to different uses of the concept "social formation." The first model seems to imply a more deterministic relation between mode of production and social formation whereas the latter model gives more relative autonomy to various aspects of social formation reproduction. The anti-evolutionistic arguments in several of the papers make it even more pressing to clarify such definitions. This clarity itself depends on specifying more carefully the ontological or "reality" status of abstract categories.

2) How do we conceive of the relationship between "culture" and physical reality? One strand of Marxist anthropology, identified with Gramsci and with critical sociology, views semiological processes as more determinant than the material processes emphasized in "traditional" Marxism. From the "culturist" point of view, anthropology's task is to provide a corrective to "economistic" Marxism. Some of the appeals to local history in this volume imply this view, placing emphasis on what used to be called "elements of the superstructure." Other writers here continue to place deterministic emphasis on political economy and to emphasize processes which used to be called part of the "base." Are such differential emphases the consequences of different ethnographic contexts, or do they reflect differences in conceptual apparatus?

3) Is Marxist anthropology a disciplined examination of distinct social formations, or a generalizing process to classify and explain types of social formations? Many authors here stress the multiple processes which must be studied to account for local differences. This multiplicity may potentially lead away from the kind of general theory conceived of by Marx and Engels. As another example, the approach to dialectics in this work still seems a very abstract one, difficult to articulate beyond the desire to integrate local and global processes. If the dialectic is at work in each social formation, is it in each case unique? To what extent is

it to be seen as a manifestation of some more general process which can be explained and described with some precision?

This particular intellectual problem is not unique to Marxist anthropology. In much mainstream anthropological work the question of whether descriptive categories are coherent and add up to some general explanatory model is secondary to vivid and accurate communication of the ethnographic situation. Certainly vivid and convincing ethnographic detail is what drew many of us to anthropology initially. However, it is not enough. The danger of abstract dialectics, of the kind visible in some of the work here, is that it can mask a re-entry, via Marxism, into the anthropology of empiricism, with all its attendant problems. One such disguised trap is the belief that appropriate analytic categories are immanent in the ethnographic experience. Yet the kind of theoretical discourse we desire is unlikely to emerge if Marxist anthropologists continue to over-stress the uniqueness of their particular ethnographic context, the familiar line of argument that begins, "In my village...."

4) Given the preoccupation of earlier Marxist anthropology with questions of evolution, we now have to ask whether it is still useful to pursue an evolutionary Marxist anthropology. Kohl, despite his criticism of "evolutionistic" perspectives, still makes a case for a general evolutionary perspective, following V. Gordon Childe. Yet Ruyle, Hakken and Babb want to develop a comparative study of something like "modes of production," without discussing questions of evolution.

In sum, to legitimate Marxism among our anthropological colleagues, we must simultaneously demonstrate the superiority of our analyses of specific social formations and justify our more abstract theorizing--the special strength of Marxism. The current volume contains pieces which, in varying degrees, do both. However we are convinced that more direct discussion will bring us further yet. We invite your comments and disagreements and urge you to send them to *Dialectical Anthropology*, to *Critique of Anthropology* or to the CMA for inclusion in possible future publications. For instance, one of the urgent research problems, as we have realized in writing this introduction, is a history of left thought and influence within U.S. anthropology, using both documentary sources and oral history collected from those who are now nearing retirement. Another sort of problem needing analysis is the detailed working-out of the relationship between U.S. imperialism and U.S. anthropology.

The preparation of this volume was carried out more collectively than most such ventures. The editors emphasize that the alphabetical arrangement of their names on the title page represents an egalitarian editorial partnership and equal contributions to the project, not a (male) senior editor and a (female) assistant to do the typing and proofreading. We are in addition enormously grateful to those whose help made the whole venture possible.

A CMA publication committee initiated the current volume in 1985: Nancy Bonvillain, Mona Etienne, Christine Gailey, David Hakken, Eleanor Leacock, Anthony Leeds, Hanna Lessinger, John Johnsen, Leith Mullings, June Nash, Frances Rothstein, Teresa Rubin, Nina Schiller, Ida Susser, Arthur Tuden and Joan Vincent attended planning meetings, solicited and later evaluated dozens of manuscripts and canvassed possible publishers. Antonio Gilman, Monica Froelander-Ulf, Antonio Lauria, William Roseberry, Merrill Singer, and Eric Wolf graciously looked at and commented on portions of this manuscript. Donna Keren, in addition to contributing a paper, undertook the monumental task of computerizing the manuscript. Working far beyond the call of duty, she is responsible for the physical appearance of this book. Any faults in presentation and interpretation are, however, the responsibility of the editors.

BIBLIOGRAPHY

Bloch, Maurice
    1983 Marxism and Anthropology. Oxford: Clarendon Press.
Cole, John and Gerald Reed
    1985 Why You Can't Find a Job. Paper delivered at the American Anthropological Association Meetings, Denver, CO. December.
    1986 The New Vulnerability of Higher Education. Thought and Action 2(1):29-40.
Engels, Frederick
    1972 The Origin of the Family, Private Property and the State. Eleanor Leacock, ed. New York: Monthly Review Press.

Fluehr-Lobban, Carolyn
   1986 Frederick Engels and Leslie White: the Symbol Versus
      the Role of Labor in the Origin of Humanity. Dialectical
      Anthropology 11(1):119-126.
Gough, Kathleeen
   1968 Anthropology: Child of Imperialism. Monthly Review
      19(11):12-27.
Hymes, Dell, ed.
   1972 Reinventing Anthropology. New York: Pantheon Books.
Harris, Marvin
   1968 The Rise of Anthropological Theory. New York:
      Thomas Y. Crowell Co.
Jacobs, Melville and Bernhard Stern
   1947 Outlines of Anthropology. New York: Barnes and
      Noble.
Lauria, Antonio
   1987 An Historical and Critical Study of a Puerto Rican Re-
      search Project: the People of Puerto Rico. Ph.D. thesis
      Department of Anthropology, New School for Social Re-
      search.
Leacock, Eleanor, ed.
   1958 Symposium on Social Stratification and Evolutionary
      Theory. Ethnohistory 5(3):103-249.
   1982 Marxism and Anthropology. *In* The Left Academy.
      Bertell Ollman and Edward Vernoff, eds. Pp. 242-276.
      New York: McGraw Hill Book Company.
Morgan, Lewis Henry
   1963 Ancient Society, or Researches in the Lines of Human
      Progress from Savagery through Barbarism to Civilization.
      Eleanor Leacock, ed. Cleveland: World Publishing Co.
Nicolaus, Martin
   1969 The Professional Organization of Sociology: a View
      from Below. Antioch Review 29(3):375-387.
Reiter, Rayna [Rapp], ed.
   1974 Toward an Anthropology of Women. New York:
      Monthly Review Press.
Sacks, Karen and Dorothy Remy, eds.
   1984 My Troubles Are Going to Have Trouble with Me:
      Everyday Trials and Triumphs of Women Workers. New
      Brunswick: Rutgers University Press.
Silverman, Sydel, ed.
   1981 Totems and Teachers: Perspectives on the History of
      Anthropology. New York: Columbia University Press.
Terray, Emmanuel
   1972 Marxism and "Primitive" Societies. New York: Monthly
      Review Press.

Vincent, Joan
    1985 Anthropology and Marxism: Past and Present. American
        Ethnologist 12(1):137-147.
Wessman, James
    1981 Anthropology and Marxism. Cambridge, MA:
        Schenkman Publishing Company.
Wolf, Eric
    1982 Europe and the People Without History. Berkeley: Uni-
        versity of California Press.

RETHINKING MARXIST ANTHROPOLOGY

Eugene E. Ruyle

When asked whether or not we are Marxists, our position is the same as that of a physicist or a biologist when asked if he is a "Newtonian," or if he is a "Pasteurian." There are truths so evident, so much a part of people's knowledge, that it is now useless to discuss them. One ought to be "Marxist" with the same naturalness with which one is "Newtonian" in physics, or "Pasteurian" in biology, considering that if facts determine new concepts, these new concepts will never divest themselves of that portion of truth possessed by the older concepts they have outdated. Such is the case, for example, of Einsteinian relativity or of Planck's "quantum" theory with respect to the discoveries of Newton; they take nothing at all away from the greatness of the learned Englishman. Thanks to Newton, physics was able to advance until it had achieved new concepts of space ("Che" Guevara, in Mills 1962:455).

The recent growth of Marxist anthropology has both positive and negative aspects. The growing recognition that Marx does indeed have something of significance to say for anthropology is a major achievement, for the mere name of Marx is, as Marx himself said of dialectics, "a scandal and abomination to bourgeoisdom and its doctrinaire professors" (Marx 1965:20).[1] But the actual results produced by Marxist anthropology have been unsatisfying. Marxist analyses within anthropology have not only failed to challenge effectively the hegemony of bourgeois modes of thought within our discipline, they have failed to enrich the revolutionary science of socialism. This dual failure, I suggest, is at root a failure of theory. While some may excuse the failure of Marxist anthropology to spread by pointing to the resistance of other theories, the real problem lies within Marxist anthropology itself. Marxist anthropology has stressed a mystical and highly nebulous concept of "structure" to the neglect of Marx's basic analytical tool, the labor theory of value. It is necessary, therefore, to "rethink" the Marxist endeavor within anthropology and reconstitute Marxist anthropology on a materialist basis so that it may better serve the working class.

Marxist Anthropology or Anthropological Marxism?

While this paper is not intended to be a direct critique of existing Marxist studies in anthropology, some critical comments are essential. First and foremost is the question of objective. In their thoughtful evaluation of Marxist anthropology, Kahn and Llobera make a number of valuable suggestions for enabling "the fruitful meeting of Marxism and anthropology...to continue to generate debate, insight and interest" (1981:300). But however important debate, insight, and interest may be as means to our ends, they are not ends in themselves. Our objective is not simply a better Marxist anthropology which uses historical materialism to provide more interesting analyses of anthropological problems; our objective rather is an anthropological Marxism which uses the facts, theories, and insights of anthropology to enrich the revolutionary science of socialism. As Marxists, our struggles within anthropology must contribute to the political maturity of the working class and assist in clarifying working-class struggle as a totality, of which ideological struggle is but one part.[2]

However, rather than being an instrument for clarifying class struggle, Marxism "has recently become for anthropologists a new source of obscurity as a result of recent work which is difficult and barbarously phrased" (Bloch 1983:v). Jargonized modes of expression are, of course, what we expect from bourgeois scholars whose social function, after all, is to obscure social reality. But they are inexcusable among Marxists. We must ask, therefore, what there is that makes it worthwhile to penetrate the obfuscating jargon so rampant in Marxist anthropology? The answer, unfortunately, is obfuscating theory.

Although space prohibits an extended theoretical critique of the Marxist literature in anthropology, two observations need to be made.

One would expect Marxist analyses of precapitalist societies to draw very heavily on the actual material remains of prehistoric civilizations as uncovered by archeologists. But archeological data

ıs conspicuous by its absence.[3] The seminal work of Childe
(1936), Steward (1949), and Flannery (1972, 1973) is virtually ignored, as are standard reviews of prehistory (e.g. Chard 1975,
Clark 1961, Daniel 1968, Fagan 1983, Wenke 1980). Perhaps this
failure to deal with prehistory is related to the particular form of
Marxism that has dominated Marxist anthropology.

In their efforts to understand precapitalist societies, Marxist
anthropologists have noted that Marx's analysis of capitalism was
concerned with uncovering the hidden structure which generates
the observed phenomena of bourgeois society. In their efforts to
find comparable structures in precapitalist societies, they have analyzed various historical and ethnographic societies using a particular reading of Marx, that of Althusser and Balibar (1970), and
drawing heavily upon the work of French structuralists such as
Levi-Strauss (1963). Now, while one may regard Marx as a structuralist if one wishes, to do so is to misunderstand both Marx and
structuralism. French structuralism is concerned with mental
structures existing in the human mind (or outside the human mind
in the nature of human thought or communication), while Marx
attempted to understand the structure of society that existed outside and independently of the human mind but which was hidden
by veils of ideology (Harris 1968:464-513).[4]

It has thus been a mystical rather than a materialist conception of structure which has dominated Marxist anthropology. To
paraphrase Marx (1965:20), Marxist anthropology is standing on its
head; it must be placed on its feet if it one wants to understand
the inner dialectic of precapitalist societies.

In accomplishing this task vis-a-vis Hegelian dialectics, Marx
used an analytical tool ignored by structural Marxism: the labor
theory of value. The labor theory of value is the central analytical
tool which enabled Marx to penetrate the ideological veils and
reveal the underlying thermodynamic structure of bourgois civilization. As Sweezy points out, "value calculation makes it possible
to look beneath the surface phenomena of money and commodities
to the underlying relations between people and classes" (1942:129).
Without the labor theory of value, one cannot understand surplus
value and the exploitative relation between ruling and ruled
classes. Without the labor theory of value, the "fundamental discussions of the concepts of mode of production, social formation,
class, relations of production, forces of production, and exploitation" (Bailey 1981:90) in Marxist anthropology lack a real
materialist base. But the labor theory of value, as developed by

Marx, was designed specifically to analyze capitalist relations of production and exploitation (Amin 1978). What is needed is a modification of Marx's value theory to enable it to be used in societies where money and markets do not play a dominating role.

Elsewhere, I have suggested ways in which Marx's labor theory of value can be generalized so that it can be a useful analytical tool for understanding precapitalist systems (Ruyle 1973b, 1975, 1976, 1977, 1985). The purpose of this paper is to summarize this approach and indicate its utility for Marxist anthropology. This will involve: 1) generalizing the labor theory of value into social thermodynamics which can analyze pre-capitalist modes of production and exploitation, 2) using this analysis to understand the prehistoric revolutions that have transformed the material conditions of life of our species, 3) using our understanding of these prehistoric revolutions to shed light on the nature of the revolutionary transformation our species is currently undergoing, thereby integrating these insights into a general societal taxonomy of systems of production and exploitation.

Clearly, only the barest outlines of such a broad enterprise can be sketched in a short paper (for a longer, but still incomplete effort, see Ruyle 1984). Such an outline may, however, be useful in placing our work in perspective.

From the Labor Theory of Value to Social Thermodynamics

In *Capital*, Marx makes it clear that the hidden secret of social structure is to be found in labor-time. In capitalism, this secret is concealed in the "fetishism of commodities," in which the products of human labor, commodities, "appear as independent beings endowed with life, and entering into relation both with one another and with the human race" (1965:72). Thus, for example, when we go to McDonalds for a Big Mac, we tend to be concerned solely with the price and utility of the Big Mac - how much it costs and how it tastes in comparison to a "Whopper" or "Jumbo Jack." We lose sight of the fact that we are involved in a definite social relationship with the workers and owners of McDonalds in which we are exchanging a portion of our labor time (embodied in our money) for the labor time embodied in the Big Mac.[5] The labor theory of value is the analytical tool developed by Marx to analyze the social relationships concealed by money and commodities in a capitalist society.

These social relations have an essential thermodynamic aspect in that definite amounts of labor energy (measured in units of time) are embodied in commodities:

> that which determines the magnitude of the value of any article is the amount of labour socially necessary, or the labour-time socially necessary for its production. Each individual commodity, in this connexion, is to be considered as an average sample of its class.... As values, all commodities are only definite masses of congealed labour-time (Marx 1965:39-40).

The exchange of commodities involves a flow of the labor-energy congealed in those commodities. The labor theory of value enables Marx to analyze the flow of labor energy between individuals and between classes in capitalist society. There is a definite amount of labor-energy embodied in the wages paid to workers, and the production of surplus value in capitalism involves forcing the worker to expend more labor energy than he or she receives in wages (Marx 1965:186-192).

To analyze the thermodynamic structure of capitalism fully, Marx had to elaborate the labor theory of value with more specific concepts, such as constant and variable capital, organic composition of capital, rates of surplus value, and so on. Although these more elaborate concepts are only applicable to capitalism, the basic insight of the labor theory of value is applicable to all human societies. All human societies, capitalist and noncapitalist, are dependent upon articles (use-values) which are produced by social labor and which therefore had definite amounts of labor energy (which can be measured in units of labor time) congealed in them.[6] In capitalism, most of these articles take the form of commodities in that they are produced for sale on the market, but, as Marx points out, a thing "can be useful, and the product of human labour, without being a commodity" (1965:40). Although Marx does not address directly the question of whether such things have value, it is certainly reasonable to say that they do and this opens the way for using the labor theory of value to analyze the relations of production and exploitation in noncapitalist societies.[7]

The use of this thermodynamic theory is simpler in noncapitalist societies because, on the one hand, these societies are themselves simpler, and, on the other hand, the thermodynamic structure of production and exploitation is more direct. As Marx puts it:

> The whole mystery of commodities, all the magic and necromancy that surrounds the products of labour as long as they take the form of commodities, vanishes therefore, so soon as we come to other forms of production....
>
> Let us now transport ourselves from Robinson's island bathed in light to the European middle ages shrouded in darkness. Here, instead of the independent man, we find everyone dependent, serfs and lords, vassals and suzerains, laymen and clergy. Personal dependence here characterises the social relations of production just as much as it does the other spheres of life organised on the basis of that production. But for the very reason that personal dependence forms the ground-work of society, there is no necessity for labour and its products to assume a fantastic form different from their reality. They take the shape, in the transactions of society, of services in kind and payments in kind. Here the particular and natural form of labour, and not, as in a society based on production of commodities, its general abstract form is the immediate social form of labour. Compulsory labour is just as properly measured by time, as commodity-producing labour, but every serf knows that what he expends in the service of his lord, is a definite quantity of his own personal labour-power. The tithe to be rendered to the priest is more matter-of-fact than his blessing. No matter, then, what we may think of the parts played by the different classes of people themselves in this society, the social relations between individuals in the performance of their labour, appear at all events as their own mutual personal relations, and are not disguised under the shape of social relations between the products of labour (Marx 1965:76-77).[8]

It is unfortunate that Marxist anthropology has not followed up Marx's suggestions here on how to analyze pre-capitalist systems of production and exploitation in terms of labor-time. Some general comments on social thermodynamics as a mode of analysis are in order.[9]

The process of capitalist production involves pumping labor energy into commodities where it is congealed and consumed when the commodities themselves are consumed. Money may also be considered to have a definite amount of labor energy congealed in it since it requires energy to obtain and gives its owner a claim on other peoples' energy.[10] The exchange of commodities and money in capitalism, therefore, involves what I have called a deep structure of energy flow in contrast to the superficial flows of energy in other aspects of daily life (Ruyle 1976). This deep thermodynamic structure is what Marx called "the economic structure of society, the real foundation, on which rises a legal and political superstructure and to which correspond definite forms of social consciousness" (Tucker 1978:4).

Productive labor is the expenditure of human energy, but other forms of human activity, such as reproductive labor, also involve the expenditure of energy and, therefore, can be measured in the same terms as labor energy, units of minutes, hours, days, weeks, months, and years. Just as bourgeois relations of exploitation and domination can be measured in thermodynamic terms, so the patriarchal relations between men and women within family structures can be analyzed thermodynamically in terms of how much time is spent, and by whom, in such activities as cleaning, cooking, and child care. Useful work along these lines has been done by feminists (e.g. Vogel 1983:17-25, Harris and Young 1981:130-134, Rubin 1975, Eisenstein 1979, Gardiner 1979), but more remains to be done. A full exploration of the social thermodynamics of domestic labor is, of course, beyond the scope of this essay, but it is worth stressing that both productive and reproductive labor require the expenditure of human energy. Social thermodynamics, in providing a linkage between feminist analyses of gender relations and the classic (sometimes seen as "gender blind") Marxian analysis of bourgeois class relations, may help improve the "unhappy marriage" of Marxism and feminism (Hartmann 1981).

Other forms of human activity also require the expenditure of human energy. Politics, law, philosophy, religion - all require definite expenditures of human energy. Churches, schools, courts, jails, and government bureaus all have definite amounts of social labor congealed in them. Thus, it is not only the economic base of society that is susceptible to thermodynamic analysis but also legal, political, and ideological superstructures. Again, it is impossible to explore this fully in a short paper, but recognition of this fact may help us better understand the articulation of infrastructures, structures, and superstructures.

Finally, Marx suggested that definite forms of social consciousness correspond to economic structures. I have suggested that this correspondence may be understood as resulting from selective pressures (analogous to those determining the structure of the gene pool) generated by thermodynamic structures (Ruyle 1973a).

Social thermodynamics, then, is a potentially powerful analytical system which builds upon Marx's own thermodynamic analysis of capitalism. In the next section, I will use social thermodynamics to analyze some of the major transformations that have occured in the prehistory of our species.

Prehistoric Revolutions

Although those who equate anthropology with the study of primitive or precapitalist societies are mistaken (as will be discussed in the next section), most Marxist anthropology does in fact focus on precapitalist systems. A fuller examination of anthropology's contribution to the understanding of precapitalist social formations is therefore in order.

The original anthropological intervention in Marxism occurred a century ago, when Marx and Engels drew upon anthropological materials, especially the work of Morgan (1963) to enrich the materialist conception of history. As Bloch (1983:10) points out, Marx and Engels used anthropological materials for two purposes. They used anthropology, first, to demonstrate that the materialist conception of history was universally valid, that all societies were constructed along the same general principles. Second, they used anthropology to show that the particular institutions of bourgeois society, such as the state, private property, and the family, were not universal, but instead were historically limited responses to the particular material circumstances of the modern epoch.

This latter point is absolutely fundamental and underlies the entire Marxian enterprise. For if the institutions of class and gender oppression in bourgeois society are simply the products of human activity within a particular set of material conditions, they can be changed by human activity. The struggle for socialism, which would be doomed to failure if class and gender oppression were inevitable concomitants of human nature, is thereby legitimized. This point, it should be noted, was made by radical thinkers long before Marx, using, quite frequently, anthropological facts and approaches (Lenski 1966, Harris 1968). Thus, the cross-cultural data professionally controlled by anthropologists is crucial to the proletarian struggle for socialism. This fact makes Marxist anthropology an important arena of ideological class struggle (and, it may be added, gender struggle).

It is impossible to understand precapitalist social formations without an understanding of prehistory and the prehistoric revolutions that have dramatically altered the material conditions of life for our species. We are currently living through a major transformation in the evolutionary development of our species, the Industrial Revolution, which began with the emergence of capitalism and which will not be completed until the establishment of a world socialist order There have been three transformations of comparable significance in prehistory: the Human, Neolithic, and Urban Revolutions.

The Human Revolution involved the emergence of humanity from pongid ancestors. It began about 5 million years ago and was not completed until about 40 thousand years ago (if, indeed, it has been completed). Before the Human Revolution our ancestors were apes; by 40 thousand years ago they were indistinguishable from contemporary humans, with hunting and gathering modes of production, and fully developed languages, religions, and family and kinship systems.

The Neolithic Revolution involved the development of plant and animal domestication and sedentary village life. Before the Neolithic Revolution, our ancestors lived in small, nomadic bands of hunter gatherers; afterwards, they lived in larger, settled villages and began to accumulate wealth. Independent Neolithic Revolutions occured in at least three areas: the Near East, about 10,000 years ago, East and Southeast Asia, about the same time or slightly later, and Central and South America, about 5,000 years ago.

The Urban Revolution involved the emergence of patriarchy and class rule (a.k.a. civilization), with cities, writing, and dramatically more powerful productive systems supporting vastly larger populations. The Urban Revolution saw the final breakup of the "liberty, equality, and fraternity" of the primitive commune and its replacement by the exploitation, oppression, patriarchy, and class struggles that have characterized all historic civilizations. Urban Revolutions occured in Mesopotamia and Egypt about 5,000 years ago, in the Indus Valley slightly later, in China about 4,000 years ago, and in Mesoamerica and Peru about 2,000 years ago.

Each of these prehistoric revolutions dramatically altered the material conditions of life for our species. They did not happen overnight; they were not events but processes which took generations or even hundreds of years for their full implications to be felt. Nonetheless, they did occur. The archeological and ethnographic records, it is true, reveal some transitional forms and also examples of settled foragers and nomadic horticulturalists. But statistical analysis also shows clearly the systemic differences between hunting and gathering societies, horticultural societies, and more complex agrarian civilizations in terms of population size and density, settlement patterns, division of labor, frequency and scale of warfare, degree of political authority, degree of inequality, kinship and marriage practices, and religious ideology (Lenski 1970:129-142). Such analysis provides cross-cultural confirmation of Marx's basic principle of historical materialism, that "the mode of production of material life conditions the social, political and intellectual life process in general" (Tucker 1978:4).

Limitations of space prevent any full discussion of these transformations, but reasonably good discussions can be found in most introductory texts in anthropology (e.g. Harris 1975, Keesing 1981, Kottak 1978) and prehistory (e.g. Chard 1975, Fagan 1983, Wenke 1980). Our concern here is to analyze thermodynamically the underlying structural transformations associated with these revolutions.

Humans, like all other animals, must expend energy to satisfy their needs. There is, however, a fundamental difference between the structure of energy expenditure of humans and non-human primates. In contrast to all other primate species, in which needs are satisfied through direct, individual appropriation of naturally occurring use values, humans satisfy their needs through production.

Every human being in every known human society is dependent upon a system of social production in which human labor energy is used to transform environmental resources into culturally acceptable use-values before they are used to satisfy human needs. Since these use-values have been produced by human labor (like the commodities of capitalist production which are but a special case of this universal human characteristic), they have a definite amount of labor energy embodied in them. Thus, when people consume the products of human labor, they are consuming a definite amount of human labor energy. More than this, since people in all known human societies produce use-values for, and consume use-values produced by, other people, all human beings are dependent upon other people's labor.

This difference is absolute. No other primate is involved in productive processes except in the most rudimentary and marginal manner (e.g. the termite fishing behavior of some chimps); all human societies are completely dependent upon the underlying flow of social labor that sustains human life by producing the goods necessary for human life, that is, upon a mode of production. It is this structural feature that differentiates humanity from all other primates. As Marx and Engels put it,

> Men can be distinguished from animals by consciousness, by religion or anything else you like. They themselves begin to distinguish themselves from animals as soon as they begin to produce their means of subsistence (1939:7).

In his paper "On the Part Played by Labour in the Transition from Ape to Man," Engels discusses this process in greater detail on the basis of data available in 1876 (1972a), and Engels' work has been updated in the light of recent work on human origins by Woolfson (1982) and myself (Ruyle 1976). This labor theory of human origins is of fundamental significance for historical materialism. It shows that not only are particular social and ideological complexes related to particular modes of production but our distinctive characteristics as humans--our bipedalism, our linguistic capabilities, our powers of reasoning--all consequences of our dependence on social production.[11]

However, although all people are dependent upon the products of labor, not all people labor. For the greater part of humanity's existence, throughout the millions of years of the Human Revolution and through the Neolithic Revolution of 10,000 years ago, our ancestors lived in conditions of communism, with an equal obligation to labor and equal access to the social product. The last 5,000 years of human history, by contrast, have been dominated by classes of people who do not participate directly in productive labor but who nevertheless are abundantly provided with the good things of life. How did such a situation come about?

To answer this question we must first understand the nature of the problem. Just as the difference between human and animal populations may be understood in thermodynamic terms, so may the difference between primitive communism and patriarchal class rule. In terms of their underlying thermodynamic structure, human societies fall into one of two categories: classless societies (primitive communism) and class-structured societies. There are, of course, differences of opinion among Marxists as to the usefulness of the concept of primitive communism which cannot be fully discussed here. (e.g. Bloch 1983:96, Keenan 1981).

Primitive communism, which occurs most typically among nomadic hunter gatherers but also among some horticulturalists, is characterized by the following: 1) all members of society, for most if not all their lives, participate directly in production through the expenditure of their own labor power, so that no one lives without working; and 2) all members of society enjoy free and equal access to the social product.

Systems of class rule, which include all historic and contemporary civilizations, are characterized by: 1) differential access to the social product, so that some people are wealthy and others poor; and 2) differential participation in production, with the wealthier classes expending little or no energy in production while the laboring classes do not enjoy the full product of their own labor. There is thus a flow of labor energy, or surplus, out of the productive classes and into the ruling class. This extraction of surplus from the direct producers is a result of the efforts of the ruling class which expends energy not in production but in a system of exploitation. All historic and contemporary ruling classes support themselves by manipulating definite modes of exploitation which include definite exploitative techniques, such as simple plunder, slavery, rent, usury, and wage-slavery, and definite institutions of violence and thought control, the state and the church, respectively (Ruyle 1973b, 1975, 1977, 1985).

Exploitation, then, does not simply "occur." It is a consequence of definite energy expenditures on the part of the ruling class. The mode of exploitation may thus be thought of as the "mode of production" of the ruling class, with the understanding that the energy expended into the exploitative system is not productive; it is not labor energy but rather exploitative energy. As a result of the efforts of the ruling class a predator-prey relationship has emerged between populations of our species similar to that existing between different animal species. The stakes involved, however, are not the food-energy locked up in animal flesh but instead the labor-energy that the human animal can expend in production (Ruyle 1973a:209).

These different thermodynamic structures--primitive communism and patriarchal class rule--are rooted in different material conditions. Primitive communism is associated typically with a hunting and gathering mode of production that supports a small, highly mobile population. Exploitative systems cannot be constructed in such conditions for several reasons, of which we shall merely mention two of the more important. First, the nomadic character of life required by hunting and gathering prevents any significant accumulation of wealth, so there is little incentive to exploit others. Second, any attempt to exploit other would jeopardize the bonds of mutual interdependence, expressed in kinship ties, upon which all members of society depend. As these material conditions change, exploitation becomes possible. With the settled village life that develops after the Neolithic Revolution, people can begin to accumulate wealth, and hence there is an incentive to exploit others. As populations become larger and denser non-kin may be exploited without jeopardizing bonds of mutual interdependence. Ambitious men can begin to develop techniques for exploiting first women, then other men, and begin to organize themselves as a ruling class (see Ruyle 1985).[12] As ruling classes develop progressively more powerful exploitative systems capable of extracting increasing amounts of surplus, this surplus is used not only to support the extravagant life style of the rulers but also to support full-time specialists in both exploitation (soldiers, scribes, priests, kings) and production (metallurgy, ceramics, weaving, and other artisans). The Urban Revolution is thus a consequence both of the progressive development of the forces of social production and of the forces of exploitation supporting the ruling class and its retainers.

The perspective sketched above is, I believe, an important elaboration of Marxian theory (see Ruyle 1975). In contrast to the more usual view which sees the class structure as determined by the mode of production, this thermodynamic view sees the class structure as determined by a mode of exploitation devised by the ruling class for its own purposes.[13] The progressive development of the forces of social production, of course, makes exploitation possible, but exploitation does not flow automaticaliy from the requisites of production. Rather, it flows from the needs of the ruling class However much the rulers may appropriate to themselves important social functions in an effort to consolidate and legitimate their rule, they are expendable and always have been.

I stress this not as an idle intellectual exercise, but as an important theoretical point related to practical politics. For by understanding what kinds of material conditions permit the development of patriarchal systems of class rule and precisely how these systems were constructed and have been maintained throughout history, we can better understand how to dismantle these oppressive systems which are causing such misery for our species.

The Industrial Revolution initiated by our modern bourgeoisie has once again radically altered the material conditions of human life, making the abolition of class rule not only possible but essential if our species is to survive.

Varieties of Modernity

As noted above, it is a mistake to equate anthropology with the study of primitive or precapitalist societies, for anthropologists have always seen our focus on such exotica as Crow kinship terminologies, subincision, potlatches, and kula rings as part of an effort to understand the the human condition in its entirety and the full range of the human experience. Morgan, it will be recalled, made some very perceptive remarks on the nature and direction of modern social change (1963:561-562), and anthropologists have never relinquished their claim on the understanding of modern societies (e.g. Boas 1928, Bodley 1985, Harris 1981, Keesing 1981, Miner 1956, Ruyle 1978, 1979a, 1979b, 1979c; Spradley and Rynkiewich 1975, Weaver 1973).

Marxist anthropology cannot, therefore, be limited to the study of precapitalist social formations. Marxist anthropology must also combine the insights of anthropology and historical materialism to better understand the nature of modern sociocultural variation. There is a particular urgency to this task, for just as popular conceptions of savages, barbarians, and backward nations were used to legitimate the colonial plunder of the non-Western world, so similar misconceptions of contemporary sociocultural phenomena are used to justify North American interventionism in the third world and the suicidal arms race. These misconceptions are subsumed by the two great myths which sustain United States imperialism: the myth of an advanced America surrounded by backward peoples, and the myth of anti-communism (Ruyle 1983).

In order to combat these myths, we need to understand both the nature of modern sociocultural variation and the dialectic of structural change in the modern world. While Marx's analysis in *Capital* remains as valid as when it was written, it must be continually updated to show how the underlying tendencies revealed by Marx are being manifested in the complex class struggles of the twentieth century. The taxonomy of modern societies diagramed in Figure 1 (below) is offered as a framework for understanding these struggles.[14]

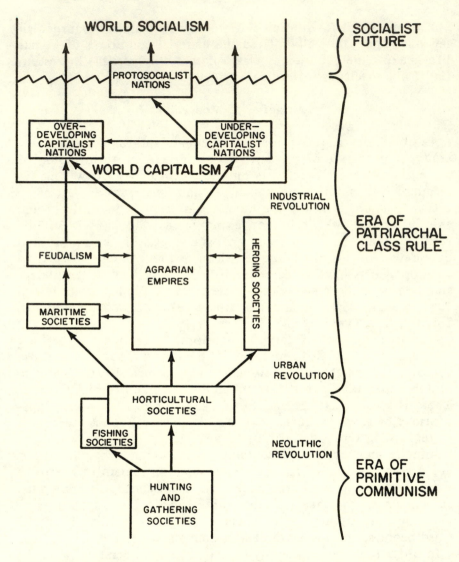

Figure 1. Evolutionary Taxonomy of Precapitalist and Modern Societies.

In one sense, capitalism is but the latest form of class rule, a form, however, in which exploitation (and the concomitant misery of the oppressed) is carried to an extreme. Capitalism, moreover, represents a universal stage in humanity's development, not in the sense that all societies are striving to become capitalist, but rather in the sense that when capitalism emerges anywhere, it must spread everywhere. As Marx and Engels noted in the *Communist Manifesto*:

> It compels all nations, on pain of extinction, to adopt the bourgeois mode of production; it compels them to introduce what it calls civilisation into their midst, i.e., to become bourgeois themselves. In one word, it creates a world after its own image (Tucker 1978:477).

But in forcing the bourgeois mode of production on all nations, capitalism does not act in a unilineal manner, with "advanced" nations forging a path for the "backward" nations to follow. There are not one but two paths into the modern bourgeois world, and social change in the modern world capitalist system is multilineal rather than unilineal.

As Marx demonstrated in his chapters on the primitive accumulation of capital (1965:713-774), the Industrial Revolution was financed by the plunder of Latin America, Africa, and Asia. Thus, although from a superficial standpoint the Industrial Revolution first occured in Europe, in a deeper, structural sense it was in reality a world historical process which transformed the social structures of the entire world: Asia, Africa, and Latin America as well as Europe and North America The result was the emergence of a single world thermodynamic system (call it what you will-- the world capitalist system, world imperialism, the great white conspiracy--the reality remains the same). Its chief characteristic is the forcible extraction of social energy as well as raw materials from third world nations (called "backward" by the imperialists) by the dominant Euro-American nations (who call themselves "advanced").

Within this global thermodynamic system, there are not one but two kinds of modern social structure. The Overdeveloping Capitalist Nations of Europe, North America, and Japan have, on the basis of their centuries of imperialist looting of the third world, developed forms of bourgeois affluence and irrationality criticized by Marxists and non-Marxists alike (for a summary of the major critiques and citations, see Bodley 1985). The Under-developing Capitalist Nations of Africa, Asia, and Latin America show the reverse side of world capitalism--the poverty and irrationality created by centuries of imperialist oppression. These are not products of backwardness as bourgeois development and modernization theories would have us believe (and, indeed, as some Marxists seem to agree), but products of modern capitalism.

Underdevelopment and Overdevelopment are thus the twin forms of capitalism in the modern world. These are not stages in a unilineal sequence, but interdependent trajectories of change within the modern world capitalist system.[15] Since 1917, as portions of the formerly colonial or semicolonial world have broken free from imperialist control, they have embarked on yet a third developmental trajectory. Under the leadership of Communist parties associated with the Third International, the Soviet Union, China, Cuba, and other nations have embarked on independent courses of development which are not capitalist but not yet fully socialist.

There is perhaps no question more divisive among Marxists than the nature of these societies, and a full consideration of the various aspects of the debate is out of the question here (for sources and discussion of the major lines of the debate, see Socialist Labor Party 1978, Line of March Editorial Board 1982). Two observations may be made, however. First, it is essential to distinguish between the particular policies pursued by the leaderships of these societies and the underlying structure of the societies themselves. An analogy may be useful. We can debate the merits of the particular style of football played by the L.A. Raiders as much as we like, but this does not alter the fact that they are playing U.S.-style football and not soccer, the football of the rest of the world. From an anthropological perspective, it is the structural differences between U.S. football and soccer that are significant; without understanding these differences one cannot meaningfully debate the pros and cons of particular styles of either football or soccer In a similar manner, bourgeois tacticians may discuss the merits and demerits of invading Nicaragua, or blockades, economic pressure, or even cooperation, as alternate ways of preserving the global system of capitalist property relations.

As Marxists, we of course need to evaluate in a critical manner the particular economic, political, and social policies pursued by the leaderships of the Soviet Union, China, Cuba, Nicaragua, and other revolutionary societies. Such criticism, however, must be analytically distinguished from the taxonomic problem of understanding the structural nature of these societies. For this, we need to understand the inner structural nature and laws of motion of the emerging socialist world.

Now, from the standpoint of social thermodynamics developed in this paper, the significant questions relate to the flows of energy in such societies. Thermodynamic analysis can provide clues as to whether these societies are in fact dismantling the systems of exploitation and oppression which have plagued humanity since the dawn of civilization, or are merely new forms of class rule. To what extent has the flow of energy out of these nations been reduced or halted? To what extent has the social energy within these nations been redirected toward meetinq more fully the basic human needs of their populations and reducing inequality?

To the extent that the extraction of social energy from these nations has been reduced or halted, they are no longer underdeveloping capitalist nations (however much they may still bear the stigmata of underdevelopment), but are rather in process of dismantling the imperialist system of exploitation. To the extent that the social energy of these nations is being redirected from elite consumption to meeting the basic human needs of their people, they are not new forms of class rule but rather emerging forms of socialism.

Unfortunately, in spite of the large amounts of conflicting evidence and opinions relating to such questions, little scientific analysis has been done. A notable exception, however, is the recent study by Cereseto on global inequality and basic human needs (1983). Cereseto uses World Bank statistics on income and the quality of life in both capitalist and socialist nations to test the two most important aspects of the Marxian paradigm: the law of capitalist accumulation, and the prediction of socialist revolution. Given the importance of Cereseto's study, I shall briefly summarize some of her findings.[16]

The Pax Americana since World War II has seen the degradation, misery, and denial of basic human needs of a large and growing portion of humanity. While the population of the world was increasing by 60% from 1950 to 1975, the total production of wealth was increasing faster, from $1 trillion in the later 1940s to over $6 trillion in 1975 and more than $9 trillion in 1978! But although wealth was increasing faster than population, poverty was also increasing, so that in one decade of rapid economic growth (1963-1973), the number of seriously poor people in the world increased by 119 million, to 1.21 billion people, or 45% of the entire capitalist world (1983:18-19). Thus the poverty and misery of third world peoples, Cereseto finds, are not caused by overpopulation or "backwardness," but rather are consequences of the fundamental law of motion of capitalism, as Marx originally noted:

> Accumulation of wealth at one pole is, therefore, at the same time accumulation of misery, agony of toil, slavery, ignorance, brutality, mental degradation, at the opposite pole, i.e. on the side of the class that produces its own Product in the form of capital" (Marx 1965:645).

The extremes of wealth and poverty that characterize the contemporary capitalist world system are continuations of the growing inequality that has marked the history of civilization since its inception (Lenski 1966), but have reached hitherto unimaginable extremes. Cereseto divides capitalist nations into three categories, based on per capita GNP: rich, middle-income, and poor.[17] She finds, not surprisingly, that the physical quality of life in rich nations is better than in poor nations.

What is surprising (not because Marxists should not have known it, but rather because no one had bothered to prove it before) is that socialism improves the physical quality of life and better meets the basic human needs of its members than does capitalism. All socialist nations fall within the middle-income category based on per capita GNP, even though many were desperately poor before their revolutions. Cereseto uses a variety of statistics on such things as inequality, infant mortality, life expectancy, literacy, and health care and finds that: 1) the socialist nations, all middle-income, do better than the capitalist nations taken as a whole in meeting the basic human needs of their members; 2) the socialist nations do far better in meeting these human needs than do capitalist nations with the same resource base (i.e. middle-income capitalist nations), and 3) socialist nations do about as well as rich capitalist nations in meeting basic human needs. Cereseto also finds that, while inequality is increasing both within and between capitalist nations, inequality is declining both within and between socialist nations.[18]

There is much more in Cereseto's careful study that merits close attention by Marxists. Her work is stressed here because it demonstrates that the elaborate thermodynamic structures of inequality that have been constructed and intensified since the beginning of civilization are in fact being dismantled by socialist revolutions of the modern era. Since the social structures and laws of motion of these societies are different from either the Over-developing or Underdeveloping forms of capitalism, they must be regarded as different kinds of society from the standpoint of societal taxonomy, irrespective of how one feels about the particular policies pursued by their leaderships. These societies are clearly part of the break-up of world capitalism. But they are not yet fully socialist, as the term has been understood in the working-class movement prior to Stalin's time. I have suggested that these societies be called Proto-socialist Nations, a term which expresses their dialectical nature and location in the world revolutionary process (Ruyle 1975, 1979c).

Concluding Remarks

As Marxists and as anthropologists, our goal cannot be simply a Marxist anthropology which uses the insights of historical materialism to provide more interesting analyses of anthropological problems. We also need an anthropological Marxism which uses the facts and theories of anthropology to enrich the revolutionary science of socialism. This dual objective can best be approached through the basic analytical tool of Marx's *Capital*, the labor theory of value.

Although Marx's specific elaborations of this theory are limited to capitalism, the underlying insight, that the social relations of production can be analyzed thermodynamically, is applicable to all human societies. I have suggested how this thermodynamic conception of social structure can shed light on such diverse social phenomena as the origin of our species, the nature of primitive communism, the origin of patriarchy and class rule, as well as the nature of capitalism and overthrow of class rule currently in progress. This thermodynamic conception can also be useful in specifying in a materialist manner the articulation of economic base with legal, political, and ideological superstructures and in understanding the transformations of structures themselves. Such work, of course, needs to be done to transform these suggestions into a useful additions to the theory which guides the working class in its struggle for socialism. As Engels notes,

To accomplish this act of universal emancipation is the historical mission of the modern proletariat. To thoroughly com-

prehend the historical conditions and thus the very nature of
this act, to impart to the new oppressed proletarian class a
full knowledge of the conditions and of the meaning of the
momentous act it is called upon to accomplish, this is the task
of the theoretical expression of the proletarian movement,
scientific socialism (Tucker 1978:717).

By providing a materialist understanding of prehistoric revolutions
and clarifying the nature of our current revolutionary epoch,
anthropology can contribute to our future.

NOTES

1   Witness the reaction of "liberal" anthropologists to the publication of *Reinventing Anthropology* (Hymes 1972), as discussed by
Scholte (1981:150-151).

2   But a very important part. In *What Is To Be Done*, Lenin
quotes Engels in support of his view that ideological struggle is
"on a par" with economic and political forms of class struggle
(1973:27). The importance of ideolgoical class struggle, of course,
does not mean that it can be carried on by specialists divorced
from other forms of class struggle. As Engels noted elsewhere,
     In our eventful time, just as in the 16th century, pure
     theorists on social affairs are found only on the side of reac-
     tion and for this reason they are not even theorists in the full
     sense of the word, but simply apologists for reaction (Engels
     1966:2).
In this connection, it would be useful perhaps for Marxist
anthropologists to discuss explicitly their involvement in the class
struggle. Perry Anderson (9184) has recently criticized the "intel-
lectualist isolation" of Western Marxism and "its sundering of all
bonds that might have linked it to popular movements for revolutionary socialism" (Lentricchia 1984:2). We do have some information on the political affiliation of some Marxist
anthropologists (See Kahn and Llobera 1981a:280-285), but little
discussion of the actual involvement of Marxist anthropologists in
the political and economic arenas of class struggle.

3   I would guess that less than 1% of the citations in Marxist
anthropology are archeological sources. A brief review of the
bibliographies of recent work (Block 1975, Godelier 1977, Hindess
and Hirst 1975, 1977; Kahn and Llobera 1981; Seddon 1978)

turned up only the following: Harris and Young (1981:133) cite Cohen (1977), and Hindess and Hirst (1975:25) cite Childe (1952), but only tangentially; Ekholm (1981) and Godelier (1977, 1978) cite several sources each and do discuss archeological data, but very incompletely. Gilman's excellent article on the "upper paleolithic revolution" is an exception to these remarks (1984).

4   For further discussion of the relationship between Marxist anthropology and French structuralism, see Copans adn Seddon (1978), Kahn and Llobera (1981a), and Bloch (1983). For discussion of the shortcomings of the French Marxist tradition, see Kahn and Llobera (1981a); of French structuralism, see Harris (1968). It may be worthwhile to quote a portion of Anderson's devastating critique of the relationship between Marxism and structuralism:

> After French Marxism had enjoyed a lengthy period of large-ly uncontested cultural dominance, basking in the remote, reflected prestige of the Liberation, it finally encountered an intellectual adversary that was capable of doing battle with it, and prevailing. Its victorious opponent was the broad theoretical front of structuralism, and then its post-structuralist successors. The crisis of Latin Marxism, then, would be the result, not of a circumstantial decline, but of a head-on defeat. The evidence of that defeat, it could be argued, is the triumphant ascendancy of structuralist or post-structuralist ideas and themes wherever Marxist ones once held sway.... But even at the peak of its productivity, Althus-serianism was always constituted in an intimate and fatal dependence on a structuralism that both preceded it and would survive it. Levi-Strauss had peremptorily sought to cut the Gordian knot of the relation between structure and subject by suspending the latter from any field of scientific knowledge. Rather than resistinq this move, Althusser radicalized it, with a version of Marxism in which subjects were abolished altogether, save as the illusory effects of ideological structures (P. Anderson 1984:33, 38).

Anderson also makes some perceptive comments on relationship between the political explosion of May, 1968, and the failures of structural Marxism, apropos our remarks in Footnote 2 (1984:38-39, 66-67).

5   More than this, the entire social relations of imperialism are embodied in the Big Mac. Consider, for example, the "Hamburger Connection": much of the beef for fast food chains comes from ranches in Central America where it is more profitable and

prestigious to raise beef for export than grow maize for the impoverished local population (W.T. Anderson 1984).

Also, the Big Mac has inspired bourgeois economists to develop the "Big Mac Index" which provides a cross-cultural comparison of the labor time necessary to purchase Big Macs, small
fries, and medium Cokes for a family of four (Banks 1984). A
bus driver in Chicago works only half as long as his London
counterpart for this culinary delight. Comparable measures could,
and should, be used to compare labor times for such things as
medical care, housing, and transportation in various bourgeois and
socialist nations.

6   It is entirely true that different societies have different conceptions of time and punctuality (Levine and Wolff 1985) and that
"the conceptualization of productive activity is totally integrated
with other social relations in pre-capitalist societies and that the
sharp boundary we draw between labour and other activities is
absent" (Bloch 1983:91). But these facts no more negate the dependence of human beings on labor than the fact that different
societies conceptualize food differently negates the human dependence on food.

7   Since there are so many dictionary definitions of the term
"value" (17 in Webster's second edition), this term is easily mis-
understood. Perhaps the term "labor-value" would be preferable
since it would be clearly materialist and not easily confused with
the metaphysical concepts of the cultural idealists.

8   Marx's entire section "On the Fetishism of Commodities and
the Secret Thereof" (1965:71-83) is an excellent statement of the
need for a thermodynamic conception of society.

9   Elsewhere I have used the term ethnoenergetics to refer to
this mode of analysis, but perhaps social thermodynamics is
preferable (Ruyle 1973b, 1975, 1977).

10   There are metaphysical complexities in this formulation, of
course, which cannot be entered into here.

11   The labor theory of human origins is thus an important arena
of struggle against the excesses of structuralism, which asserts
        the outright primacy of the communicative over the produc-
        tive functions in the definition of humanity and the develop-
        ment of history alike: that is, in Habermas's terms, of "lan-
        guage" over "labour".... Whereas hominids practised labour
        with tools, revealing it as a pre-human activity, homo sapiens

as a species was characterized by the innovation of language and the family that it alone could institute. Moreover, this privilege of communication over production is not simply constitutive of what it meant to become fully "human"; it continues to operate as the dominant principle of historical change thereafter (P. Anderson 1984:61).

It is, however, the human dependence on labor activities that serves to distinguish humans from tool-using apes (Ruyle 1976:140). Those familiar with the first law of dialectics, the transformation of quantity into quality and vice versa (Engels 1940:26), should have no problems with this.

12   Contrary to what I suggested earlier (Ruyle 1973b), it appears that the emergence of exploitation was closely linked with the emergence of patriarchy. Engels, in discussing the earliest form of exploitation, remarked,

> It was not long then before the great "truth" was discovered that man also can be a commodity, that human energy can be exchanged and put to use by making man into a slave (1972:234).

What Engels did not know is that the first slaves were not men but women. References to slave women appear in the earliest protoliterate tablets in Sumeria, centuries before references to male slaves, and slave women were more numerous than slave men throughout early Sumerian history (Adams 1966:96ff). The economic role of women slaves in the early stages of the development of civilization was comparable to that of women workers in the textile mills of early capitalism. As Adams notes:

> Their economic role was a much more significant one, however, in connection with great estates and temples, of which the Bau archive furnishes so richly documented an example. In the Bau community of some 1200 persons, there were from 250 to 300 slaves, of whom the overwhelming proportion were women. One tablet alone lists 205 slave girls and their children who probably were employed in a centralized weaving establishment like one known archeologically at the site of ancient Eshnunna; other women are known to have been engaged in milling, brewing, cooking, and similar interior operations permitting close supervision (1966:102).

For further discussion of the subjugation of women and the rise of Sumerian civilization, see Rohrlich (1980). While there are disagreements among both feminists and Marxists as to the degree of female subordination in primitive communism (for the major opposing views, see Rosaldo 1974, Leacock 1972), it is clear that women's oppression increased with the rise of class rule. While, as Harris and Young stress, it is incorrect to see women as a uniformly oppressed category (1981:111-112), systems of class rule are universally patriarchal in that 1) the most oppressed people are women, and 2) the major institutions of class rule are almost exclusively staffed by men. Feminist scholars are increasingly aware that "the state is male in the feminist sense" (MacKinnon 1983:644) and are exploring the relationship between the state and women's oppression (Sacks 1976, Rapp 1978, Rohrlich 1980, Gailey 1985).

13   For an evaluation of this view, see Moseley and Wallerstein (1978:273-274).

14   My formulation here has been shaped by a variety of sources, of which the most important are: Amin (1976), Baran (1957), Baran and Sweezy (1966), Domhoff (1967), Frank (1969a, 1969b), Magdoff (1969), and Wallerstein (1974a, 1974b).

15   Marx noted in 1853 that capitalism took on a different appearance in underdeveloping nations than in the overdeveloping nations:

> The profound hypocrisy and inherent barbarism of bourgeois civilization lies unveiled before our eyes, turning from its home, where it assumes respectable forms, to the colonies, where it goes naked (1969:137).

16   It appears that some of the most important work (i.e. Cereseto 1983, Lenski 1966, 1970) in anthropological Marxism has been done by sociologists rather than anthropologists. Perhaps the reasons for this situation are similar to those suggested by Anderson who, after observing that some of the best ethnographies are written by non-anthropologists, wrote (1984:1002):

> It is partly because anthropologists choose to write in sesquipedalian jargon, and choose to focus their books on arcane and frequently absurd points of theory. There is, however, a deeper failure. Don't anthropologists care about people anymore?

Similarly, we may ask, don't Marxists care about revolution anymore?

17   There is no contradiction, incidentally, between Cereseto's three categories and the two I specified above (Overdeveloping Capitalist Nations and Underdeveloping Capitalist Nations). Cereseto's categories are based on the observed data on per capita income, which forms a continuum from the richest nation to the poorest. My categories are based on underlying structural features (energy flow) which are analytically distinct (comparable to Weberian "ideal types), even though the surface manifestation (per

capita income) may form a continuum. This does not negate the reality of the underlying distinction.

18 Not only has income inequality been increasing in the capitalist world, but also institutional violence, political assassinations, and state-sponsored torture have increased since World War II (Chomsky and Herman 1979). By contrast, the proto-socialist nations, and specifically the Soviet Union, have become less repressive since Stalin's time (Chomsky and Herman 1979:8, Szymansky 1979, 1984).

BIBLIOGRAPHY

Adams, Robert McC.
   1966   The Evolution of Urban Society: Early Mesopotamia and Prehispanic Mexico. Chicago: Aldine-Atherton.
Althusser, L., and Balibar E.
   1970 Reading Capital. London: NLB.
Amin, Samir
   1976 Unequal Development: An Essay on the Social Formations of Peripheral Capitalism. New York: Monthly Review Press.
   1978 The Law of Value and Historical Materialism. New York: Monthly Review Press.
Anderson, E.N., Jr.
   1984 Review of William Hinton, Shenfan. American Anthropologist 86:1002.
Anderson, Perry
   1984 In the Tracks of Historical Materialism. Chicago: University of Chicago Press.
Anderson, Walter T.
   1984 Chewing up the Forests of Central America. Long Beach Press-Telegram, August 1984.
Bailey, Anne M.
   1981 The Renewed Discussions on the Concept of the Asiatic Mode of Production. *In* The Anthropology of Precapitalist Societies. Joel S. Kahn and Josep R. Llobera, eds. Pp. 89-107. London: The Macmillan Press, Ltd.
Baran, Paul A.
   1957 The Political Economy of Growth. New York: Monthly Review Press.
Baran, Paul A. and Paul M. Sweezy
   1966 Monopoly Capital: An Essay on the American Economic and Social Order. New York: Monthly Review Press.
Bloch, Maurice, ed.
   1975 Marxist Analyses and Social Anthropology. New York: Wiley.

Bloch, Maurice
1983 Marxism and Anthropology: The History of a Relationship. Oxford: Clarendon Press.
Boas, Franz
1928 Anthropology and Modern Life. New York: Norton.
Bodley, John H.
1985 Anthropology and Contemporary Human Problems. 2nd edition. Palo Alto: Mayfield Publishing Company.
Cereseto, Shirley
1982 Capitalism, Socialism, and Inequality. The Insurgent Sociologist 11(2):5-38.
Chard, Chester S.
1975 Man in Prehistory. 2nd edition. New York: McGraw-Hill Book Company.
Childe, V. Gordon
1951 (orig. 1936) Man Makes Himself. Revised edition. New York: Mentor.
1952 The Birth of Civilisation. Past and Present II.
Chomsky, Noam, and Edward S. Herman
1979 The Washington Connection and Third World Fascism. Boston: South End Press.
Clark, Grahame
1961 World Prehistory: An Outline. Cambridge: Cambridge University Press.
Cohen, M. N.
1977 The Food Crisis in Prehistory. New Haven: Yale University Press.
Copans, Jean, and David Seddon
1978 Marxism and Anthropology: A Preliminary Survey. *In* Relations of Production: Marxist Approaches to Economic Anthropology. David Seddon, ed. Pp. 1-46. London: Frank Cass.
Daniel, Glyn
1968 The First Civilizations: The Archaeology of Their Origins. New York: Thomas Y. Crowell.
Domhoff, G. William
1967 Who Rules America? Englewood Cliffs, NJ: Prentice-Hall.
Eisenstein, Zillah
1979 Developing a Theory of Capitalist Patriarchy and Socialist Feminism. *In* Capitalist Patriarchy and the Case for Socialist Feminism. Zillah R. Eisenstein, ed. Pp. 5-40. New York: Monthly Review Press.

Ekholm, Kajsa
  1981 On the Structure and Dynamics of Global Systems. *In*
    The Anthropology of Pre-capitalist Societies. Joel S. Kahn
    and Josep R. Llobera, eds., Pp. 241-261. London: Macmil-
    lan.
Engels, Frederick
  1940 (Orig. 1882) Dialectics of Nature. New York: Interna-
    tional Publishers.
  1966 Preface. *In* Capital: A Critique of Political Economy.
    Volume III. By Karl Marx, Pp. 1-21. Moscow: Progress
    Publishers.
  1972 (Orig. 1884) The Origin of the Family, Private Proper-
    ty and the State. New York: International Publishers.
  1972a (Orig. 1876) The Part Played by Labor in the Transition
    from Ape to Man. *In* The Origin of the Family, Private
    Property and the State. Frederick Engels, Pp. 251-264.
    New York: International Publishers.
Fagan, Brian M.
  1983 People of the Earth: An Introduction to Prehistory. 4th
    edition. Boston: Little, Brown and Company.
Flannery, Kent V.
  1972 The Cultural Evolution of Civilizations. Annual
    Review of Ecology and Systematics 3:399-426.
  1973 The Origins of Agriculture. Annual Review of
    Anthropology 2:271-310.
Frank, Andre Gunder
  1969a (Orig. 1966) The Development of Underdevelopment.
    In Latin America: Underdevelopment or Revolution. Pp.
    3-17. New York: Monthly Review Press.
  1969b (Orig. 1967) Sociology of Development and Under-
    development of Sociology. *In* Latin America: Under-
    development or Revolution. Pp. 21-94. New York:
    Monthly Review Press.
Gailey, Christine Ward
  1985 The State of the State in Anthropology. Dialectical
    Anthropology 9:65-89.
Gardiner, Jean
  1979 Women's Domestic Labor. *In* Capitalist Patriarchy and
    the Case for Socialist Feminism. Zillah R. Eisenstein, ed.
    Pp. 173-189. New York: Monthly Review Press.
Gilman, Antonio
  1984 Explaining the Upper Paleolithic Revolution. *In* Mar-
    xist Perspectives in Archaeology. Mathew Spriggs, ed. Pp.
    115-126. Cambridge: Cambridge University Press.

Godelier, Maurice
   1977 Perspectives in Marxist Anthropology. Cambridge: Cambridge University Press.
   1978 The Object and Method of Economic Anthropology. *In* Relations of Production: Marxist Approaches to Economic Anthropology. David Seddon, ed. Pp. 49-126. London: Frank Cass.
Harris, Marvin
   1975 Culture, People, Nature: An Antroduction to General Anthropology. 2nd edition. New York: Thomas Y. Crowell.
   1968 The Rise of Anthropological Theory. New York: Thomas Y. Crowell.
   1981 America Now: The Anthropology of a Changing Culture. New York: Simon and Schuster.
Harris, Olivia and Kate Young
   1981 Engendered Structures: Some Problems in the Analysis of Reproduction. *In* The Anthropology of Pre-capitalist Societies. Joel S. Kahn and Josep R. Llobera, eds. Pp. 109-147. London: Macmillan.
Hartmann, Heidi
   1981 The Unhappy Marriage of Marxism and Feminism: Towards a More Progressive Union. *In* Women and Revolution: A Discussion of the Unhappy Marriage of Marxism and Feminism. Lydia Sargent, ed. Pp. 1-41. Boston: South End Press.
Hindess, Barry and Paul Q. Hirst
   1975 Precapitalist Modes of Production. London: Routledge & Kegan Paul.
   1977 Mode of Production and Social Formation. London: Routledge & Kegan Paul.
Hymes, Dell
   1972 Reinventing Anthropology. New York: Pantheon.
Kahn, Joel S., and Josep R. Llobera, eds.
   1981 The Anthropology of Pre-capitalist Societies. London: Macmillan.
Kahn, Joel S., and Josep R. Llobera
   1981a Towards a New Marxism or a New Anthropology. *In* The Anthropology of Pre-capitalist Societies. Joel S. Kahn and Josep R. Llobera, eds. Pp. 263-329. London: Macmillan.
Keesing, Roger M.
   1981 Cultural Anthropology: A Contemporary Perspective. 2nd edition. New York: Holt, Rinehart and Winston.

Keenan, Jeremy
    1981 The Concept of the Mode of Production in Hunter-Gatherer Societies. *In* The Anthropology of Pre-capitalist Societies. Joel S. Kahn and Josep R. Llobera, eds. Pp. 2-21. London: Macmillan.
Kottak, Conrad Phillip
    1978 Anthropology: The Exploration of Human Diversity. 2nd edition. New York: Random House.
Leacock, Eleanor
    1972 Introduction. *In* The Origin of the Family, Private Property and the State. By Frederick Engels, Pp. 7-67. New York: International Publishers.
Lenin, V.I.
    1973 (Orig. 1902) What Is To Be Done? Burning Questions of Our Movement. Moscow: Progress Publishers.
Lenski, Gerhard E.
    1966 Power and Privilege: A Theory of Social Stratification. New York: McGraw-Hill.
    1970 Human Societies: A Macrolevel Introduction to Sociology. New York: McGraw-Hill.
Lentricchia, Frank
    1984 Forward. *In* In the Tracks of Historical Materialism. By Perry Anderson, Pp. 1-5. Chicago: University of Chicago Press.
Levine, Robert, and Ellen Wolff
    1985 Social Time: The Heartbeat of a Culture. Psychology Today 19(3):28-35 (March 1985).
Levi-Strauss, Claude
    1963 Structural Anthropology. New York: Basic Books.
Line of March Editorial Board
    1982 Symposium on Paul Sweezy's Theory of Post-revolutionary Society. Line of March 10:43-108 (Jan-Feb 1982).
MacKinnon, Catharine
    1983 Feminism, Marxism, Method and the State: Toward Feminist Jurisprudence. Signs 8:635-658.
Magdoff, Harry
    1969 The Age of Imperialism: The Economics of U.S. Foreign Policy. New York: Monthly Review Press.
Marx, Karl
    1965 (Orig. 1867) Capital: A Critical Analysis of Capitalist Production. Volume 1. Moscow: Progress Publishers.
    1969 (Orig. 1853) The Future Results of British Rule in India. *In* Karl Marx on Colonialism and Modernization. Shlomo Avineri, ed. Pp. 132-139. New York: Anchor Books.

Marx, Karl, and Friedrich Engels
  1939 The German Ideology. New York: International Pub-
    lishers.
Mills, C. Wright
  1962 The Marxists. New York: Dell Publishing Company.
Miner, Horace
  1956 Body Ritual Among the Nacirema. American
    Anthropologist 58:503-507.
Morgan, Lewis Henry
  1963 (Orig. 1877) Ancient Society. Cleveland: World Pub-
    lishing Company.
Moseley, K.P. and Immanuel Wallerstein
  1978 Precapitalist Social Structures. Annual Review of
    Sociology 4:259-290.
Rapp, Rayna
  1978 Gender and Class: An Archaeology of Knowledge Con-
    cerning the Origin of the State. Dialectical Anthropology
    2:309-16.
Rohrlich, Ruby
  1980 State Formation in Sumer and the Subjugation of
    Women. Feminist Studies 6(1):76-102.
Rosaldo, M.
  1974 Woman, Culture and Society: A Theoretical Overview.
    In Woman, Culture and Society. M. Rosaldo and L.
    Lamphere, eds. Pp. 17-42. Stanford: Stanford University
    Press.
Rubin, Gayle
  1975 The Traffic in Women: Notes on the "Political Econo-
    my" of Sex. *In* Toward an Anthropology of Women.
    Rayna R. Reiter, ed. Pp. 157-210. New York: Monthly
    Review Press.
Ruyle, Eugene E.
  1973a Genetic and Cultural Pools: Some Suggestions for a
    Unified Theory of Biocultural Evolution. Human Ecology
    1:201-215.
  1973b Slavery, Surplus, and Stratification on the Northwest
    Coast: The Ethnoenergetics of an Incipient Stratification
    System. Current Anthropology 14:603-631.
  1975 Mode of Production and Mode of Exploitation: The
    Mechanical and the Dialectical. Dialectical Anthropology
    1:7-23.
  1976 Labor, People, Culture: A Labor Theory of Human
    Origins. Yearbook of Physical Anthropology 20:136-163.
  1977 Energy and Culture. *In* The Concepts and Dynamics of
    Culture. Bernardo Bernardi, ed. Pp. 209-237. The Hague:
    Mouton Publishers.

Ruyle, Eugene E. (cont'd)

1978 A Socialist Alternative for the Future. *In* Cultures of the Future. Magoroh Maruyama and Arthur Harkins, eds. Pp. 613-628. The Hague: Mouton Publishers.

1979a Capitalism and Caste in Japan. *In* New Directions in Political Economy: An Approach from Anthropology. Madeline Barbara Leons and Frances Rothstein, eds. Pp. 201-233. Westport, CT: Greenwood Press.

1979b Conflicting Japanese Interpretations of the Outcaste Problem (buraku mondai). American Ethnologist 6:55-72.

1979c China: A Protosocialist State. Paper presented at the 21st Annual Conference of the American Association of Chinese Studies, Long Beach, November, 1979.

1983 The Great American Myth: Anti-communism and the Preservation of Empire. Paper presented at the Annual Meeting of the Southwestern Anthropological Association, San Diego, March 25, 1983.

1984 Anthropology for Marxists: Prehistoric Revolutions. Paper presented at the West Coast Marxist Scholars Conference, Berkeley, April 26-29, 1984.

1985 On the Origin of Patriarchy and Class Rule (a.k.a. civilization). unpublished Ms.

Sacks, Karen

1976 State Bias and Woman's Status. American Anthropologist 78:565:569.

Scholte, Bob

1981 Critical Anthropology Since its Reinvention. *In* The Anthropology of Pre-capitalist Societies. Joel S. Kahn and Josep R. Llobera, eds. Pp. 148-184. London: Macmillan.

David Seddon, ed.

1978 Relations of Production: Marxist Approaches to Economic Anthropology. London: Frank Cass.

Socialist Labor Party

1978 The Nature of Soviet Society. Palo Alto, CA: New York Labor News.

Spradley, James P, and Michael A. Rynkiewich, eds.

1975 The Nacirema: Readings on American Culture. Boston: Little, Brown and Company.

Steward, Julian

1949 Cultural Causality and Law: A Trial Formulation of Early Civilization. American Anthropologist 51:1-27.

Sweezy, Paul M.

1968 (Orig. 1942) The Theory of Capitalist Development. New York: Monthly Review Press.

Szymanski, Albert
> 1979 Is the Red Flag Flying? The Political Economy of the Soviet Union Today. London: Zed Press.
> 1984 Human Rights in the Soviet Union. London: Zed Press.

Tucker, Robert C. ed.
> 1978 The Marx-Engels Reader. New York: Norton.

Vogel, Lise
> 1983 Marxism and the Oppression of Women: Toward a Unitary Theory. New Brunswick, NJ: Rutgers University Press.

Wallerstein, Immanuel
> 1974a The Rise and Future Demise of the World Capitalist System: Concepts for Comparative Analysis. Comparative Studies in Society and History 16:387-415.
> 1974b The Modern World System. New York: Academic Press.

Weaver, Thomas, ed.
> 1973 To See Ourselves: Anthropology and Modern Social Issues. Glenview, IL: Scott, Foresman and Company.

Wenke, Robert J.
> 1980 Patterns in Prehistory: Mankind's First Three Million Years. New York: Oxford University Press.

Woolfson, Charles
> 1982 The Labour Theory of Culture: A Re-examination of Engels's Theory of Human Origins. London: Routledge & Kegan Paul.

STUDYING WORK:
ANTHROPOLOGICAL AND MARXIST
PERSPECTIVES

David Hakken

The aim of this article is to illustrate the value of a strongly materialist, Marxist approach in anthropology. The reader's general familiarity with recent Western Marxist anthropology, and the critique of this trend as over structuralist, is presumed. The article begins with discussion of a recent articulation of this critique by Joel Kahn and Josep Llobera, who are perhaps more responsible than any others for the introduction of French Marxist anthropology into the English-speaking world. After a brief examination of the "Hegelian" alternative to structural Marxism proposed by Kahn and Llobera, a third Marxist approach is presented, one which is still dialectical and yet more overtly materialist than that generally popular in contemporary Marxism. This approach is then illustrated conceptually by discussion of a central issue in Marxist anthropology, the analysis of work. The materialist Marxist approach is first illustrated negatively, via critiques of work anthropology, Marx's discussion of work in *Capital*, and neo-Marxist approaches to work, and then positively, through the articulation of an ethnological approach to work. The ultimate intent is to show both how anthropology can be dialectical and materialist, as well as why Marxism must be more anthropological.

The Critique of Recent Marxist Theory in Anthropology

In a review of French Marxist anthropology, Kahn and Llobera (1981) are fundamentally negative about its theoretical productivity. In brief summary, they trace the project of Meillassoux, Godelier, Terray, etc., to an admonition by Althusser and Balibar (1970) to extend explicitly the theoretical construct "mode of production" to precapitalist social formations. Kahn and Llobera conclude that much of the controversy which characterizes the ensuing project is misguided, the result of applying numerous theoretical elements inappropriately, such as "...the projection of an atomostic [sic] conception of the social totality and...the persistence of an economistic infrastructure/superstructure metaphor" (1981:312). They go on to argue,

> What this critique of French Marxist anthropology implies is the need for a *theory* of pre-capitalistic forms of accumulation and not a semantic debate over whether or not some particular capitalistic category, for example, exploitation, is present in any specific pre-capitalistic social formation....The problem can be resolved only in the context of a *theory* which refuses to separate the notion of surplus and its distribution on the one hand from the social constitution of the categories of productive and unproductive labour on the other (1981:313; emphasis added).

In their critique, Kahn and Llobera discuss how theoretical constructs (e.g., "infrastructure metaphors") derived primarily from consideration of industrial social formations are applied uncritically in the analysis of other types. They identify a need for constructs derived from a more general theory, one capable of accounting for the development of all social forms. Moreover, such a theory must more fully integrate diverse moments of social reproduction, both semiotic and political economic.

However, the specific theory to replace the French Marxist problematic, one which Kahn and Llobera describe only briefly, appears to reject cross-culturally applicable categories. This rejection is based on an essentially negative materialism:

> It might be added, then, that to adopt a materialist, as opposed to an idealist, standpoint is not to assign the primacy to the economic but to renounce the use of metaphysical principles like Hegel's absolute spirit to explain history. This in turn might lead us to reject the inherent atomism of the structural interpretation of the Marxist social totality, by accepting that the 'atom' of a mode of production is incapable of universal definition and there are no autonomous spheres

termed 'economic,' 'political,' and 'ideological' in capitalist society, but only apparently autonomous institutions.... [We hope to] produce an analysis which recognizes the organic nature of classes even under capitalism and the dialectical relation between class struggle on the one hand and mode of production on the other (1981:312,314).

Such an anthropology would come close to denying the possibility of comparative study of social formations (traditionally called ethnology). This is because it appears to advocate an ontological relativism--the presumption that no external world is apprehensible except through a given, culturally relative set of constructs: "the atom of a mode of production is incapable of universal definition." There is also an apparent contradiction here, for to continue to use "mode of production" as an important analytic device, Kahn and Llobera must have some theory which will allow us to identify "production" when we encounter it; likewise for "accumulation" and "class." Unfortunately, Kahn and Llobera say that "This is not the place for a detailed discussion of the positive implications of the approach outlined..." (p. 312); so the reader is left with unclear notions of the Marxist anthropology which they would advocate.

Dialectics and Materialism in Contemporary Marxism

Consideration of Kahn and Llobera's work raises a fundamental problem in contemporary Marxism, the appropriate relationship of dialectics and materialism in the analysis of the reproduction of social formations. Sartre (1976) conceptualizes social process as a developing dialectical reason, a "totalizing totality" composed of multiple, internal dialectical relations, including the relationship between the analyst and what is being analyzed. In contrast, Habermas conceives of social process as a relationship between different forms of reality, a material process or "system" and the "life world" of ordinary social situations, where people interact and create culture (1981; Hohendahl 1985). The difference between these two views might be characterized as that between unitary and relational dialectics. For Sartre, the analytic stress is on the dynamics of various unique but unified processes, whereas for Habermas, the problem is to identify the various structures which mediate relations between "relatively autonomous" processes, material on the one hand, semiotic on the other.

In Marxist anthropology, one finds implicit analogues of both Sartrean and Habermasian dialectics. "Sartrean" views of social formation reproduction conceive of this process "holistically," while "Habermasian" views distinguish ontologically between cultural or semiotic processes and political economic ones; these are said to "interact" in social reproduction.[1] These differences in Marxist anthropologies are related to a traditional distinction within the discipline regarding culture. The Sartrean view corresponds to the historical particularist view of culture as a "seamless web," encompassing all of social life, while the Habermasian perspective corresponds to a Parsonian/semiotic approach, one which views culture as a particular aspect of human action, to be distinguished from the psychological, the social, etc. This latter view has become increasingly popular within anthropology in the United States (Wolf 1980), where an analytic equation of "the cultural" with "the semiotic" or "the symbolic" is hegemonic.

For the anthropologist concerned with general theoretical issues, such as accounting for the dynamics of similar social formations, transformations from one type of social formation to another, or articulations among social formations, some conception of fundamental units is necessary. The problem here is not one of making analytic distinctions; there is little doubt that for heuristic purposes, it may make sense to distinguish a political economic from a semiotic moment. Rather, the problem is about what is real (ontology) and therefore how our basic analytic categories should be constituted.

There are dangers for Marxist anthropology in both the Habermasian and the Sartrean approaches to dialectics. In our desire to legitimate Marxist approaches within anthropology, and in our critique of the economism of Third International social theory, Marxist anthropologists may have been too quick to reduce the theoretical preeminence of the political economic moment and, in the process, given undue emphasis and autonomy to the semiotic. At the same time, one must avoid the particularist dialectics implicit in Sartre's approach, wherein the dynamics of each social formation are viewed as so unique that a general understanding of social reproduction, let alone social transformation, is theoretically impossible. The key task in avoiding both these problems is to attain clarity about the meaning of the theoretical constructs which we employ in our analyses. Our constructs must be both grounded in the general characteristics of social reproduction and flexible enough to illuminate the dynamics of particular social formations. Such theoretical constructs can be grounded in a Marxist realist ontology; that is, a dialectics which grounds basic analytic categories in the discernible material processes characteristic of human life.[2]

A Marxist Realist Ontology and the Anthropology of Work

To illustrate what can be accomplished with a realist dialectics, we shall consider the problem of work. The reasons for addressing work or production are numerous, including the centrality of "mode of production" to the Althusserian project and the importance of "subsistence activities" to ecological approaches and Harris-style materialism in anthropology. Even Sahlins chooses "production" as the arena of social life through which to illustrate his semiotics in *Culture and Practical Reason* (1976).

Concern with the problems involved in studying work anthropologically arises from the author's comparative study of worker's education, industrial work culture, and the social correlates of computerization. Much speculation about the last, for example, identifies the disappearance of work as a likely consequence of new information technology (e.g., Bell 1973, Schaff 1982). In attempting to find a way to evaluate such claims, it has been necessary to develop an ethnological notion of work; that is, to identify a set of substantive activities which can both be recognized as work in all existing cultural systems and which could conceivably disappear with computerization.

Concern with these issues is also stimulated by attempts within Marxist studies to expand the notion of work, in order to take account of the feminist critique of a "workerist" or "productionist" bias within Marxism.[3] There is a direct connection between the intellectual issue of sorting out a way to talk clearly about work and the solution of major political issues facing progressive movements.

Problems with Current Work Constructs in Anthropology

If it is true that some cross-culturally applicable concept of work is desirable, we might expect to find it in the writing of anthropologists studying work, a growing area of interest within the discipline.[4] Unfortunately, the new work anthropology has failed to develop such a work construct. The constructs used are either overly broad, tied too closely to the semiotics of industrial social formations, or theoretically underdeveloped. For example, Frederick Gamst, President of the Society for the Anthropology of Work, defines work generally as "...purposeful exertion of physical and mental abilities to accomplish something" (1984:58). It seems clear that in a desire to avoid a narrow identification of work with wage labor, Gamst has opted for extreme breadth. The problem with such breadth is that the subject of work anthropology is made indistinguishable from general anthropology; any hope of a systematic study of work as a distinct or distinctive human activity is lost. Also lost is any social dynamics theory--be it Marxist, mechanistic materialist (e.g., Harris 1979, Hunter 1985), or empiricist (e.g., Applebaum 1984a)--which gives causal importance to work institutions. Further, there are major epistemological problems with qualifiers like Gamst's "purposeful." Such criteria appear to require us to ascertain the particular way the people involved feel about their activity before we decide if it is work, a difficult task. Further, such qualifiers are clearly related to industrial notions of "rationality" or "intentionality"; are they necessary or useful cross-cultural notions?

Gamst appears to feel the need to limit his broad conceptualization to make it serviceable. In his essay he does this simply by offering an alternative definition (making no effort to clarify its theoretical relationship to the first definition): "More narrowly considered, work refers to being engaged in a gainful occupation such as being cultivator, craftsman, or administrator" (1984:58). Clearly some criterion to distinguish work from non-work is necessary to any conceptualization, but the criterion selected should make ethnological sense and be theoretically coherent. Gamst's criterion of "gainful" work is relevant in wage-labor society, but how would one distinguish "gainful" from non-gainful activity among gathers and hunters? Such difficulties are best understood as deriving from the tendency criticized by Kahn and Llobera--the generalization of ideologically laden notions from industrial society in an uncritical and inappropriate manner.

There are clearly some occasions when, for justifiable rhetorical reasons, we wish to use criteria derived from one social formation to differentiate among activities in others. Lee (1979), Sahlins (1972), and Johnson (1982) all engage in such an activity (see the review article by Gross 1984): the cross-cultural comparison of the amount of time allocated to subsistence activities in order to evaluate a claim often made about industrial social formations. This is the claim that industrialism had lightened the intensity of human productive activity. To evaluate this claim, one needs to operationalize some notion of work, and for this purpose, the specifics of the activities to be labeled "work" are not as important as the consistent cross-cultural application of the criteria used. Unfortunately, the authors of such studies occasionally pass unconsciously beyond the identification of critical counter-examples and write as if their studies constitute a basis for ethnological generalization. Rutz (1984), for example, argues that these studies generally pay too little attention to the semiotic presumptions built into descriptive categories; consequently, their ethnological value is questionable.

An example of theoretical underdevelopment is the editorial commentary of Herbert Applebaum in his two readers in the anthropology of work (1984a, 1984b). Applebaum's approach to work is empiricist in that he takes the meaning of work as self-evident, requiring no consistent conceptualization. In the second volume, Applebaum offers what may be a definition of work: "Work is productive activity which alters the physical environment to meet human needs..." (1984b:2). This could be read as merely a description, but if it is a definition, one would need to know how productive activity and human needs are to be identified; Applebaum doesn't address such issues. This does not prevent him from making generalizations: "Work exists everywhere because people must solve the problems of subsistence in order to meet their human needs" (1984a:1), and "Work and its organization is the principle force in the building of civilizations; without its efficient use no society or culture can have any future" (1984a:x). Such statements may indeed have some validity, but they are not formulated in a rigorous enough manner to allow for falsification.

Wallman's work (1979) implies the possibility of a kind of emic or semiotic empiricism as a way to a theory of work. This is the idea of constructing a grand list of all the activities in all cultures which are called "work" or described as "worklike" (e.g., "homework"). The problems with this approach are monumental. First, there is the scale of the activity; the *Oxford English Dictionary*, for example, contains over fifteen pages of work and work-related entries. One would imagine that comparable situations may exist in non-English speaking cultures. Second, there is the problem of translation--finding adequate equivalents to the concept "work" which are not, like the notion "purposive activity," slightly masked ways of imposing an industrial "rationality" criterion. Third, there is the problem of how to deal with metaphor. In industrial social formations, the term "work" is used in a variety of other senses, as in "workout" (e.g., running) and "housework" (unpaid household labor). Are such uses to be labeled "merely metaphoric" and thus excluded from the work construct? If so, what is the boundary criterion to be used? If not, at least in Anglo-American societies, almost any activity will turn out to be work, because comparisons to work are virtually omnipresent linguistically. Again, the anthropology of work has become general anthropology.

A different and initially more promising approach is offered by Richard Lee, for whom "...work is defined as those activities that contribute to the direct appropriation of food, water, or materials from the environment" (1979:252). Lee goes on to specify which activities are work, including subsistence activity, manufacture of subsistence tools, and housework, thereby giving a good indication of how his work construct might be used cross-culturally. This is a work construct defined in terms of activities and physically identifiable consequences rather than mental states. However, Lee also argues that consulting oracle disks or listening to reports of game sighting are not work, "...because these activities are carried out in a pleasurable context" (1979:252). He does not justify the introduction of this mentalist qualifier into his physicalist definition, but one might reasonably infer that it is related primarily to the separation of "work" from "play" in industrial society. The operational separation of work from anything pleasurable is of doubtful ethnological validity.

To put the matter positively, what is needed is a concept of work which permits all social analysts, no matter what the social formation which they study, to be reasonably sure that they are talking about the same thing--an ethnological work construct. First, such a work construct should be based on the analysis of activity, not states of mind. Second, the activities to be considered work must be present in all social formations. Third, it should be relatively easy to distinguish work activity from other kinds of activity. Fourth, the criteria to be used to distinguish work from other kinds of activity should make cross-cultural sense and not be tied too closely to one type of social formation (e.g., industrialism). It follows from this that fifth, our work theory must involve a critique of the work constructs of the industrial social formations within which we, both anthropologists and Marxists, have become human ourselves. Sixth, the construct employed should be based on a developmental theory of work, one which helps us account for the underlying similarities and differences in the work institutions manifest in different cultures.

Marxist Approaches to Work

There are at least two good reasons for turning to Marxism in our search for a usable work construct. First, the Marxist tradition of study generally places work or the institutions of production at the center of social theory, which means that a great deal of theorizing about work has already been done. Second, Karl Marx could reasonably be credited with initiating the critical study of work in industrial social formations; to the extent, then, that the problems encountered above are attributable to unrecognized ties to industrialism, the Marxist tradition should help us overcome these difficulties. It is also true, however, that the Marxist tradition is responsible for some of the difficulties described above as well.

The fact that the first volume of Karl Marx's *Capital* (1967) is entitled *A Critical Examination of Capitalist Production* indicates the theoretical importance he gave to the examination of work. One can summarize Marx's basic approach to work in the following propositions:

1. That the activities which make the construct "commodity" key to the analysis of capitalist social formations are important to other social formations as well;
2. That these activities produce things which share a condition of having value, due to the fact that they all contain human labor;
3. That these things have value because they are produced for other people; and therefore
4. That human activity is only work if it results in the production of things which have value for others, the creation of "social use-values."

Marx describes work in the following manner: "Productive activity, if we leave out of sight its special form, viz., the useful character of the labour, is nothing but the expenditure of human labour-power" (1967:44).

Next, Marx introduces a clear developmental dimension to his description of work, by focusing on what happens to social formations where social use-values become commodities:

> Every product of labour is, in all states of society, a use-value; but it is only at a definite historical epoch in a society's development that such a product becomes a commodity, viz., at the epoch when the labour spent on the production of a useful article becomes expressed as one of the objective qualities of the article, i.e., as its value ....[T]he gradual transformation of such products into commodities proceeds *pari passu* with the development of the value form (1967:61).

Later, he appears to argue that value becomes an "objective quality" of the article at that point in history at which the possibility of exchanging one use-value for another use-value enters into the conscious thought of the first producer before production begins. Here, the mentalist component of Marx's theory of production is evident. After developing the key concept "mode of production," Marx moves from identification of analytic categories to the demonstration of how to use these categories to *explain* history.

In addition to providing the basis for a theory of historical development, Marx's discussion of production has a philosophical anthropological side; that is, work is presented as the human essence:

> But coats and linen, like every other element of material wealth that is not the spontaneous produce of Nature, must invariably owe their existence to a special productive activity, exercised with a definite aim, an activity that appropriates particular nature-given materials to particular human wants. So far therefore as labour is a creator of use-value, it is useful labour, it is a necessary condition, independent of all forms of human society, for the existence of the human race; it is an eternal nature-imposed necessity, without which there can be no material exchanges between man and Nature, and therefore no life (1967:42-43).

Elsewhere, Marx refers to labor as "the normal activity of living [human] beings" and is critical of Smith for treating labor as "the mere sacrifice of rest, freedom, and happiness" (p. 46). "Marx calls productive activity 'the life of the species'; it is man's (sic) life activity...and it is common to people in all societies" (Ollman 1975:101).

There are several positive aspects to Marx's work construct. It is largely physicalist, with a focus on a particular range of distinct activities. It is conceived as a concept which is to be applicable cross-culturally and universally. His work construct is clearly based on a critique of work in industrial society. It is also theoretical--that is, while the distinctive features of work are constant, its specific form changes with social evolution; moreover, the changes in productive activity are held to be intimately connected with broader social change.

Nonetheless, there are substantial difficulties with Marx's work construct. One is the ambiguity in his argument about the appropriate place of semiotic process in the analysis of work. Initially, the reader is told that the nature of the needs being satisfied by the product of work (the use of the product) is irrelevant to whether or not it is work. Later, however, Crusoe's prayers are not to be considered work, because he enjoys praying. (This may well be the origin of Lee's qualifier pointed out above.) Yet Smith is criticized for defining work as the opposite of leisure. While Marx finds it impossible to ignore states of mind, his ways of handling the relationship of semiotic processes to the nature of work are not consistent enough.

Such essentially terminological ambiguities are of no great importance to the analysis of work in capitalism, which is probably why Marx was not bothered by them. Yet, as documented by Kahn and Llobera, a great deal of effort has been expended on attempting to extend Marx's analysis to a broader range of social forms. Because Marx's general theory of social dynamics is dependent upon a theory of production, flaws in the theoretical construction of the relationship between semiotic and material moments in production may undermine the development of general theory.

Even greater difficulties follow from the way in which Marx identifies production with human essence. Balbus has argued that Marx's productionist human ontology is an inappropriate inversion of Hegel's idealist anthropology. Marx is not just giving recognition to the empirical importance of production; rather,

> In Marx's hands, then, labor becomes an ontological category; it is that activity which constitutes the Being of human

beings. Put otherwise, production is the one constant, un-changing structure within which human history unfolds and on which the flux of human history depends (1982:13).

Balbus proceeds to link this ontology to French Marxist anthropology's difficulties in using "mode of production", tying them to Marx's uncritical use of categories taken from industrial social formations:

> When Marx argues that 'the way and mode in which they gained their living explains why in one place politics played the decisive role and in another, Catholicism,' he takes refuge in the notion that it is possible in all places to distinguish the activity of gaining a living, i.e., production, from nonproduc-tion activities....With his notion of a trans-historical 'gaining a living,' then, Marx is guilty of doing precisely what he ac-cuses his bourgeois theoretical opponents of doing, i.e., projecting the specific logic of bourgeois society back into the past and thus reading the past entirely in terms of the cate-gories of the present (1982:34-35).

Thus, Balbus identifies the conceptual problems encountered above among both French Marxist and work anthropologists as existing already in Marx's productionist ontology. This stance interferes with the ability of Marxists to take pre-commodity-based social formations as serious objects of study in their own right; instead, such social formations are analyzed mostly for the presence or ab-sence of events of interest primarily because of their importance to industrialism. For example, in Mandel's work (1962), the focus on the discovery of "surplus" leads to the creation of a pre-capitalistic "just so" story about the economic marginality of simple societies.

Following Foucault, some Marxists (e.g., Barnett in Barnett and Silverman 1979) argue that primary emphasis should be placed on the social constitution of categories. The problems with this approach, both epistemological and explanatory, are essentially the same as with the semiotic approaches to work anthropology dis-cussed above (e.g., Wallman). However, the general tendency of contemporary Marxist approaches to work appears to be to avoid the dangers of either semioticist or political economist reduc-tionisms by opting for an extremely broad concept of work. Wit-ness, for example, the approach to production which informs the work of Roy Bhaskar in an otherwise strong philosophical defense of *The Possibility of Naturalism* (1979):

> [F]ollowing Marx, one can regard social activity as consisting, analytically, in *production*, that is, in work on (and with), entailing the transformation of...material causes....[P]raxis is both work, that is, conscious *production*, and (normally unconscious) reproduction of the conditions of production, that is, society....[S]ocial activity consists analytically in production; that is, in work on and the transformation of given objects...(1979:43,44,47).

There are a number of important ambiguities here, such as whether the reproduction of the conditions of production (society) is a social activity, and the relation of material causes to objects. These ambiguities harm Bhaskar's overall project, which is an attempt to reestablish a realist or materialist foundation for social science. What is intended nonetheless appears to be a very broad concept of work, but as with the work anthropologists, by making *everything* work, it becomes impossible to explain anything in terms of work.[5]

In summary, this analysis of Marxist work constructs has aimed to establish the importance of Marxism to a critical, developmental, ethnological theory of work, even if there are problems with those generated thus far. What follows is an attempt to construct a more serviceable notion of work and give it as firm a materialist foundation as possible.

An Ethnological Work Construct

A summary of several semiotic points already made, about the way "work" is used in industrial societies, provides an important clue to grounding a viable ethnological work construct. Although the term "work" is used in numerous ways in the United States, these uses can usually be reduced to one of three basic types. First, North Americans use the term "work" to refer to activity exchanged for income--wage/salary labor. Second, they use it to refer to a wide range of often mutually exclusive activities which are work-like, in that they involve qualities like planning, effort, purpose, boredom, self-expression, self-fulfillment, and so on. All of these are associated with paid labor, and since the experience of paid work is extremely varied, the activities to which this comparative use of "work" is applied are equally varied--virtually any activity can be presented as "work-like." Third, the term is used more narrowly to refer to activity which is necessary to the day-to-day, physical reproduction of the conditions for life, the quality of life, or the life-style of people in one's intimate social networks, such as growing food, making tools, driving the family car to the supermarket, preparing the family dinner, cleaning the house, or gathering wood for a cooking fire. As N!ai says, "Even if you hadn't worked, if hunger grabbed you, you still got something to eat." When children in the United States are taught "the meaning of the value of work," this is, among other things, an attempt to make them conscious of the necessity of participating in certain collective, physical activities which result in a collective benefit, including both activities like keeping the house clean and finding a way to earn an income which makes sense in relation to the needs of others in their interdependence networks.

Ethnologically, the first "job" use of "work" is clearly not cross-culturally appropriate. The second, "work-like," is too broad. "Work" in the third sense, as social activities which contribute directly to the material well-being of one's social networks, does take place in all social formations and is relatively distinguishable from other human activities.

Leila Liebowitz, shortly before her untimely death, was developing a theory which gave work in this third sense a strategically important place in human evolution. From her point of view (1981), it was the habit of obtaining the predominant proportion of subsistence in and for a social group which provided proto-hominids with the crucial adaptive advantage. This pattern therefore constitutes the distinctive (as opposed to essential) behavioral feature of the human genus. (Among non-human primates, only a small portion of subsistence activity is carried out in groups and the results shared (Tanner 1981, Galdikas and Telecki 1981). It is thus logical to suggest that later fundamental transformations of such activity or "work"--the mediation of subsistence activity by the commodity form, for example--would be intimately related to general transformations in human history. Liebowitz's perspective also helps to explain the wide distribution of a social construct like this third use of "work," in that it corresponds to an important and distinctive human activity and is likely an early and enduring focus of human symboling.

Following physical anthropology's lead, the physical and semiotic aspects of work can be related analytically; there is good reason to believe that an analyst could identify some comparable group of activities and symboling in any past, present or future social formation. Thus, work can be defined ethnologically as follows: *the social production of social subsistence use-values.* This involves the social extraction and manipulation of physical materials to fulfill some collective human need or problem of day-to-day physical reproduction, like food, shelter, and clothing-- needs whose existence follows from our condition as life forms.

Such a work construct meets the requirements outlined above: it is focused on activity; the activities focused on are present in all social formations. And, because the construct focuses on what results from the activities, work is relatively easy to distinguish from other activities. Further, the activities have distinguishing features which make cross-cultural sense, both emically and etically; they are easily connected to an evolutionary, developmental theory of social formations. Finally, because the construct is developed out of an analysis of the way work takes place in industrial social formations, it can avoid the inappropriate implications of which Kahn and Llobera are so critical.

Possible criticisms of this ethnological construct

What follows is an attempt to show how such a work construct might be used by anticipating several criticisms which could possibly be made of it:

1. While clearly based on a realist ontology, is this construct also dialectical--that is, does the theory of social causation embedded within it allow sufficient scope for human agency, drawing attention to primary areas of social dynamism? For example, embedded in the construct is a distinction between activities resulting in tangible things, like food, and intangible "production" or "reproduction" of "things" like "emotional support" or "social relations." Yet, as modern feminists have argued, one of the workerist aspects of traditional Marxism and its focus on the industrial proletariat is the devaluation of forms of activity which are both necessary to reproduction of the social system *and* traditionally female. Shouldn't one choose analytic categories which break down, rather than reinforce, analytic distinctions between material and non-material activities?

The work construct outlined accepts much of the feminist argument. For example, it places activities like housework, meal preparation, laundry, and food shopping at the center of work concern; because they all involve the manipulation of physical materials for subsistence needs, they are as much work as coal mining and steel making. While separating these activities analytically from other major processes, like emotional support, it does this for justifiable theoretical reasons. Such a step allows development of theory which can explain social transformation in terms of unitary types of activity.

2. Yet doesn't such a theory mean that several activities which often result in income are probably best *not* thought of as work? Extreme examples include the "production" of pet rocks or the provision of summer camp experiences for Cabbage Patch dolls. Less extreme cases include the activity which goes into protecting trade secrets, public relations, and advertising-- activities which are more clearly related to the reproduction of capitalist social relations of production, and the "production" of surplus value, than to the provision of physical subsistence. Indeed, a good case could be made that teaching, journalism, and anthropology itself would often not qualify as work under this definition. Can we really use a definition of work which doesn't include the things many of us do for wages/salaries?

The construct proposed does encourage distinguishing between activities which are directly involved in meeting physical needs and those which make more sense in relation to the imperatives of the reproduction of social relations in the social formation within which the work is taking place. This has the benefit of focusing attention on the justness of such social relations, rather than presuming their legitimacy.

3. Yet if some substantial part of the activity mediated by the commodity form in contemporary social formations is no longer to be considered work, then what is to come of the notion "mode of production," surely an element central to any analysis which wants to be called Marxist? Does it make sense to abstract production analysis from much of what we normally think of as capitalism?

The ethnological work construct is designed to enhance the utility of the mode of production notion. It does this by avoiding the problems of extreme breadth alluded to above as often characteristic of both work anthropology and neo-Marxist conceptions of production, like that of Bhaskar. It is also designed to allow causal analysis of the basic dynamics of any social formation. Consequently, any analysis of work in a specific social formation would only *begin* with description of the items produced socially to provide subsistence. It would also require knowledge of the technology of their production, the social relations within which production takes place, and the cultural constructs through which these material and social relations are perceived.

The overall aim of such specific studies of work would be comparative, to differentiate those aspects of work activity whose imperative is mostly material from those whose imperative lies elsewhere in the social totality. The approach outlined above would allow a more dialectic understanding of mode of production, and the dynamics of social formation reproduction, to be constructed on the comparisons. Comparative analysis of specific cases would identify different relationships among basic elements in different social formations. An ethnology of work based on this approach would likely indicate a more or less straightforward connection between technical work relations and social reproduction in earlier social formations (e.g., gathering and hunting). In contrast, a looser relationship between techniques of production and reproduction, one of greater relative autonomy, might be found to be characteristic of later social formations. Mode of production in more complex social formations is probably less determined by technical relations than by social and cultural ones (e.g., accumulation of surplus value, exploitation). As each of these increases in internal complexity, the imperatives of subsistence are more highly mediated.

Illustrations of the Ethnological Work Construct

At this point, the standard anthropological argument would proceed by establishing a particular ethnographic context and demonstrate how the construct developed illuminates this context better than competing constructs. However, such single case arguments tend to deflect attention from the kind of general conceptual problems which are the focus of this essay. The only way to test adequately the value of the argument developed above--to present an account of work which spans all known types of social formations--is clearly beyond the scope of this article. Consequently, two brief illustrations of how the construct might be applied will be presented, one which shows how the construct developed reverberates with and generalizes a particularly insightful example of insurgent anthropology, and a second which demonstrates how the approach outlined helps deal with a contemporary political issue.

First, consider Taussig's discussion of *The Devil and Commodity Fetishism in South America* (1983). He argues that the semiotics of certain Colombian peasants and Bolivian tin miners contain a plausible critique of both capitalist analytic categories and social relations, and that these critical semiotics should be treated as a viable alternative to capitalist analysis, not as some pre-scientific "myth." There is a fundamental similarity between the semiotics he describes and those of North American workers, who often distinguish between a "real" job, one "where you get your hands dirty," and "paper-pushing" and other forms of labor felt to be less real. Now clearly, such semiotics are often manipulated, as when tied to invidious gender distinctions, just as peasant self-consciousness can become a block to the development of solidarity with wage laborers. Nonetheless, these Latin and North American "ethno-semantics" capture an important sense in which capitalistic labor is "unproductive" in a material sense. It is precisely this anti-productive aspect of industrialism which is highlighted by the ethnological work construct. The dimension underlying these two situations is the difference between activities which contribute directly to the well-being of social networks and those which separate people--indeed, are often in contradiction to this well-being, because they reproduce social relations of exploitation.

Second, consider again an issue raised early on: the social correlates of new information technology. Many futurists envision a "post industrial" crisis; some like Adam Schaff see this crisis centering on profound psychological consequences, due to "the end of work as we know it" because of "total automation" (1982). Others, like socialist planner Mike Cooley of the Greater London Enterprise Board, also feel there is a crisis correlated with new information technology, but they see the crisis as a social one, stemming from the inability of contemporary capitalism to insure that activity necessary to the provisioning of society is performed. Cooley calls this latter activity "production for social need" (1985:5), and he sees its absence as a consequence of counterproductive tendencies inherent in the current industrial social formation.

Underlying these contrasting analyses are different work constructs. Shaff's conception equates work and wage labor, while Cooley's conceives of work in terms consonant with "social production of social use-values." In identifying the main problem as one of self-identity, Shaff sidesteps the problem most obvious to those currently unemployed--how to get an income if you haven't a job. "Total automation" is presumed, but this is only possible if production is treated as a completely technical matter. It is the fallacy of technicism (Hakken 1985) to abstract production from the complex social relations within which it is embedded, such as the necessity of worker consumption to the realization of profit. Further, Shaff's analysis even obscures understanding of the psychological consequences of information technology. This is because the psychological consequences of any new technology depend upon the nature of worker behavioral response, both individual and collective, to it (Clawson 1979, Shaiken 1985). In short, Shaff's analysis mystifies the issue of new technology, and this mystification follows from the nature of his work construct.

In contrast, Cooley's approach draws attention precisely to the extent to which institutions of work and other social relations may be in conflict. He sees the trajectory of his industrial social formation in contradiction to meeting fundamental human and social needs. His writing demonstrates that the critique of industrial work notions, and the development of alternative ways to think about work, are an essential precondition to the development of a political program adequate to the current crisis of capitalist social formations. If Cooley is right, and we need to dissociate our concept of work from the dynamics of capitalist economies, there is clearly an important role for work anthropology. This role is to develop a way of thinking about work which is equally applicable to past, present, and future social formations. This work anthropology will have much to contribute to both general anthropology and left politics. Further, if a truly dialectical materialist Marxism can provide the framework for the ethnology of a process so distinctive of humans as the social production of social subsistence use-values, then such a theory is likely to be relevant to other problems as well. The future for Marxist anthropology is both more materialist *and* more dialectical.

NOTES

1   Both these approaches should be kept separate from those which claim to be inspired by Marxism but are less concerned about being dialectical. These latter may be political economically

reductionist, tending to see human behavior, whether symbolic or "practical," as a more or less straightforward consequence of political economic process and allowing little room for human agency (e.g., Elling 1985). It is also possible to be reductionist in a more "cultural" direction, placing causal emphasis almost exclusively on semiotic rather than material processes (e.g., Barnett in Barnett and Silverman 1979).

2   "Marxist realism" or "realist materialism" is a philosophical position being developed in response to the relativistic ontologies and epistemologies which dominate analytic philosophy (Quine 1969) and the philosophy of social science. Among Marxist realism's advocates are David-Hillel Rubin and Roy Bhaskar (1979). Gregor McLennan attempts to apply the perspective to history (1981).

3   Feminists are often critical of the tendency of Marxists to equate "work" with "wage labor" and "workers" with "the industrial proletariat" (Campbell 1984). Besides obscuring the importance of women's work, such tendencies are an impediment to the development of an adequate theory of social transformation, especially as some bid *Farewell to the Working Class* (Gorz 1982). Important current debates in Britain, for example, center on the related issues of who is in the working class and the relative agency of the working class and other social groups in the revolutionary process.

4   Work anthropology, through its stress on participant observation, made a substantial methodological contribution to the post-Braverman (1974) revival of the sociology of work. The general ethnography of earlier anthropologists, much of which is relevant to work, provides some useful rhetorical examples to political economists as well as substantive economic anthropologists in their battles against neo-classical economics. Nonetheless, work anthropology has not made a substantial contribution to significant current theoretical debates in the social study of work. These debates include not only the issue of the future of work alluded to above; they include the question of skill degradation (Wood 1982) and labor market segmentation (Gordon, et al. 1982). This failure to contribute to theory is yet another reason to clarify the core concerns of work anthropology (Greaves 1985).

5   These comments are found within Bhaskar's attempt to specify the scientific object of social science, and they should not be taken as a developed theory of work. They do illustrate a way of talking very broadly about production--e.g., to include uncon-

scious activity--which seems to equate work and most general social activity. This same way of talking is manifest in Nash's (1984) and Gamst's (1984) notions of work as respectively "purposeful activity" or "purposive activity," and especially in Weltfish's very general "expenditure of life energy." Given such definitions, to talk about the character of production as influencing or determining the character of other social activity is tautological: the bulk of social activity influences all of social activity. Such comments probably draw some inspiration from Marx's own rhetoric, as in the *Philosophical Manuscripts of 1844*: "Religion, family, state, law, morality, science, art, etc., are only *particular* forms of production and fall under its general law" (Easton and Guddat 1967:304).

BIBLIOGRAPHY

Althusser, Louis, and Etienne Balibar
  1970 Reading Capital. New York: Pantheon.
Applebaum, Herbert, ed.
  1984a Work in Non-Market and Transitional Societies. Albany: State University of New York Press.
  1984b Work in Market and Industrial Societies. Albany: State University of New York Press.
Balbus, Isaac D.
  1982 Marxism and Domination: A Neo-Hegelian, Feminist, Psychoanalytic Theory of Sexual, Political, and Technological Liberation. Princeton: Princeton University Press.
Barnett, Steve and Martin G. Silverman
  1979 Ideology and Everyday Life. Ann Arbor: University of Michigan Press.
Bell, Daniel
  1973 The Coming of Post-Industrial Society. New York: Basic Books.
Bhaskar, Roy
  1979 The Possibility of Naturalism. New Jersey: Humanities Press.
Braverman, Harry
  1974 Labor and Monopoly Capital. The Degradation of Work in the Twentieth Century. New York: Monthly Review Press.
Clawson, Dan
  1979 Bureaucracy and the Labor Process. New York: Monthly Review Press.

Campbell, Beatrix
1984 Wigan Pier Revisited. London: Virago.
Cooley, Mike
1985 The Cost of Social Need. Guardian, August 3rd.
Easton, Lloyd, and Kurt Guddat, eds.
1967 Writings of the Young Marx on Philosophy and Society. Garden City, N.Y.: Anchor Books.
Elling, Ray
1985 Cross-National Study of Health Systems: Is Socialism Hazardous to Health? Paper presented to the Eighty-seventh annual meeting, American Anthropological Association, Washington, D.C.
Gamst, Frederick C.
1984 Two Considerations for an Anthropology of Work. *In* Work in Non-Market and Transitional Societies. H. Applebaum, ed. Pp. 56-61. Albany: State University of New York Press.
Galdikas, Birute M.F., and Geza Teleki
1981 Variation in Subsistence Activities of Female and Male Pongids: New Perspectives on the Origins of Hominid Labor Division. Current Anthropology 22(3):241-256.
Gordon, David, et al.
1982 Segmented Work, Divided Workers. Cambridge: Cambridge University Press.
Gorz, André
1982 Farewell to the Working Class: an Essay on Post-Industrial Socialism. London: Pluto.
Greaves, Tom
1985 What Is the Anthropology of Work? Paper presented to the Eighty-seventh annual meeting, American Anthropological Association, Washington, D.C.
Gross, Daniel
1984 Time Allocation: A Tool for the Study of Cultural Behavior. *In* Annual Review of Anthropology. B. Siegal, ed. Pp. 519-558. Palo Alto, CA: Annual Reviews.
Habermas, Juergen
1981 Theorie des Kommunikativen Handelns, (Vol.2). Frankfurt: Surkamp.
Hakken, David
1985 Studying the Future of Work. Paper presented to the Eighty-seventh annual meeting, American Anthropological Association, Washington, D.C.
Harris, Marvin
1979 Cultural Materialism: The Struggle for a Science of Culture. New York: Random House.

Hohendahl, Peter
  1985 Habermas' Critique of the Frankfurt School. New German
     Critique 35:3-26.
Hunter, David
  1985 Subsistence Strategies and the Organization of Social Life.
     In Anthropology: Contemporary Perspectives. David K.
     Hunter and Phillip Whitten, eds. Pp. 175-180. Boston:
     Little, Brown.
Johnson, Allen
  1985 In Search of the Affluent Society. *In* David K. Hunter
     and Phillip Whitten, eds., Anthropology: Contemporary
     Perspectives, Pp. 201-206. Boston: Little Brown.
Kahn, Joel, and Josep Llobera
  1981 Towards a New Marxism or a New Anthropology. *In*
     The Anthropology of Pre-Capitalist Societies. Kahn and
     Llobera, eds. Pp. 263-329. London: The MacMillan Press.
Lee, Richard
  1979 The !Kung San: Men, Women, and Work in a Foraging
     Society. New York: Cambridge University Press.
Liebowitz, Leila
  1980 Double Entendre: or, Yet Another Model of the Origins
     of the Division of Labor along Sex Lines Which Tries to
     Integrate Biological and Social Factors. Paper presented to
     the Twenty-first annual meeting, Northeastern
     Anthropological Association, Saratoga Springs, New York.
Mandel, Earnest
  1962 Marxist Economic Theory (Vol. One). New York:
     Monthly Review Press.
Marx, Karl
  1967 Capital: A Critique of Political Economy (Vol. One).
     New York: International Publishers.
McLennan, Gregor
  1981 Marxism and the Methodologies of History. London: New
     Left Books.
Nash, June
  1984 The Anthropology of Work. *In* Work in Non-Market
     and Transitional Societies. H. Applebaum, ed. Pp. 45-56.
     Albany: State University of New York Press.
Ollman, Bertell
  1975 Alienation: Marx's Conception of Man in Capitalist
     Society. New York: Cambridge University Press.
Quine, W.V.
  1969 Ontological Relativity and Other Essays. New York:
     · Columbia University Press.
Ruben, David-Hillel
  1979 Marxism and Materialism. Sussex: Harvester Press.

Rutz, Henry
1984 Units of Time Budget Analysis: The Social Construction of Time and Its Allocation by Fijian Households. Clinton, N.Y.: Department of Anthropology, Hamilton College.
Sahlins, Marshall
1972 Stone Age Economics. Chicago: Aldine.
1976 Culture and Practical Reason. Chicago: University of Chicago Press.
Sartre, Jean Paul
1976 Critique of Dialectical Reason. London: New Left Books.
Schaff, Adam
1982 Occupation vs. Work. *In* Microelectronics and Society. Friedriche, Gunter, and Adam Schaff, eds. Pp. 322-334. New York: New American Library.
Shaiken, Harley
1984 Work Transformed: Automation and Labor in the Computer Age. New York: Holt, Rinehart, and Winston.
Tanner, Nancy M.
1981 On Becoming Human: A Model of the Transition from Ape to Human and the Reconstruction of Early Social Life. Cambridge: Cambridge University Press.
Taussig, Michael
1983 The Devil and Commodity Fetishism in South America. Chapel Hill: University of North Carolina Press.
Wallman, Sandra, ed.
1979 Social Anthropology of Work. London: Academic Press.
Weltfish, Gene
1974 Work, an Anthropological View. Saratoga Springs, NY: Empire State College.
Wolf, Eric
1980 They Divide and Subdivide and Call it Anthropology. New York Times, November 30th.
Wood, Stephen, ed.
1982 The Degradation of Work? Skill, Deskilling, and the Labour Process. London: Hutchinson.

SUMER AND THE INDUS VALLEY CIVILIZATION COMPARED: TOWARDS AN HISTORICAL UNDERSTANDING OF THE EVOLUTION OF EARLY STATES

Philip L. Kohl

Late nineteenth century evolutionary writings, such as Engels' *Origin of the Family, Private Property, and the State*, depicted a social world that had continually transformed itself since the early hominids first diverged from an unknown ancestral ape. Change was not only characteristic of natural and social reality, but it was marked by sudden, disjunctive, qualitative leaps and transformations in which, to adopt the modern biological terminology, periods of relative equilibrium were interrupted or punctuated by short intervals of rapid development, which, in turn, led to the emergence of qualitatively new social formations. Given the task of attempting to order and explain the countless non-Western societies, which were first systematically described at this time, as well as to account for preindustrial, historically documented societies, early evolutionary works necessarily adopted a typological and comparative perspective that attempted to order diversity, in part, through elaborate systems of classification. Also implicit within this ambitious attempt was a search for and an unquestioning belief in the reality of cross-cultural regularities among societies often widely separated in space and time. Thus, as in Engels' study, features of pre-classical Greek gentile organization could be perfectly paralleled to structural characteristics found among the Iroquois.

These late nineteenth century characteristics of what in the West were termed unilinear evolutionary models are well-known and, to some extent, also appear in neo-evolutionary writings, which are currently experiencing almost a renaissance in Western anthropology and archeology. Yet there are subtle differences between the nineteenth century evolutionary view and contemporary neo-evolutionary Western writings which, in a sense, radically alter the utility, validity, and, above all, political import or consequences that follow from adherence to a cultural evolutionary perspective. Firstly, what was a legitimate task in the late nineteenth century--ordering an inchoate mass of data--can degenerate into a formulaic listing of commonly accepted features, themselves now almost platitudes, that distinguish one evolutionary level from another, as, for example, state from pre-state societies. The search for regularities, understandable enough in the late nineteenth century, can lead today, given our far greater ethnographic and prehistoric knowledge, to a deliberate refusal to examine interesting differences or variations among early class societies. As I have argued elsewhere (Kohl 1984:128-129), a valid, scientifically demonstrable cultural evolutionary perspective should be distinguished from an evolutionistic approach that engages in trite, tautological typological exercises that do not advance our understanding of either past or present social reality.

More insidiously, neo-evolutionary writings often adopt a continuous, gradualistic adaptive vision of social change that is sometimes even explicitly contrasted with a revolutionary approach that insists upon rapid, punctuated periods of qualitative transformation. Evolution becomes the antithesis of revolution, hardly the outcome envisioned by Engels in 1884. R. Cohen (1981:207), for example, in discussing human values associated with an evolutionary epistemology, explicitly states: "... evolutionary theory applied to human affairs leads to conservatism", a conclusion that he admits to feeling "uncomfortable" with but one that he feels follows inescapably from his understanding of evolution. Similarly, H.J.M. Claessen's recent attempt (1984:365) to distinguish the early from the mature state begins his essentially typological exercise on this rather flat and listless note:

> Though the evolution of sociopolitical organization is a *continuous* series of processes in the course of which one form more or less *gradually* develops out of another, it still seems possible to classify sociopolitical phenomenon in terms of stabilized forms.... The state, however it may be defined...is certainly one such *stabilized* form (emphasis added).

A literary critic, totally unfamiliar with the theoretical literature on the origin of the state, would experience little difficulty in contrasting the unthreatening, managerially functional, and even natural state referred to above with Engels' insistence that the emergence of the state means that society "has involved itself in insoluble self-contradiction and is cleft into irreconcilable antagonisms which it is powerless to exorcise" (1973: 229). According to the latter vision, the emergence of the state is not just a natural process, inextricably linked to gradually growing complexity, but also a conscious act by which more powerful groups with specific economic interests attempt to extend and perpetuate their control over the entire society by creating a supposedly external, neutral power, the state, to maintain order. To quote Engels directly:

> The lowest interests--base greed, brutal appetites, sordid avarice, selfish robbery of the common wealth--inaugurate the new, civilized, class society. It is by the vilest means-- theft, violence, fraud, treason--that the old classless gentile society is undermined and overthrown (1973:161).

In other words, neo-evolutionary or, as I prefer, evolutionistic, writings eliminate that great motor of social change, class struggle, from their analyses and predictably produce overly general, uninteresting, banal, and scarcely credible accounts of the development of complex society.

Another problem, related in that reality is ignored, concerns the appropriate use of sources for understanding cultural evolution. When Morgan and Engels were writing in the late nineteenth century, it seemed perfectly legitimate to juxtapose Iroquoian development with that historically documented for the ancient Greeks. Today, it is becoming increasingly clear, as Eric Wolf has brilliantly demonstrated in his *Europe and The People Without History* (1982), that ethnographically documented societies, all of which have come into direct or indirect contact with an expanding, technologically superior industrial order, experience profound and sudden changes that radically alter their livelihoods or internal evolutionary trajectories. While they remain a source of analogy, such societies cannot themselves be considered examples of any cultural evolutionary process distinct from the historically specific but global process largely defined and directed by the expansion of the capitalist world system. For all its faults, the prehistoric record remains our only (and, consequently, our best) source for the emergence of state society. To extend the argument further, analysis of the prehistoric record for purposes of determining the development of complex society also must take into account larger historical processes--analogous, though of course not identical, to the expansion of capitalism--which disrupt and alter the internal evolutionary trajectories of societies that become caught up in or incorporated within these processes. In other words, adoption of an evolutionary perspective can never supplant broadly conceived *historical* analyses of processes affecting all societies that find themselves directly or indirectly involved in the relevant webs or networks of interaction. Evolutionary and historical explanations should not be opposed, but signify complementary, if not, at times, synonymous types of analyses. The rest of this paper will attempt to illustrate this central thesis by contrasting the nature of early complex society in South Asia, the so-called Indus Valley or Harappan civilization, with the earlier, and, therefore, necessarily influential Sumerian state that emerged in southern Mesopotamia.

The Indus Valley Civilization and Ancient Mesopotamia Compared

Before we begin, it is useful to recall that Western neo-evolutionists, like E. Service (1975), list the Indus Valley civilization as an example of an early, archeologically documented state formation, according it the same evolutionary status as that granted to Sumer, pharaonic Egypt, and Shang China. Traditional reconstructions of the Indus Valley civilization have always attempted to explain its enigmatic remains by reference to historically recorded features of ancient Sumer or Egypt. Thus, for example, Sir Mortimer Wheeler (1968:35) compared the so-called granaries at Mohenjo-daro and Harappa with unexcavated storage facilities mentioned in cuneiform documents from Ur and with the White House or treasury of Upper Egypt. Such a comparison not only was meant to elucidate the presumed function of these public buildings of the Indus cities, but also was intended to illustrate how the Indus Valley civilization was ruled by priest-kings who paid their dependent labor force in barley rations or in a manner roughly identical to that known from Mesopotamia. Although Wheeler argued that the "idea" of civilization may have diffused from Mesopotamia to the East, both he and later neo-evolutionists insisted that the Harappan civilization essentially followed its own evolutionary path which remarkably resembled that of contemporary complex societies farther west.

Similarity between organizational features of Harappan society and those better documented to the west were stressed, while, at the same time, many scholars noted certain obvious distinctions. Briefly, the relative uniformity of Harappan materials from their standardized ceramics, burnt bricks with invariant dimensions (28X14X7 cm.), repetitively designed square stamp seals with inscriptions, and common utilitarian metal tools--has been contrasted with the more striking diversity apparent in similar classes of materials from Mesopotamia. Writing, which developed principally for accounting purposes in Mesopotamia, contrasts functionally with what is known of the enigmatic Indus Valley inscriptions, those of which survived apparently serving primarily as individual or familial markers. The relative abundance of monumental art and statuary in Mesopotamia contrasts sharply with the dozen or more relatively small modeled objects from all of the excavated Harappan sites. The absence is too striking and consistent not to reflect basic differences in craft organization and productive activities between Harappa and Mesopotamia.

The public temples within walled sacred precincts in Sumerian cities can be distinguished from the public architecture within the raised or platformed walled citadels at Mohenjo-daro and Harappa. It should also be noted that some scholars (Shaffer 1982) today question the identification of the large structure at Mohenjo-daro as a granary. It is a structure which does not resemble the so-called granary or storage facility at Harappa. The exact function of the Great Bath and associated complex at Mohenjo-daro remains an enigma, and nothing structurally similar or perhaps functionally identical to the temples and palaces of Mesopotamia has been uncovered on Indus sites, save possibly for the partially excavated Assembly or Pillared Hall situated south of the the Great Bath.

The regular, orthogonally intersecting, and well-drained streets of Harappan sites, cities and villages, contrast sharply, of course, with the twisting lanes and *cul de sacs* of the organically developing cities of southern Mesopotamia--at least to the extent that one can generalize from the Larsa period plan of Ur and the Sargonid remains from Eshnunna. However, the northern Mesopotamian site of Tell Taya, although still incompletely published, apparently was better planned than Ur or Eshnunna. The site, consisting of a walled inner town surrounded by extensive rings of suburbs covering 155 ha., expanded dramatically during the second half of the third millennium and, subsequently, was displaced by Rimah as the dominant city in the area during the second millennium (Reade 1982:77). In other words, unlike Ur or Eshnunna, Taya developed suddenly. Its town plan reflects this history more than it demonstrates rigid governmental direction. Cities built by the same culture, like Boston and New York or Moscow and Leningrad, may exhibit markedly different town plans that primarily relate to each city's specific history of development. What remains anomalous about Harappan town planning is that villages, as well as cities, exhibit similar features of layout and evident municipal administration (see below).

The problem of non-comparability limits generalizations about differences in individual house forms. Slums or poorer residential and industrial quarters have not been extensively excavated in Mesopotamia. A huddle of reed huts enclosed by a double wall was uncovered at Uruk (Crawford 1977:36), and Woolley (Hawkes and Woolley 1963:425) noted the occurrence of slums and "shoddy' 1-story houses northwest of the Temenos at Ur. Regional and/or chronological differences, such as the lack of open courts in the Sargonid houses at Eshnunna (Frankfort 1934:17), appear to distinguish the more substantial excavated private dwellings within Mesopotamia. The spacious, well-built Larsa period houses at Ur differ from one another but are said to have all been constructed along the same lines (Woolley and Mallowan 1976:23); that is, generally 2-storied houses built around a central courtyard onto which the rooms opened. Businesses or shops sometimes were attached, and nearly all these well-built houses had what was identified as a "domestic chapel" at their rear away from their entrance; familial burial vaults often were constructed under the brick pavement of the chapel. For Old Babylonian Nippur, E. Stone (1981) recently has utilized archeological, textual, and ethnoarcheological data to argue that virilocal extended family and nuclear family residences co-existed in the same area and period depending upon life-cycle and generational events within families. The former extended family structures were significantly larger than the single living and two subsidiary room arrangements for nuclear families, although the small size of the Nippur houses, in general, should be noted, ranging from around 16 sq.m. to around 93 sq.m. per house with an estimated *roofed* area per average nuclear family of 23 sq.m. (Stone 1981, table 5).

The lower city at Mohenjo-daro contained both domestic structures and what appears to have been commercial buildings or artisans' workshops (DK-G area, block 1). Five slightly different structural modules or basic types, differing primarily in the position of the courtyard, recently have been defined for the domestic houses at Mohenjo-daro (Sarcina 1979:437). This study showed that most houses encompassed an area of slightly more than 100 sq.m., though interesting exceptions occurred for three of the five modules with some houses exceeding 250 sq.m. Additional variation within Indus Valley remains may be suggested by the excavations of the so-called workmen's quarter or barracks-like structures immediately north of the citadel at Harappa. Inter- or intra-mural burials were not typically observed within the houses of the Indus cities.

The environmental setting of Sumer, of course, differed from that occupied by the misnamed, spatially extensive "Indus Valley" civilization. Tremendous regional diversity across the vast area dotted with Harappan sites makes generalizations about the ecological constraints of the latter civilization hazardous, while environmentally-based difficulties, such as salinization and recurrent flooding during spring harvest, broadly characterized the entire southern alluvial plain of Mesopotamia.

Both civilizations, of course, practiced irrigation agriculture, and the Indus, like the Euphrates, is an aggrading river that in Sind flows above the level of the plain. Its flood-plain may extend to a width of 16 km., and in times of high water the river may carry 20 to 40 times its normal flow (Thapar 1982:7). Unlike the Euphrates, the Indus receives two periods of inundation: one in March-April when the snows melt in the Himalayas; and the other in late summer when the lower mountains receive the southwestern monsoon. This double peaking meant that both summer *(kharif)* and winter *(rabi)* crops could have been sown. B. and R. Allchin (1982:192) suggest that the Harappans' principal food grains, wheat and barley, were grown during the winter and that cotton and sesame were harvested in early autumn. More intriguingly, L. Constantini (1981:274-277) argues that rice, sorghum, and millet were introduced into the agricultural cycle towards the end of the Harappan period in the early second millennium B.C. Double-cropping ensued and output expanded enormously, perhaps contributing to the crisis of the old social order. That is, probably for reasons best explained in terms of Harappan social structure, the tremendous agricultural productivity ushered in by the new foods and expanded double-cropping practices led to further deconcentration, rather than accumulation, of wealth, facilitating the demise of Harappan cities.

Diversity in precipitation patterns within the Indus Valley is striking. M. Fentress (1978:411) estimates that 1.5 to 12.5 cm. fell annually at Mohenjo-daro, while rainfall ranged from 5 to 55 cm. at Harappa, located 650 km. farther north. The rural hinterland which supported the two best known cities differed greatly. Harappa, located on the well-embedded, comparatively small Ravi River, experienced far fewer problems with flooding and water control than Mohenjo-daro, situated along the middle course of the Indus. The second most important river along which Harappan sites have been located, the now dry Gaggar-Hakra River to the east, received less rainfall than the Indus and cut a degrading course with a well-defined bed. The greatest concentration of Harappan sites along the Hakra has been found on recent surveys by M.R. Mughal in Bahawalpur. Most of the Mature Harappan sites are clustered near Derawar where the Hakra river formerly fanned out to form an inner delta reminiscent of such formations in Central Asia, such as the Serakhs and Inkhlab deltas along the Tedjen. The settlement data for "Indus" sites, referred to below, is derived from these surveys along the dried-up Hakra.

Differences in mortuary remains between Sumer and the Indus Valley civilization are noteworthy. The basic problem in their interpretation, of course, consists of the fact that semi-autonomous belief systems affect the distribution of materials in graves, making it difficult at times to reconstruct aspects of social structure. This *caveat* noted, however, most archeologists (for instance Alekshin 1983) still assume some rough correlation between distributional mortuary evidence and degree of social stratification.

Data from the Early Dynastic cemeteries of Ur and Kish, in particular, are well-known and exhibit clear differences in the distribution of materials per grave, culminating in the spectacular "royal tombs" and associated death pits at Ur, which, at the very least, hardly suggest an egalitarian social order. The Harappan evidence is far less substantial, and scholars like Wheeler have argued that similar evidence for sharp social stratification would have been forthcoming had Mohenjo-daro's cemetery, presumably buried beneath some 10 meters of alluvium, been located. But the 57 Mature Harappan graves from the R37 cemetery at Harappa suggest otherwise. Differences among grave lots, of course, occur with some burials containing as many as forty pots, but, relative to the earlier Mesopotamian burials, the degree of social stratification evident in the burials appears to be almost minimal. Cemeteries also have been excavated at the small towns of Kalibangan and Lothal that essentially duplicate the evidence from Harappa. Some graves consisted of brick chambers or cists and some contained several ornaments, but the general contrast with the Mesopotamian pattern is manifest and socially meaningful, not a product of the accidents of archeological research.

Another interesting difference between the two civilizations concerns the nature of the archeological evidence relating to long-distance trade. For example, a striking contrast can be drawn between the Harappan trading colony or outpost at Shortughai, the earliest levels of which contained an *unmixed* Harappan assemblage, on the one hand, and the Assyrian trading outpost at Kultepe (Kanesh) in Central Anatolia where the excavator T. Ozguc (1963) admitted that the Mesopotamian presence would have gone undetected had not the tablets been recovered, on the other. This difference must reflect fundamentally distinctive ways of organizing and maintaining far-flung trading networks, which, in turn, probably relate to basic structural differences between the two civilizations. Recently, Lamberg-Karlovsky (n.d.) has developed the arresting idea that the Harappan civilization may have been structured by some incipient caste principles that assigned different productive tasks to specific endogamous social groups. From this perspective, assimilation to the local society did not occur at Shortughai since the kin-related traders maintained a rigid separation based on their primary identification as members of a specific trading caste.

Clearly, a list of unweighted differences--some possibly significant, others trivial--between these early states could be extended almost indefinitely; ceramic and lithic technology, seal manufacture and use, or any aspect of material culture possibly could be contrasted in a way that would illuminate basic structural differences. This paper cannot hope to be inclusive, but will concentrate on two additional axes or parameters which should highlight important differences between ancient Mesopotamia and the Indus Valley civilization: regional settlement data; and urban/rural distinctions.

Settlement Patterns

Environmental features obviously help shape, but do not exclusively determine, regional settlement patterns, which thus must be examined in greater detail from several perspectives. Unfortunately, the studies which have been undertaken in Mesopotamia and for the Harappan civilization are not directly comparable, so our conclusions must be tentative. We will attempt to contrast the settlement studies primarily conducted by R.McC. Adams in southern Mesopotamia with those now completed by M.R. Mughal in the Cholistan Desert, Bahawalpur. It also should be noted that data roughly comparable to that for the Harappan civilization is now also available in Central Asia, specifically Margiana or the lower Murghab region, thanks to the precise surveys of I.S. Masimov and V.I. Sarianidi.

Adams' studies are well-known. He has emphasized regional differences within southern Mesopotamia as regards the timing and extent of urbanization, and his recently published study, *Heartland of Cities*, clearly shows how patterns of settlement in one region at one time were affected by patterns in adjacent regions. Uruk and its countryside waxed as the Nippur-Adab area waned in the late fourth millennium B.C., leading Adams inescapably to conclude that "literally tens of thousands of small villagers appear to have abandoned their homes and moved southward" (1981:70) at this time, a clear example of a disjunctive and sudden large-scale historical event. This conclusion is consistent with another major discovery of Adams, namely, that the cities in southern Mesopotamia grew at the expense of their rural hinterlands. Villages were abandoned in the Uruk countryside between the Jemdet Nasr/E.D. I and E.D. II/III periods on an equally remarkable scale, prompting Adams (1973:343) to reflect on:

> the essentially artificial character of early Mesopotamian cities, at least from a socio-economic viewpoint. They were amalgams brought together to increase the economic well-being and offensive and defensive strength of a very small, politically conscious superstratum.

Do similar patterns emerge when one considers settlement data from South Asia? Considerable fluctuations or sharp disjunctions from one period to another seem to emerge from considerations of shifts in settlements along the Ghaggar-Hakra system east of the Indus, but it is unclear whether the processes by which populations moved (or were forced to move) and new settlements established were roughly the same as those directing such shifts in Mesopotamia. A detailed analysis of the Harappan settlement data suggests interesting, though still not entirely explicable, contrasts with those available from southern Mesopotamia.

Firstly, there appears to have been considerably more diversity within the regional patterning of settlements in the Indus Valley than has been observed in southern Mesopotamia. This observation is not surprising given the far greater and more diversified area over which Harappan sites have been located. But settlement pattern contrasts for classic Indus Valley sites are still striking. W. Fairservis (1979:57) has commented upon the striking density of small villages surrounding the city of Mohenjo-daro. Unlike the Uruk countryside, village density increased as one approached the city. He concludes:

> ...the Indus farmers were villagers through whose labors the urban centers were nourished. It [this pattern] may also indicate that there were probably no large canal systems or other monumental engineering works that required strong central control. Quite the contrary, it would appear that the flood waters of the Indus and the broad alluvium of the valley permitted widespread settlement requiring only limited irrigation and did not provide the impetus to centralization.

An exactly opposite pattern has been noted at Harappa, leading to speculations about the special functions of this isolated "gateway city" within the Harappan polity (Possehl 1982:17) or "major northern supply center to Mohenjo-daro" (Fentress 1982:250). This paper cannot present in detail the subtle analyses of Fentress (1978) and Shaffer (1982) that have helped place in perspective the overstated claim of uniformity between the two best documented "capital" cities. Suffice it to note that three times the number of stamp seal impressions were found at Harappa as compared to Mohenjo-daro or just the reverse of the expected ratio calculated from the amount of excavated area/site. Similarly, in five metal categories the ratios of Mohenjo-daro examples to Harappan ranged from 4-33 to 1, and certain metal tool types were mutually exclusive between the two sites. Yet, on the other hand, although such distributional variations exist and must be meaningful in terms of how the two best-known urban sites interacted with one another, it is perhaps more noteworthy that one is forced to use differential distributions of the *same artifact types* to detect any differences at all. The picture of relative Harappan homogeneity remains one's most striking impression, even granted the regional variations that can be documented. To paraphrase D. Miller (n.d.:18), the resistance to such attempts at regional differentiation underscores the unusual nature of Harappan remains.

More complete and quantifiable settlement data comes from the work of M.R. Mughal (1982) in Bahawalpur. Most of the 174 Mature Harappan sites are located near Derawar dispersed across an area where the Hakra river fanned out into several separate channels, forming an inner delta. Noteworthy, in particular, are the profusion of what are termed industrial sites that are identified by *unmixed* surface indications of brick, ceramic, or metallurgical production. Seventy-nine such sites or roughly 45% of the total number of Mature Harappan sites consisted of such industrial centers; another 33 sites (or 19% of the total) were classified as settlements containing kilns. The contrast could not be greater with what is recorded in Mesopotamia where Adams (1981:47-50) explicitly mentions the difficulty of determining special purpose sites. He writes:

> Surface indications support an occasional suggestion about specialized activity at a particular site - for example, walled enclosures that may have served as fortified khans or storage facilities, sites preponderantly composed of the debris of glass - brick-making, clay cones suggesting wall mosaics on early public buildings, remains of pottery kilns, or unusual concentrations of chipped stone tools. *But such observations pertain to only a tiny minority of the sites catalogued...* (emphasis added)

To extend this contrast further, in a recent paper on craft specialization in what is termed the "Turanian basin", M. Tosi (1984:27-34, fig. 3) estimates that roughly one-quarter to one-third of the total surface area of four sites in "prehistoric Turan" (Tepe Hissar, Altyn-depe, Shahdad, and Shahr-i Sokhta) was devoted to different craft activities. The silence from Mesopotamia is deafening and unlikely to be an artifact of differential observation alone. Industrial activity areas, particularly related to flint working, have been traced in the extensive outlying suburban rings of Tell Taya (see above), and texts, of course, refer to numerous craft specialists in Mesopotamia as early as the late fourth millennium.

Craft activities clearly were pursued in Sumer. The difference must be relative, not absolute, but it is the relative lack of such observed surface remains in Mesopotamia which suggests that Mesopotamia's major non-agricultural productive activities, presumably its textile industries, qualitatively differed from those on sites located in resource-rich areas across the Iranian plateau to the east.

Another interesting contrast emerges when one calculates the total estimated area of urban relative to non-urban settlements (defined exclusively by their spatial dimensions) for Bahawalpur and compares them to figures calculated and published by Adams. To summarize the results - the Mature Harappan sites break down as follows:

Mature Harappan Settlement Distribution:

0-5 ha.	111.7 ha. or 25% of total estimated area
5-10 ha.	136.4 ha. or 31% of total
10-20 ha.	113.6 ha. or 26% of total
20+ ha.	81.5 ha. or 18% of total from the single urban site of Ganweriwala Ther

If these figures then are compared to Adams' data (1981:138, table 12), the following results emerge:

Mesopotamia to Harappa Compared:

	% Non-Urban (10 ha. or less)	% Urban (40 ha. or more)
E.D. II/III	10.0	78.4
Akkadian	18.4	63.5
Ur III/Larsa	25.0	55.1
Cassite	56.8	30.4
Middle Babylonian	64.2	16.2
Bahawalpur	56.0 %	18.0%

That is, the so-called urban phase of settlements in South Asia corresponds, in terms of the presumed relative proportions of their populations living in cities to villages, to the period of precipitous urban decline in Mesopotamia, which was initiated during Cassite times. Or to drive the point home further, the percent of Harappans in Bahawalpur who lived in "urban " communities larger than 10 ha. (44%) is roughly comparable to the number of such urban dwellers in both the Uruk and Nippur-Adab areas during the Early to Middle Uruk period or during the first half of the fourth millennium B.C., roughly 1500 years prior to the emergence of the early Indus state (see Adams 1981:75). As M. Gandhi observed for a much later period, his was a land of villages, not cities, and in this respect it fundamentally differed from the distinctive Mesopotamian pattern.

Urban/Rural Distinctions

What is interesting is not just the areal dominance of small villages in South Asia but their character or nature as revealed by excavations. The 4-hectare site of Chanhu-daro shows evidence for metal production, bead working, and the manufacture of stone weights, seals, and shell artifacts (Mackay 1943). Allahdino, an even smaller site, does not seem to have produced itself such a wide range of artifact types, but its excavators (Shaffer 1982:45) have commented on how nearly every major artifact type, including seals with Harappan inscriptions (implying some degree of literacy on the part of at least some of its inhabitants), were found at this small village. An equally small village site in southern Turkmenistan, Taichanak-depe, almost duplicates the evidence for considerable local craft production (Shchetenko 1968) at non-urban sites documented at Chanhu-daro and recalls our above discussion on the extent of craft production evident on surface examinations of sites stretching from eastern Iran to Central Asia and the Indus Valley. The obvious implication is that Indus Valley and probably Central Asian and "Turanian" Bronze Age sites were characterized by a pattern of decentralized craft production (see Miller n.d.:19), which, nevertheless, yielded assemblages of remarkably similar artifact types. To what extent such universally produced objects were circulated by internal trading mechanisms or, perhaps, by itinerant endogamous groups assigned specific productive tasks and how this pattern should be compared to what must have been an entirely different system of internal exchange and redistribution within Mesopotamia form subjects for future research.

Finally, it is noteworthy that the feature of town planning referred to above as one of the characteristic traits of Indus Valley sites is manifest both at the major centers and on small villages.

In many respects, the small towns and villages almost seem to duplicate the layout of the larger centers, including the features of dual areas (or double mounds), orthogonally laid out streets, and the like. D. Miller (n.d.:11-12) even has suggested that the smaller sites "emulate the same pattern" as the larger sites and feels that such imitation must have social and ideological significance, likening this feature to one still evident in contemporary Indian villages with small houses maintaining the same purity/impurity distinctions on a reduced scale as is present in larger structures. He writes:

> ...all excavations show a regularity of layout that is quite different from our image of the peasant "village". This means not only that tiny sites are emulating larger ones, but secondly, that contrary to our expectations, the proportion of the site given over to public buildings may increase with a decrease in the size of the site itself. A site such as Lothal may have a larger proportion of public buildings than the "citadel" to lower town ratio of Mohenjo-daro.

To summarize, contrasts between Mesopotamia and the Indus Valley civilization have been demonstrated on the basis of substantial archeological evidence. An urban civilization, characterized by the *dominance*, not occasional presence, of urban sites, emerged only in Mesopotamia during the third millennium B.C. Sharp class distinctions have been reconstructed from the archeological evidence and have been confirmed by countless texts describing a society hierarchically organized along class lines. Some scholars recently have attempted to interpret the puzzling features of the Harappan civilization by extrapolating backwards principles of social organization documented for historic India. That is, one can attempt to detect certain incipient caste principles that assigned specific productive activities to particular endogamous social groups (Lamberg-Karlovsky n.d.) or, alternatively, view the relative lack of materials suggestive of sharp social distinctions as indicative of a social order analogous to those formed by major ascetic or monastic movements, such as Buddhism, in later Indian history (Miller n.d.:30). Such a type of ascetic order may have forbidden through embargoes on imports or sumptuary laws any sizable statues or luxuries suggestive of conspicuous consumption or sharp material manifestations reflective of differential accumulation of wealth. The latter thesis, of course, does not postulate a classless Harappan society but a highly ordered one that did not have significant material correlates helpful to later prehistorians.

Our concern in this paper is not to offer a definitive explanation for the Harappan state formation but to insist that it fundamentally and qualitatively differed from that which developed in ancient Mesopotamia and to evaluate all attempts at lumping the Indus Valley civilization with Sumer as examples of early pristine state societies as uninformative and potentially misleading and obfuscating. Whatever the exact nature of Harappan society, we are certain that it reached its mature urban state at least a millennium later than cities and state society first arose in Sumer. This consideration also must be factored into any solution to the nature of the Harappan state for it introduces not only the dimension of time, but *history*, and forces us to consider the momentous changes that swept throughout the ancient West Asian "world system." When the bonds with gentile social organization were first dissolved, classes, kingship, and the institutionalized monopoly of force termed the state made its presence felt far beyond the narrow confines of the plain watered by the Tigris and Euphrates rivers. It is impossible here to consider archeologically demonstrable interregional connections that linked vast regions of the Old World by the second half of the third millennium B.C. That they existed cannot be questioned; what they meant for influencing the evolution of secondarily developing and, consequently, to some extent, derived complex social formations, such as the Indus Valley civilization, requires further elucidation. V. Gordon Childe of course argued that the progressive features of European society were related to their initial formation in the eastern Mediterranean on the periphery or in the shadow of the ancient Orient:

> The urban revolution in the Orient liberated craftsmen and specialists from the necessity of procuring their own food, but only at the cost of complete dependence on a court or a temple. It gave them leisure to perfect their skills but no encouragement to do so along progressive lines; for the last thing to interest a divine king or high priest would be labour-saving devices.... The more progressive character of Aegean industry and craftsmanship is legitimately explicable by reference to the social and economic structures within which

they functioned. Craftsmen had not been reduced, as in the Orient, to an exploited lower class because no class division had as yet cleft Aegean societies (1957:8-9).

Irrigation-dependent societies in Central Asia and the Indus Valley demand an analogous, though not identical, explanation. The high level of technical sophistication evident in what are now popularly termed Bactrian bronzes from the Margiana and Bactrian plains superficially attain the same high standard evident in Aegean crafts; technologies in the ancient world diffused easily and often were more advanced nearer the sources of raw materials than on the resource-poor alluvial plains of the great riverine civilizations. The organizational skill evident in the construction of large platforms and planned settlements, which are hallmarks of the Indus Valley civilization, could not have been produced by an undifferentiated society. But the divisions that ordered this society and created these works did not resemble those historically recorded for ancient Mesopotamia and pharaonic Egypt. Set in a distinctive setting and dependent upon a diverse subsistence base and utilitarian technologies structured around decentralized principles of craft production, the Indus Valley civilization developed a social organization that was highly distinctive and, undoubtedly, extraordinarily influential for the subsequent evolution of South Asian civilization. It developed and expanded in response to a different set of historical imperatives that included the prior existence of the Sumerian state.

In conclusion, the *evolution* of the Indus Valley civilization must be explained *historically*; that is, by reference to those larger processes of change and technological development that all interacting societies of West Asia were experiencing in the latter half of the third millennium B.C. The same universal historical perspective, although clearly structured by different imperatives, must be invoked today to understand the distinctive evolution of specific societies struggling throughout the world to progress beyond the dominant world system of the late twentieth century. That is, one should not expect third world societies to "take off" according to the classic developmental model based on England's historically specific evolution of an industrial state any more than one should maintain that all secondary ancient Bronze Age states duplicated the structural features of ancient Sumer; the modernization-development paradigm in North American economics and political science is analogous to cultural evolutionism in anthropology--a misleading simplification of reality.

Both in the ancient and modern era chronologically earlier developments alter the broader historical context in which cultural evolution and social progress occur. Some developmental paths are blocked, while potentially novel ones lead off into uncharted terrain. General evolution takes place when the broader context itself changes, a process that is both unintentional and willed. More egalitarian Iron Age societies, for example, supplanted the archaic states of the Bronze Age, developing subsequently either into democratic *poleis* or despotic multi-ethnic empires. The future course of cultural evolution is uncertain, but, if ancient history is at all a guide, a relatively safe assumption would be that former peripheral societies will--sooner or later--develop into centers and vice versa, that dominant states which at one time control their less technologically advanced neighbors through bewilderingly complex and powerful economic and military means will, at another time, collapse.

NOTES

The original version of this paper will be published in German by the Akademie der Wissenschaften der DDR in the collected volume: *Grundprobleme vorkapitalischer Gesellschaftsentwicklung*, currently in press, Berlin, DDR.

BIBLIOGRAPHY

Adams, R. Mc.C.
    1972   Patterns of Urbanization in Early Southern Mesopotamia. *In* Man, Settlement, and Urbanism. P.J. Ucko, R. Tringham, and G.W. Dimbleby, eds. Pp. 735-749. London: Duckworth.
    1981   The Heartland of Cities. Chicago: University of Chicago Press.
Alekshin, V.A.
    1983   Burial Customs as an Archaeological Source. Current Anthropology 24:137-149.
Allchin, B. and R. Allchin
    1982   The Rise of Civilization in India and Pakistan. Cambridge: Cambridge University Press.

Childe, V.G.
  1957   The Bronze Age. Past and Present 12:2-15.
Claessen, H.J.M.
  1984   The Internal Dynamics of the Early State. Current
          Anthropology 25:365-379.
Cohen, R.
  1981   Evolutionary Epistemology and Human Values. Cur-
          rent Anthropology 22:201-218.
Constantini, L.
  1981   Palaeoethnobotany at Pirak: A Contribution to the
          2nd Millennium B.C. Agriculture of the Sibi-Kaachi
          Plain, Pakistan. *In* South Asian Archaeology. H. Hartel,
          ed. Pp. 271-277. Berlin: Dietrich Reimer Verlag.
Crawford, H.E.W.
  1977   The Architecture of Iran in the Third Millennium
          B.C. ('Mesopotamia 5, Copenhagen Studies in Assyri-
          ology,' vol. 5). Copenhagen: Akademisk Forlag.
Engels, F.
  1973   The Origin of the Family, Private Property, and the
          State, edited and with an introduction by E.B. Leacock.
          New York: Monthly Review Press.
Fairservis, W.A.
  1979   The Harappan Civilization: New Evidence and More
          Theory, Ancient Cities of the Indus. *In* Ancient Cities of
          the Indus. G. Possehl, ed. Pp. 49-65. New Delhi: Vickers
          Publishing House PVT, Ltd.
  1982   Allahdino: An Excavation of a Small Harappan Site. *In*
          Harappan Civilization. G.L. Possehl, ed. Pp.107-112. New
          Delhi: Oxford and IBH Publishing Co.
Fentress, M.A.
  1978   Regional Interaction in Indus Valley Urbanization: The
          Key Factors of Resource Access and Exchange. *In* Amer-
          ican Studies in the Anthropology of India. S. Valuk, ed.
          Pp. 399-424. Delhi: Manohar.
  1982   From Jhelum to Yamuna: City and Settlement in the
          Second and Third Millennium B.C. *In* Harappan Civiliza-
          tion. G.L Possehl, ed. Pp. 245-260. New Delhi: Oxford and
          IBH Publishing Co.
Frankfort, H.
  1932-33 Iraq Excavations of the Oriental Institute. Third
          Preliminary Report. (Oriental Institute Communications,
          no. 17). Chicago: University of Chicago Press.
Hawkes, J. and L. Woolley
  1963   Prehistory and the Beginnings of Civilization. (History
          of Mankind, vol. 1). New York: Harper & Row.

Kohl, P.L.
    1984   Force, History and the Evolutionist Paradigm. *In*
    Marxist Perspectives in Archaeology. M. Spriggs, ed. Pp.
    127-134. Cambridge: Cambridge University Press.
Lamberg-Karlovsky, C.C.
    n.d.   Caste or Class Formation within the Indus Civilization.
    Forthcoming *In* A Felicity Volume for Beatrice de Cardi
    on the Occasion of Her 70th Birthday. E.C.L. During-
    Caspers, ed. Leiden.
Mackay, E.
    1943   Chanhu-daro Excavations 1935-36. New Haven:
    American Oriental Society.
Miller, D.
    n.d.   Ideology and the Harappan Civilization. Manuscript
    cited with permission of author.
Mughal, M.R.
    1982   Recent Archaeological Research in Cholistan Desert.
    In Harappan Civilization. G.L. Possehl, ed. Pp. 85-96. New
    Delhi: Oxford and IBH Publishing Co.
Ozguc, T.
    1963   An Assyrian Trading Outpost. Scientific American.
    Reprinted (1979) *In* Hunters, Farmers and Civilization: Old
    World Archaeology. C.C. Lamberg-Karlovsky, ed. Pp.
    234-241. San Fransisco: Freeman.
Possehl, G.L.
    1982   The Harappan Civilization: A Contemporary
    Perspective. *In* Harappan Civilization. G.L. Possehl, ed. Pp.
    15-30. New Delhi: Oxford and IBH Publishing Co.
Reade, J.
    1982   Tell Taya, Fifty Years of Mesopotamian Archaeology.
    J. Curtis, ed. Pp. 72-78. London: British School of Ar-
    chaelogy in Iraq.
Sarcina, A.
    1979   The Private House at Mohenjo-daro. *In* South Asian
    Archaeology 1977. M. Taddei, ed. Naples: Instituto Uni-
    versitario Orientale.
Service, E.
    1975   Origins of the State and Civilization. New York:
    Norton.
Shaffer, J.
    1982   Harappan Culture: A Reconsideration. *In* Harappan
    Civilization. G.L. Possehl, ed. Pp. 41-50. New Delhi: Ox-
    ford and IBH Publishing Co.
Shchetenko, A.Ya.
    1968   Raskopki poseleniya epokhi bronzi Taichanak-depe.
    Karakumskie Drevnosti, II:18-24.

Stone, E.C.
  1981   Texts, Architecture and Ethnographic Analogy:
  Patterns of Residence in Old Babylonian Nippur. Iraq
  XLIII:19-33.
Thapar, B.K.
  1982   The Harappan Civilization: Some Reflections on Its
  Environments and Resources and Their Exploration. *In*
  Harappan Civilization. G.L. Possehl, ed. pp 19-33. New
  Delhi: Oxford and IBH Publishing Co.
Tosi, M.
  1984   The Notion of Craft Specialization and Its
  Representation in the Archaeological Record of Early
  States in the Turanian Basin. *In* Marxist Perspectives in
  Archaeology, M. Spriggs, ed. Pp. 22-52. Cambridge: Cam-
  bridge University Press.
Wheeler, R.E.M.
  1968   The Indus Civilization, third ed. Cambridge: Cam-
  bridge University Press.
Wolf, E.
  1982   Europe and The People Without History. Berkeley:
  University of California Press.
Woolley, L. and M. Mallowan
  1976   The Old Babylonian Period. *In* Ur Excavations,
  Vol.20 (VII). T.C. Mitchell, ed. London: British Museum
  Publications Ltd.

NINETEENTH-CENTURY MORMONISM AS A PARTIAL "ASIATIC" SOCIAL FORMATION

Hans A. Baer

Following a long period of dormancy, which was only broken by Wittfogel's (1957) mechanical treatment of "Oriental despotism," Marx's concept of the Asiatic mode of production has undergone a recent revitalization (Bailey and Llobera 1981, Dunn 1982). The concept of the Asiatic mode of production (AMP) is being used more and more to understand the nature of archaic state societies not only in Asia but also in Europe, Africa, Mesoamerica, and South America (Godelier 1977, Coquery-Vidrovitch 1978). As Krader (1975:8) correctly notes, the Asiatic mode of production is a construct that can be applied to the analysis of social formations in both the Old and New Worlds. Furthermore, various scholars have attempted to apply this concept to contemporary social formations (Bahro 1978, Gouldner 1980:343-344).

Marx and Engels never explicitly defined nor adhered to a static interpretation of the Asiatic mode of production. Lowe (1966:14) maintains that at least three different models of the AMP appear in their writings:

> The 1853 version used the self-enclosed village community and state water works to explain the persistence of the political phenomenon of Oriental despotism. The *Capital* version used the self-enclosed village community and the state consumption of surplus value to explain the economic phenomenon of underdevelopment in commodity exchange. The *Anti-Duhring* version emphasized the self-enclosed village community, but pointed to the eventual transition from communal land ownership to small-peasant land ownership.

Despite inconsistencies, largely due to faulty ethnographic evidence in Marx and Engels' application of the concept, a growing number of scholars have come to regard the AMP in its broad outlines as a useful device for understanding the structure of certain pre-capitalist social formations. In answering his own query as to whether the AMP concept that Marx proposed in 1858 should be revived, Maurice Godelier (1977:119) responds, "Not if the concept is to be revived just as Marx constructed it. Yes, if we can remove the *dead parts* and *change* it into a new concept, using the knowledge and learning of our time."

According to Godelier (1978a:212), the

> very essence of the Asiatic mode of production is the existence of primitive *communities* in which ownership of land is communal and which are still partly organized on the basis of kinship relations, combined with the existence of *State* power, which expresses the real or imaginary *unity* of these communities, *controls* the use of essential economic resources, and *directly appropriates* part of the labour and production of the communities which it dominates.

He calls for the creation of a typology of various forms of the Asiatic mode of production in order to shed light upon the trajectories by which social stratification was introduced into classless societies. While I will not undertake such an ambitious endeavor in this paper, I will attempt to apply the AMP concept, at least with some modifications, to one social formation. It will be demonstrated that 19th century Mormonism constituted a social formation which articulated several modes of production. This social formation, particularly during the period 1847-1890, combined a quasi-communal mode of production, an Asiatic mode of production, and a capitalist mode of production.

While Mormonism did not evolve directly out of a classless society as apparently did many earlier Asiatic formations, it was an outgrowth of a quasi-communal religious experiment (Krader 1975). Mormonism emerged in the 1830s as a utopian sect that was only one of many communitarian experiments responding to the social strains and contradictions of the new industrializing capitalist order in the United States. Early Mormonism emphasized egalitarian and cooperative ideals, and actually implemented some of them. Thus, it may be argued that the theocratic state that came to full maturity in the American West followed an evolution roughly analogous, although greatly compressed in time, to that of various archaic civilizations. I am by no means the first to recognize the state-like quality of 19th century Mormonism. Thomas O'Dea (1954:227) argues that the Mormons evolved from "near sect to near nation" and that they, "in a word had become a people, with their own subculture within American culture and their own homeland as a part of the American homeland." Anthropologist Mark Leone (1979:4) describes 19th century Mormonism as a "religious commonwealth comparable to city-states in Southern Mesopotamia." In this essay, I would like to expand upon these interpretations by elaborating on the complexity of 19th century Mormonism as a social formation existing on the periphery of a more powerful formation which spawned and eventually reincorporated its offspring. I will argue that the Mormons established a partial Asiatic social formation in the Intermountain West that was administered by a priesthood bureaucracy exerting control over governmental, agricultural, financial, and industrial activities. This historically unique social formation posed an impediment to the expanding political economy of the United States second only to that of the Southern plantation economy prior to the American Civil War. The expansionist nature of American industrial capitalism contributed to the transformation of Mormonism from a relatively independent theocratic state into a respectable religious denomination which today exhibits many of the characteristics of a modern transnational corporation.

The Development of Mormonism as a Nineteenth-Century Social Formation

Godelier (1978a:212) suggests that the Asiatic mode of production "constitutes one of the possible forms of *transition* from classless to class societies, perhaps the most ancient form of this transition, and contains the *contradictions* of this transition, i.e. the combination of communal relations of production with embryonic forms of the exploiting classes and of the State." While indeed this claim may be correct, we should not overlook the possibility that the AMP may in certain unique situations develop indirectly out of a class society, including one dominated by the capitalist mode of production.

As has been repeatedly shown, cultural evolution is not a unilinear process, and it is possible that under certain conditions a simpler social formation may emerge out of a more complex one.

Segments of class societies have throughout history challenged their subordinate position by attempting to recreate desired features of the primitive or communal mode of production. During the 19th century, largely in response to the dislocations induced by the rapid growth of industrial capitalism, literally dozens of communal or utopian groups emerged in the United States. The most durable of these novel social experiments was the Mormon Church. While Mormonism began as a utopian sect highly committed to egalitarian and communal ideals, it rapidly evolved into a complex social formation which exhibited internal contradictions as well as contradictions in its relationship with its parent society. Despite the fact that Mormonism eventually became fully incorporated into the expanding capitalist economy of the United States, it existed for several decades of the 19th century as a partial or semi-Asiatic mode of production. In this section I will examine the development of Mormonism through the following five stages: 1) a quasi-communal stage, 2) an incipient Asiatic stage, 3) a mature Asiatic stage, 4) a declining Asiatic stage, and 5) a corporate church stage. In each of these phases, Mormonism exhibited an articulation of several modes of production.

The Quasi-Communal Stage

The Church of Jesus Christ of Latter-Day Saints (popularly known as the Mormon Church) has its roots in the revivalistic fervor of the Burned-Over District of western New York during the 1820s (Cross 1950). Although the religious activities and the social conditions of the area had an important impact on the emergence of Mormonism, it is extremely important to note that the new church had only some 70 members when its prophet-founder, Joseph Smith, Jr., decided to move its headquarters to Kirtland, Ohio, in late 1830. Despite reference to the notion of "all things in common" in the Book of Mormon, the legendary record of New World civilizations, there is no indication that the Mormon prophet intended to convert his church into a communal society until he met Sidney Rigdon. Rigdon, a former Campbellite preacher who became Smith's first lieutenant in the early years of the church, was the leader of a tiny communitarian group in Kirtland. Shortly after the two men met, Smith received a revelation referred to simultaneously as the "Law of Consecration," the "United Order," and the "Order of Stewardship" (O'Dea 1957:188).

The Law of Consecration attempted to combine communalism and private enterprise. Production was still kept on an individual or family basis. Individuals or families transferred or "consecrated" their property to the church, but retained use of it under a "stewardship" (Gardner 1924:142-143). The bishop of the congregation or ward held the title or possessions as common property of the church, but returned these to members, in the form of a stewardship, what he felt they required for their livelihood. In addition to each family receiving a building lot in town, farmers were granted a parcel of cropland and craftsmen the necessary tools and materials. The "surplus," defined as the amount earned over and above that required for the support of the member and his dependents, was to be returned to the bishop. This surplus was to be used "first, in supplying the deficiency where stewardships fail to yield sufficient income for the necessities of those who possess them; second, to form or purchase new stewardships for such as have not received any; third, to supply those with means additional resources for the improvement or enlargement of their respective stewardships; fourth, the purchase of lands for the public benefit, to establish new enterprises, develop resources, build houses of worship, temples, send abroad the Gospel or anything else that looks to the general welfare and founding of the Kingdom of God on earth" (B.H. Roberts, as quoted in Gardner 1924:144).

Joseph Smith's Law of Consecration ran into problems in both Ohio and Jackson County, Missouri, during 1831-1834 for a variety of reasons. There were disputes over transfer of property to the church, over the collection of surplus, and over the size of stewardship. The collapse of the United Order in Jackson County was finalized by the expulsion of the Mormons and their resettlement in other areas, particularly Clay County, Missouri. In June, 1834, Smith received a revelation calling for the withdrawal of the United Order on the grounds that the Mormons were not yet prepared for it (Doctrine and Covenants 1963, Section 105:188-190). The Mormon settlement in Ohio came to an abrupt end shortly after Joseph Smith fled for Missouri in January, 1838. He left in order to avoid financial difficulties resulting from the demise of the church-owned Kirtland Safety Society Anti-Banking Company, which had been forced to close during the Panic of 1837. While at the new Mormon settlement of the Far West in Caldwell County, Missouri, Smith received a revelation, often referred to as the "lesser law," requiring that Mormons tithe or "pay one-tenth of all their interest annually" to the church (Doctrine and Covenants 1963, Section 119:212).

Despite its emphasis on cooperative efforts and egalitarianism, Mormonism exhibited a contradiction between its espoused ideals and its social structure from its very beginning. On the one hand, Mormonism was partially democratized in that virtually every adult male could be ordained a priest. On the other hand, oligarchic control of the church was established during the 1830s with the creation of an elaborate hierarchy of ecclesiastical offices, quorums, and councils. This hierarchical structure contributed to the association between ecclesiastical position and social status that emerged within the church:

> New members of the hierarchy tended to be drawn from economic levels that were above the average of the Mormon population from which they came, and once in the hierarchy their economic status tended to remain at inertia until opportunities for economic betterment came to them by virtue of their ecclesiastical office. These opportunities for economic improvement were structured by the hierarchy: the greatest improvements in income and wealth came with service as the President of the Church, then as his counselors, then as the Presiding Bishop and Quorum of Twelve, then as counselors to the Presiding Bishop, and to the least degree, if at all, with service as Council of Seventy and Presiding Patriarch (Quinn 1976:155).

In part, the hierarchy reproduced itself from generation to generation in that many of its members were recruited from closely related families. According to Quinn (1976:42), "of the 123 men appointed to the hierarchy between 1832 and 1932, 53 (43.1%) sustained a kinship relation to one or more living General Authorities. Several of these kinship ties were distant cousin relationships but of the 123 men appointed, 37 (30.1%) were connected to living General Authorities in a kinship relation of second cousin or closer."

Incipient Asiatic Stage

As an emerging social formation, it was inevitable that Mormonism would encounter conflict with the surrounding society. As Flanders (1965:3-4) notes, a "burgeoning, centralized, corporate sect" such as Mormonism, which "exhibited power--

power enough perhaps to establish social, economic, and political dominion wherever it was located by the Prophet," was bound to invite opposition. Nauvoo, which served as the center of Mormon settlement in western Illinois and southeastern Iowa, grew to a city of about 10,000 people, making it, next to Chicago, the largest city in Illinois within a few years. According to O'Dea (1957:52), the liberal charter which the state legislature granted the Mormons in December, 1840, made Nauvoo an "almost independent city-state, and Joseph Smith's interpretation of it would make the Mormon city even more of a separate, self-sufficient unit." Joseph Smith and the Mormon hierarchy served as the civil officials of the city and officers of the Nauvoo Legion, a semi-autonomous militia which fell more under the jurisdiction of federal law than state law. On March 11, 1844, the Mormon prophet established the Council of Fifty, a secret organization during the Nauvoo period, to serve as the governing body of the Kingdom of God on earth. Since it was believed the non-Mormons or Gentiles would be among the subjects of the Kingdom, a distinction was made, at least in theory, between the Council of Fifty (which included some Gentiles) and the General Authorities or the upper echelons of the Mormon priesthood hierarchy.

Nauvoo's economy combined communitarianism, church-sponsored public works projects, and petty capitalist entrepreneurship, particularly in land speculation and trade. The Mormon Church was the largest purchaser of land in the Nauvoo area; Smith was elected to serve as Trustee-in-Trust for the church in January, 1841. As Flanders (1965:121) indicates, however, church and personal affairs were intricately intertwined:

> Nauvoo was by definition a speculation, if not for private, then for community gain. Professional speculators would have slipped past armed patrols to reach Nauvoo. Attracted by its spectacular growth, many of these professional speculators joined the Church, and some were accorded to the honors of successful businessmen. Smith justified his own trading in land as profiting the common good...

Although some apparently joined the church with the hope of earning a handsome profit, the church distributed many town lots and farm lands to the needy who migrated to Nauvoo. Various cooperative industries and stores were established, and much trade was based upon barter, a practice which was considered compatible with communal ideals. As is typical of other Asiatic formations, the principal means of appropriation of surplus in Nauvoo as well as in Utah took the form of tribute, either in agricultural produce, tithes, or labor services (Wessman 1981:213-228). Since Nauvoo's economy was relatively undeveloped, various public work projects, particularly the erection of the Nauvoo Temple, mitigated in part a serious unemployment problem while at the same time giving the Mormon people the sense that they indeed were God's chosen people. It must be noted, however, that the "erection of numerous public buildings and the bureaucratization of the corporate life of Church and Kingdom provided a kind of patronage which was apparently divided among favored and deserving Churchmen" (Flanders 1965:159). Another contradiction of some of these public works projects was that they diverted funds away from endeavors that were essential if the Mormons were to develop a self-sufficient economy. The emergence of a more fully developed Asiatic society among the Mormons had to await their exodus to the Intermountain West. A mob's assassination of Joseph Smith on June 27, 1844, hastened the migration to a remote area of the American West anticipated by the Mormon prophet.

The Mature Asiatic Stage

When the Mormons arrived in the Salt Lake Valley in 1847, the area was still part of Mexico but soon became U.S. territory following the Mexican War. Church leaders had anticipated this possibility and made plans for a full-fledged state over which they would have jurisdiction. Their proposed state of Deseret, which never was recognized as such by the federal government, was to include present-day Utah, all of Nevada, parts of Idaho, Wyoming and New Mexico, most of Arizona, and even a section of southern California. Nevertheless, the Mormon commonwealth, which was developed under Brigham Young's leadership, remained relatively politically autonomous until the late 1880s.

After Utah became a U.S. territory in 1850, members of the Mormon hierarchy conspicuously occupied offices in territorial, county, and municipal governments. Brigham Young became governor of the territory with his two counselors serving as secretary and chief justice. Despite the presence of Gentile federal officers in Utah, the territory was for the most part headed up by the First Presidency and the Quorum of Twelve Apostles during the

mature Asiatic stage. The Mormon commonwealth grew to en-
compass a far-flung but tightly integrated network of planned
towns. In the Great Basin as well as other areas of the western
United States,

> Mormons established an entire social environment, complete
> with schools, courts, irrigation systems, exchange networks,
> price controls, systems of weights and measures, a monetary
> system including specie, a network of roads, maps, an ex-
> ploration plan, land, timber and water rights management,
> and printing facilities. Everything from the founding of basic
> agrarian industries to the invention of a new alphabet sprang
> into existence as much from necessity as from conscious fore-
> thought... (Leone 1979:18).

The backbone of the Mormon religious state in the Intermountain West was a far-flung network of essentially and, in a
few cases, communal villages. These villages were characterized
by the concentration of inhabitants in a central locus with individual stewardships of arable land and common grazing and timber lands on their periphery. The Mormon settlement pattern
resembled that of earlier Asiatic societies in that each community
was engaged in basically the same activities. While it does not appear that, due to their reliance on purchases from the East and
heavy recruitment of outsiders, most Mormon villages developed
the economic self-reliance and insularity of archaic Asiatic communities, a portion of their surplus was appropriated by the
church-state in the form of tribute or tithes. Leone (1979:53)
contends that the tithing system was the "key to harnessing variation" by the Mormons in the Intermountain West.

According to Arrington (1958:134-137), there were five forms
of tithing:

1. *Property tithing* consisted of the 10% capital levy on property owned by the individual at the time he began to pay
   tithing,
2. *Labor tithing* consisted of donations of every tenth day
   toward various church projects such as the construction of
   forts, meeting houses, irrigation canals, roads, and other
   public enterprises,
3. *Produce and stock tithing* was a tenth of the yield of
   household, farm, ranch, factory, or mine,
4. *Cash tithing* included donations of U.S. coin and currency,
   local coin currency and scrip, and gold dust, and

5. *Institutional tithing* was a levy on the profits of stores, shops and factories.

Even during the period of its greatest political autonomy, Mormonism constituted only a partial or semi-Asiatic society. Social formations often articulate several modes of production with one of them dominant over the others. While arguing that the AMP was the primary mode of the Inca empire, Godelier (1977:65) maintains that this social formation also included a pre-Inca tribal mode based on common ownership of land and an embryonic mode based upon "personal ties between aristocratic families and peasant families or subject cattle herders." Elsewhere, Krader (1975:126) refers to the presence of incipient capitalist relations, such as usury, in ancient Babylon, Greece, Rome, China, and India. In a similar vein, Mormonism during its first decades in the Intermountain West articulated a quasi-communal mode at the village level, an Asiatic mode which rested upon the appropriation of tribute by the General Authorities, and aspects of a capitalist mode inherited from its parent society. In reality, as we have already seen, the articulation of these three modes existed in Mormonism prior to the Utah period. It was in Utah, however, that Mormonism came to more clearly resemble the collective bureaucratic formations of archaic times--a pattern which will be described more fully later in this paper.

Mormon economic enterprises during the 19th century have often been described as "mixed" in that they combined cooperative and private ownership. Nearly all Mormon communities held water and timber resources in common. Most trade among Mormon communities was for use-value, but also involved "some selling of produce on the open market for profit and some wage labor" (Leone 1979:24). The church often awarded favored individuals with contracts and extra plots of land, in essence encouraging the development of a small Mormon business class. While in theory, as Arrington (1958:130) maintains, the Mormon businessman was to serve as an "overseer of a part of the Kingdom," in reality Mormon religious leaders during the mature Asiatic stage constituted an incipient capitalist class. According to one study, the wealth of the General Authorities increased sevenfold between 1850 and 1859 whereas that of rank-and-file Mormons improved only slightly (Quinn 1976:101).

Even during the period between 1847 and 1865, the capitalist mode associated with the parent society penetrated and at times articulated with the Mormon economy. Mormons were heavily involved in servicing and re-outfitting emigrants headed for the California Gold Rush of 1849-1850 (Arrington 1958:68-71). The Brigham Young Express and Carrying Company transported U.S. mail, freight, and stagecoach passengers between the Missouri River Valley and Salt Lake City. The Mormons sold food supplies to the booming mining communities in the Intermountain West.

The Declining Asiatic Stage

Despite its status as a relatively autonomous agrarian state for several decades, Mormonism was increasingly threatened by the westward expansion of the political economy of the United States. The end of the Civil War and the completion of the transcontinental railroad in 1869 portended the eventual absorption of the Mormon state into its parent society. A steady stream of Gentile merchants, bankers, prospectors, and mining companies flocked to the Intermountain West. In attempting to halt the impact of their onslaught, Brigham Young urged his people to engage in home industries and to minimize the purchase of outside products. Since the boycott of eastern goods was not totally effective, it enabled Gentile merchants to establish a virtual monopoly in commerce. In response, Young encouraged Mormons to enter commerce in order to squeeze out the intruders. This development, however, enhanced the prosperity of Mormon merchants, and widened the gap between them and the rank-and-file Mormons.

During the 1870s and 1880s Mormonism increasingly faced two interrelated contradictions--one internal and the other external. The internal contradiction involved two dimensions: 1)20the coincidence of community structures and an emerging class structure and 2) the coincidence of theocratic position and private ownership. According to Godelier (1978a:243), the existence of such a contradiction in the Asiatic mode of production results in an evolution "toward forms of class societies in which community-based (communal) relations have less and less reality because of the development of private property." Within several years of Brigham Young's death in 1873, the Mormon hierarchy had significantly altered its position on communal living or United Order (which Young had tried to revive in the early 1870s) and other forms of cooperative enterprise. By 1878 President John Taylor instituted the Zion's Central Board of Trade for purposes of coordinating the church's market-related activities. This organization involved a "type of mild economic planning and social experimentation consistent with prevailing capitalistic tendencies," made extensive use of Mormon businessmen and specialists, and completely excluded labor representatives (Arrington, Fox and May 1976:317).

The external contradiction faced by 19th century Mormonism was its coexistence with a more powerful social formation in the same geographical territory. The encroachment of the Eastern political economy into Utah in essence relegated the Mormon theocracy to the status of an internal colony. Krader (1975) argues that the AMP is destroyed by or articulated to the capitalist mode during the latter's colonial expansion. As we have seen in the case of Mormonism, a dialectical relationship exists between the Asiatic and the capitalist modes. The capitalist mode stands to the "Asiatic mode of production as a development out of it and as its antagonist. The capitalist practices were imposed by force in the lands of the Asiatic mode of production, which became their colonies" (Krader 1975:293-295). Federal legislation attacking Mormon polygamy served as a ruse for completing the absorption of the Mormon religious state into the Union. When such legislation failed to completely subordinate Mormon society, the United States government embarked upon a program, backed up with the use of armed federal troops, of confiscating church property, disincorporating the church, and imposing a Gentile-controlled government in Utah. The Mormon state symbolically conceded its sovereignty to the United States in 1890 when Wilford Woodruff, the President of the church, issued the Proclamation Manifesto--a policy designed to end the practice of plural marriage in federal territory.

The Corporate Church Stage

After Utah obtained statehood in 1896, the Mormon Church accommodated itself to the political and economic institutions of American society. Individualism, capitalism, and social stratification increasingly were regarded as acceptable patterns by members of the Mormon hierarchy. Despite the ideological commitment to egalitarianism and communalism, particularly during the first decade of the Mormon Church, such a development should not be surprising in light of the fact that the Mormon hierarchy constituted an economic elite almost from the beginning. Mormon religious leaders generally became conservative Republicans who spoke out against trade unionism and welfare programs. As the

20th century advanced, the Mormon Church expanded its financial investments or created new ones in agriculture, mercantilism, publishing, communications, real estate, insurance, mining, banking, and other economic endeavors. Mormon religious leaders came to increasingly sit on the boards of church-owned businesses as well as ones in which the church had large investments (Turner 1966:102-136). Despite the initial setbacks following 1890 which subordinated the church to the political economy of the larger society, the Mormon Church not only has become one of the fastest growing religious organizations, but also the richest church per capita in the world (Stark 1984). Data gathered by various analysts demonstrate that its assets rank it among the 50 largest organizations in the U.S. (Morgan 1962, Lang 1971, Beecham and Briscoe 1976). According to Leone (1979:28), the "business and social practices of the modern church--the use of tithing as investment capital, the presence of church officials on boards of large corporations, opposition to labor, church patronage of favored businesses...and church investment in large enterprises like sugar refining--have combined with other practices to regenerate its wealth and sustain its growth."

Twentieth-century Mormonism has created an elaborate and complex bureaucracy to administer its financial, educational, missionary, building, welfare, and genealogical research programs. The church headquarters are now housed in a modern 25-story skyscraper which overshadows the adjacent Salt Lake Temple. Pictures of the First Presidency and the Quorum of Twelve Apostles depict elderly and some middle-aged men in conservative business suits who give the viewer the distinct impression that he is looking at the board of directors of a thriving corporation instead of the leaders of a religious organization per se. Other large religious organizations, both in this country and abroad, own large amounts of stock in and even occasionally have representatives on the boards of national and transnational corporations; yet the Mormon Church appears to best exemplify a merger of ecclesiastical and entrepreneurial objectives. The Mormon Church, on the congregational level and particularly the level of the General Authorities, actively selects leaders who have proven themselves competent in business affairs.

Bearing in mind that the Mormon Church in many ways operates like any other business corporations, it may be argued that it constitutes an excellent example of what might be termed a "theocratic corporation" or "corporate church". Like the modern business corporation, the Mormon Church is structured as a classical pyramidal bureaucracy in which all major decision-making processes and power are centralized at the apex. In the case of the Mormon Church, policies of corporate investment and expansion are intricately intertwined with more explicitly religious undertakings, such as proselytism, the construction of chapels for worship services, and religious instruction. In his discussion of the economic transition of Mormonism between the 19th and 20th centuries, White (1980:107) notes that "while it is extremely difficult...to determine the extent of Mormon capitalism, there can be no doubt the contemporary church is a multinational corporation in the most profound sense."

The resemblance between the Mormon church and the transnational corporation is exemplified by the warm relations that the church has developed since the 1970s with repressive right-wing regimes in various Latin American countries in which it has invested, including Argentina, Brazil, Chile, Paraguay, and Uruguay. Various influential Mormons with strong business and political ties in Latin America "represented the Mormon church not only as an American-based, conservative church but as one that stresses, in doctrinal terms, the *depoliticization* of its membership" (Gottlieb and Wiley 1984:144).

Discussion

It is important to reiterate that even during its mature Asiatic stage, Mormonism articulated several modes of production and was never completely independent of its parent society. Following a world-systems perspective, it may be argued that Mormonism as a social formation existed at the periphery of another social formation well on its way to becoming part of the core (Wallerstein 1979). While there is often a tendency to treat specific social formations as if they are isolated entities, in reality they are to a greater or lesser degree units of a world political economy. This point aside, the concept of the Asiatic mode of production is a valuable one for comprehending the nature of 19th century Mormonism. Conversely, Mormonism provides us with yet another case study for elucidating the nature of the AMP. Bearing this thought in mind, a review of the literature on the AMP suggests considerable concern with three of its dimensions: 1) property relations, 2) the nature of the ruling stratum, and 3) the presence or absence of large-scale hydraulic works.

During the course of correspondence with Engels in 1853, Marx, who had been reading of the work of François Bernier, came to the conclusion that the "*king is [the] one and only proprietor of all the land* in Oriental society" (quoted in Sawer 1977:43). This pattern is in keeping with the notion that the Mormon prophet-president served as the Trustee-in-Trust of church property. In addition to serving as the titular head of the church, the prophet-president, as Hansen (1967:66) observes in the following remarks, was regarded as a monarch:

> The scriptures indicated that Christ would rule as king over the kingdom of God. Smith took this idea quite literally and thought it only logical that he, as predecessor of the Savior, should enjoy certain prerogatives of royalty. Consequently, shortly before his death, the prophet apparently had himself ordained as "King on Earth." Brigham Young upon his arrival in the Salt Lake Valley, likewise reportedly had this ceremony performed in the Council of Fifty.

Marx a few years later argued that the self-sufficient villages, regardless of the "official veil of State property of land," practiced actual ownership of traditional lands (Anderson 1974:479). In time, however, Marx came to make a distinction between nominal ownership and traditional rights of possession or usufruct, and essentially returned to his original contention that ultimate ownership of land rested in the State--that higher community which linked and regulated the productive activities of all the local communities.

Members of the church hierarchy, from the General Authorities down to the bishops of the wards, served as the economic managers of an elaborate system of water control and distribution, cooperative stores, industries, agricultural enterprises, and public works projects, including the construction of the ornate Salt Lake Temple and Tabernacle. In light of the central role played by tribute in social formations such as 19th century Mormonism, it is not surprising that some scholars have recommended that the term "tributary mode of production" be substituted for the geographically misleading term "Asiatic mode of production" (Amin 1974:140-141, Banu 1981, Currie 1984:263-264). Largely because Amin (1980:46-70) lumps the Asiatic and feudal modes under the single rubric of the "tributary mode of production," I have hesitated in this paper to substitute this designation for the more widely-used one of the "Asiatic mode of production."

Analysts of the Asiatic formation offer contrasting interpretations of their ruling strata. Sawer (1977:62) contends that Marx did not really regard the bureaucratic elite of Asiatic society as a ruling class per se since state ownership of land was "antithetical to the real development of the private ownership of the means of production, on which his definition of class rested." L.S. Vasil'ev, a Soviet scholar, discusses the nature of the ruling elite of Asiatic society in an 1968 article focusing on Chinese civilization. He is "careful to describe the bureaucratic elite as assuming the *functions* (including that of economic exploitation) of a ruling class rather than actually *being* a ruling class; he does this because in Marx's mode of Asiatic society social stratification stems from social inequality (status differences) rather than property differences, and there is an absence of (private-property based) classes or class antagonism in the Western sense" (cited in Sawer 1977:101). French Marxists have also tended to view the AMP as a transition between the primitive communal mode and modes present in state formations. Conversely, Melotti (1977:58), in citing Marx's assertion that the state is "the organ of class rule, an organ for the oppression of one class by another," rejects the notion that Asiatic society is not a true class society but merely a transitional stage. Marx himself may have minimized the presence of social classes in the Asiatic society by emphasizing the supposed existence of primitive economic egalitarianism in its rural communities. Particularly in his discussion of Indian villages, it appears that Marx overlooked the caste system that dictated much of daily life. As Anderson (1974:490) aptly notes, "wherever a powerful central state occurs, advanced social differentiation exists, and there is always a complex skein of exploitation and inequality reaching into the lowest units of production themselves." This last point is particularly well illustrated in the case of 19th century Mormonism.

Although much of the surplus collected by the Mormon religious states was redistributed among rank-and-file members, the growing pattern of social inequality that characterized 19th century Mormonism strongly suggests that church leaders benefitted considerably from the system of tithing. General Authorities were able to draw upon general funds for travels and clerical expenses, serving in the territorial legislature and, after the Manifesto, received salaries for services rendered to church businesses. It is important, however, to note that, despite the existence of a variety of social sanctions which were largely carried out by ecclesiastical courts, the appropriation of tithes was not generally viewed as a coercive practice. According to Leone (1979:3-4), Mormonism was able to develop into a "genuine theocracy" primarily because "everybody believed in the same version of the supernatural." This observation supports Godelier's (1978b:8) contention that "in religion, we find the foundation of a non-violent form of violence, the ideal material for a relation of exploitation of man by man." It should be noted, however, that the hegemony of Mormon ideology was never complete as is apparent from the emergence of various schismatic sects, such as the Morrisites and the Godbeites, which challenged the "one man rule" of the Mormon church. Joseph Morris, who spoke out several times against what he regarded as the excessive materialism, gathered about 500 followers in a United Order community at the mouth of Weber Canyon near Ogden, Utah, in the early 1860s. In contrast, the Godbeites were a group of prosperous Mormon merchants who in 1869 opposed Brigham Young's economic boycott on trade with non-Mormons. The church took full measures, including military force, to repress such dissident groups.

During its incipient Asiatic stage, the Mormon state was not based on a large-scale hydraulic system. The location of Nauvoo on the bottom lands of the Mississippi River and the rich Midwest prairie did not necessitate extensive irrigation. If the land in Illinois settled by the Mormons had not been situated in the midst of an already relatively densely populated area, Mormonism might have developed into a mature Asiatic formation without a large-scale irrigation system. Conversely, as Leone (1979:86) observes, "the history of water control provides a firm basis for understanding 19th century Mormon communities since such control was one of the contexts for the development of Mormon society in the West and one where the shaping of Mormonism can be plainly seen." The Mormon religious state in the Intermountain West rested upon a "complex irrigation complex involving fickle streams, frail dams, easily washed-out canals, and the hugh labor force needed to operate the whole system successfully" (Leone 1979:24). In contrast to the centralized hydraulic systems often associated with the AMP, the Mormon complex, at least once it was set in place, functioned in a relatively decentralized manner. Water control was administered by highly autonomous irrigation districts which were under the legal jurisdiction of the county courts. According to Arrington (1958:53), "even today, farmer-owned 'mutual' companies control virtually all the irrigation canals in Mormon communities in the West." The Mormon case illustrates the increasingly accepted argument that the AMP may or may not be, depending on local environmental conditions, associated with a large-scale hydraulic system.

Conclusion

The significance of the Mormon case lies in the fact that it challenges certain commonly held assumptions about the nature of the Asiatic mode of production and the evolution of social formations. Perhaps the most significant of these is the notion that the AMP always preceded the slave, feudal, and capitalist modes of production. During the better part of the 20th century, a deterministic Marxism has tended to regard evolution as a rather rigid historical process in which one stage gave way to another stage according to certain universal laws. In some of his writings, such as the *German Ideology* and in the preface to *Critique of Political Economy* (in which he included the "Asiatic" stage), Marx outlined a relatively fixed evolutionary trajectory. In time, the sequence of primitive communism, ancient society, feudalism, and capitalism became canonical. Adherence to such a scheme, modified perhaps by inclusion of the Asiatic stage, has continued to the present day. Yet, in the *Grundrisse* Marx appeared to be groping with an evolutionary pattern which he recognized to be far more complex. Melotti (1977), Godelier (1978a), and others have called for the construction of a multilinear evolutionary scheme which recognizes Asiatic society as one stage.

In that many have tended to view the earliest social formations as having been Asiatic societies, the Mormon case indicates the possibility of the AMP resurfacing as an outgrowth of historically altered modes of production. In contrast to archaic societies, the period during which the Asiatic mode served as the dominant mode of production in Mormonism was extremely brief. On the one hand, the rapidity by which the Asiatic mode emerged and declined in Mormonism appears to support Krader's (1975:185) contention about the lack of validity in Marx's view of Asiatic society as a stagnant formation in the evolutionary sense. On the other hand, Mormonism as a partial Asiatic society functioned as transitional formation primarily because it was unable to sever its ties with the capitalist mode. As opposed to Asiatic formations prior to European colonialism in which the capitalist mode existed at a very rudimentary level, Mormonism, both during its quasi-communal stage and mature Asiatic stage, found itself closely articulated with relatively developed capitalist mode. The same political economy that indirectly fostered the emergence of a utopian sect, which quickly transformed into a partial Asiatic society, alter absorbed it. Despite the relative political independence of the Mormon theocratic state, the brief existence of Mormonism as an Asiatic formation was related to its inability to completely sever economic ties with its parent society.

BIBLIOGRAPHY

Amin, Samir
  1974   Accumulation on a World Scale: A Critique of the Theory of Underdevelopment, Volume I. New York: Monthly Review Press.
  1980   Class and Nation: Historically and in the Current Crisis. New York: Monthly Review Press.
Anderson, Perry
  1974   Lineages of the Absolutist State. London: New Left Books.
Arrington, Leonard J.
  1958   Great Basin Kingdom: An Economic History of the Latter-Day Saints. Chichago: University of Chicago Press.
Bahro, Rudolf
  1978   The Alternative in Eastern Europe. London: Verso.
Bailey, Anne M. and Josep R. Llobera, eds.
  1981   The Asiatic Mode of Production: Science and Politics. London: Routledge & Kegan Paul.
Banu, Ioan
  1981   The 'Tributary' Social Formation. *In* The Asiatic Mode of Production. A. Bailey and J. Llobera, eds. Pp. 278-80. London: Routledge & Kegan Paul.
Beechem, Bill and David Briscoe
  1976   Mormon Money and How It's Made. Utah Holiday, March 22.
Coquery-Vidrovitch, Catherine
  1978   Research on an African Mode of Production. *In* Relations of Production: Marxist Approaches to Economic Anthropology. David Seddon, ed. Pp. 261-88. London: Frank Cass.

Cross, Whitney
    1950   The Burned-Over District. Ithaca, New York: Cornell University Press.
Currie, Kate
    1984   The Asiatic Mode of Production: Problems of Conceptualizing State and Economy. Dialectical Anthropology 8:251-68.
Doctrine and Covenants
    1963   Salt Lake City: Church of Jesus Christ of Latter-Day Saints.
Dunn, Stephen P.
    1982   The Fall and Rise of the Asiatic Mode of Production. London: Routledge & Kegan Paul.
Flanders, Robert Bruce
    1965   Nauvoo: Kingdom on the Mississippi. Urbana: University of Illinois Press.
Gardner, Hamilton
    1922   Communism Among the Mormons. Quarterly Journal of Economics 37:134-74.
Godelier, Maurice
    1977   Perspectives in Marxist Anthropology. Cambridge: Cambridge University Press.
    1978a   The Concept of the "Asiatic Mode of Production" and Marxist Models of Social Evolution. *In* Relations of Production: Marxist Approaches to Economic Anthropology. David Seddon, ed. Pp. 208-57. London: Frank Cass.
    1978b   Infrastructure, Societies, and History. Current Anthropology 19:763-68.
Gottleib, Robert and Peter Wiley
    1984   America's Saints: The Rise of Mormon Power. New York: G.P. Putnam's Sons.
Gouldner, Alvin W.
    1980   The Two Marxisms: Contradictions and Anomalies in the Development of Theory. New York: Seabury.
Hansen, Klaus J.
    1967   Quest for Empire: The Political Kingdom of God and the Council of Fifty in Mormon History. Lansing: Michigan State University Press.
Hindess, Barry and Paul Hirst
    1975   Pre-capitalist Modes of Production. London: Routledge & Kegan Paul.
Lang, Francis
    1971   The Mormon Empire. Ramparts, September, Pp.37-43.
Leone, Mark P.
    1979   Roots of Modern Mormonism. Cambridge, MA: Harvard University Press.

Lowe, D.M.
    1966   The Function of China in Marx, Lenin and Mao.
    Berkeley: University of California Press.
Melotti, Umberto
    1977   Marx and the Third World (translated by Pat Rans-
    ford). London: MacMillan.
Morgan, Neil
    1962   Utah: How Much Money Hath the Mormon Church?
    Esquire, August, Pp. 86-91.
O'Dea, Thomas F.
    1954   Mormonism and the Avoidance of Sectarian Stagna-
    tion: A Study of Church, Sect, and Incipient Nationality.
    American Journal of Sociology 6:285-93.
    1957   The Mormons. Chicago: University of Chicago Press.
Quinn, Dennis Michael
    1976   The Mormon Hierarchy, 1832-1932: The American
    Elite. Ph.D. Dissertation, Yale University.
Sawer, Marian
    1977   Marxism and the Question of the Asiatic Mode of
    Production. The Hague: Martinus Nijhoff.
Stark, Rodney
    1984   The Rise of a New World Faith. Review of Religious
    Research 26:18-27.
Turner, Wallace
    1966   The Mormon Establishment. Boston: Houghton Mifflin.
Wallerstein, Immanuel
    1979   The Capitalist World-Economy. Cambridge: Cam-
    bridge University Press.
Wessman, James W.
    1981   Anthropology and Marxism. Cambridge, MA:
    Schenkman.
White, O. Kendall
    1980   Mormon Resistance and Accommodation: From Com-
    munitarian Socialism to Corporate Capitalism. *In* Self-
    Help in Urban America. Scott Cummings, ed. Pp. 89-112.
    Port Washington, New York: Kennikat Press.
Wittfogel, Karl A.
    1957   Oriental Despotism. New Haven: Yale University
    Press.

ETHNIC IDENTITY AND NON-CAPITALIST RELATIONS OF PRODUCTION IN CHIMBORAZO, ECUADOR[1]

Barbara Schroder

Introduction

This paper is about the maintenance of non-wage labor relations on haciendas in highland Ecuador in the early 1980s. It addresses several issues in anthropological approaches to third world economic development. One is the role of the masses of third world indigenous peoples--those characterized by Eric Wolf (1982) as "the people without history"--in the process of capitalist development. Secondly, it addresses the issue of the importance, in our models of economic development, of cultural factors. And thirdly, it documents the complex class position of many Andean rural peoples--people who are neither "peasants" nor "proletarians", but something of both. The first part of the paper will touch on these theoretical issues; the second will present some of the economic and inter-ethnic history of the study region, the Riobamba area of Chimborazo Province, and the third will describe the results of field work conducted there between 1980 and 1982.

A Historical Social Class Approach

The most popular anthropological models for understanding third world economic development in the 1970s were world systems (Wallerstein 1974), dependency (Frank 1966) and articulation of modes of production (Meillassoux 1972). In the 1980s an increasing number of scholars have sought to correct for a tendency common to all of these "globalist"[2] approaches; a tendency to assign *all* causality to the world capitalist system, and, in the pro-

cess, to ignore the impact of local-level actors.[3] In throwing out
the bath water of bourgeois modernization theory, they thus
threatened to dispose of the baby--a vision of people "at the bottom" who are capable of acting according to their own interests,
contrary to the desires of capitalism, and who, when they do so,
may in fact alter the shape that economic development takes in
their part of the world.

The position taken here is one which, while it acknowledges
the very important impact of capitalist development in the world's
core upon events in the periphery, also maintains that part of the
dynamic of peripheral socio-economic systems is to be found, not
in the capitalized core, nor in the logic of capitalist accumulation,
but rather, in the local histories and inter-class struggles of the
periphery. In this, it attempts to restore a notion of dialectic to
globalist approaches to economic development. Further, it holds
that an understanding of peripheral areas such as the Andes must
go beyond strict analysis of class conflicts, to also consider conflicts based on other social cleavages, such as religion and eth-
nicity.

This "historical social class approach"[4] has been developed in
the works of Nicos Mouzelis, Joel Kahn, and Carol A. Smith. In
"Modernization, Underdevelopment, Uneven Development: Prospects for a Theory of Third World Formations," Mouzelis (1980)
discusses the epistemological basis for the functionalism inherent
in globalist approaches. He traces it to our Western assumption, or
"telos", concerning the inevitability and somehow, for us, naturalness of the process of modernization, or capitalist development.
Mouzelis describes how, in our attempts to analyze peripheral social formations through this model, we often misunderstand the
social processes that we observe.

Joel Kahn (1980) argues against the functionalism of articulation of modes of production and world system theories in his
*Miningkabau Social Formations: Indonesian Peasants and the
World Economy.* Implicit in these theories is the assumption that
non-capitalist modes of production exist because they are functional to the needs of capitalism. However, in the case that he is
examining, the emergence of petty commodity production in In-
donesia after its incorporation into the world capitalist economy,
Kahn finds that this functional approach does not hold up; he can
demonstrate no logical reason why the "needs of capitalism" would
have dictated this particular development at this particular point
in Indonesian history. Rather, he contends, a better understanding

is arrived at by considering the motives and rationales of local social classes, acting to some extent outside of and in opposition to
the needs of expanding world capitalism.

Carol A. Smith (1984) develops the argument further in "Local
History in Global Context: Social and Economic Transitions in
Western Guatemala," concerning a part of the world similar in geographical and historical context to highland Ecuador. In examining the history of "closed corporate communities" in western
Guatemala, she finds that Guatemala's indigenous peasants were
active shapers of Guatemala's history, affecting both the kind of
capitalist development that occurred there as well as the delayed
timing of Guatemala's entrance into the world market. A second
important finding of Smith's work is that it was through an essentially *cultural* institution, the indigenous "parcialidad," that
Guatemala's indian peasants exercised this influence.

Juan Martinez-Alier's work on Peruvian sheep haciendas
(1977) in the period from the 1940s to the 1960s was one of the
first works to point out the role of Andean peasant resistance to
proletarianization in the maintenance of non-capitalist relations of
production there. His work counters the contention that these relations of production are best explained by the needs of capitalism. Exploring the archives of hacienda correspondence,
Martinez-Alier documents the (largely unsuccessful) efforts of
hacienda owners to modernize their enterprises by, among other
things, converting to wage labor. The main source of opposition
to the process came from the efforts of indigenous workers to
maintain their sheep herds on hacienda pastures as part of their
wage. Their struggle was to maintain an economic base independent of wage labor. Martinez-Alier documents one other important issue--how indigenous workers on Andean haciendas combine
both "proletarian" and "peasant" strategies in their actions. They
form unions, hold strikes, and agitate for higher wages, at the
same time that they fight to maintain their independent economic
base through continuing non-capitalist labor forms. The findings
of the present study of Ecuadorian haciendas[5] and their indigenous workers in many ways resemble Martinez-Alier's findings for Peruvian haciendas of an earlier period.

It was with this "historical social class" approach that I approached the question of the maintenance of non-capitalist labor
forms on haciendas in highland Ecuador. No one familiar with
the history of this area could easily ignore the tremendous importance there of international and national forces, linked to the de-

velopment of international capitalism. However, as will be shown, an understanding of the history of capitalist agricultural development in this region must go beyond an examination of the "needs of capitalism," to look as well at the motives and actions of the area's indigenous population.

An Introduction to Chimborazo's Agrarian Sector

Ecuador in the 1970s saw a rapid expansion of its economy, due to the production of petroleum for export. This economic growth, in addition to increasing external dependence on both the international market and on foreign capital, also promoted dramatic internal socio-economic changes, including increased urbanization and the growth of urban middle and working classes. Significant changes in that sector of society providing food for internal consumption had been underway since the 1950s with the development of a modernizing agrarian bourgeoisie. Those changes were further propelled by agrarian reform laws in the 1960s and 1970s.

This agrarian reform legislation aimed at equalizing land tenure--1.15% of landowners owned 64.3% of agricultural land in 1954--to reduce the threat of social and political instability caused by campesino[6] pressure for land. However, because of the opposition of a still-powerful landed oligarchy, the effects of the legislation were diluted. For example in 1984, 1.12% of landholders still controlled 48.2% of agricultural land (Handleman 1980). Agrarian reform did, however, generally succeed in transforming the old hacienda labor systems. Under these arrangements, campesinos, the majority of them indigenous, paid for usufruct rights over agricultural plots, grazing lands, water and firewood by providing a stipulated amount of labor to the hacienda. The success of this aspect of agrarian reform is often credited to the support it received from a "modernizing capitalist" fraction of hacendados, who wanted to rid their properties of unwanted internal peons.

The above processes--greater dependence on foreign markets and capital, the growth of a middle class, agrarian reform legislation--indicate the increasing development of Ecuadorian society along capitalist lines. However, at the same time, in the countryside, haciendas were continuing to employ a large number of non-capitalist labor forms, including sharecropping and payment in kind, although these arrangements had been outlawed since 1964. This juxtaposition of capitalist development and non-capitalist forms of labor is particularly evident in the highland province of Chimborazo, where a survey of 127 haciendas in the four counties of Riobamba, Guamote, Colta and Guano was carried out. (These four counties are hereafter referred to as the Riobamba area.) According to the 1974 census, there were 283 properties larger than 50 hectares in this area. If we assume a 10% decrease in this number between 1974 and 1980, when this survey was conducted, this sample represents approximately 50% of all haciendas in the area.

Since the Spanish conquest of 1532, Chimborazo Province has played an important role in the nation's economy as a supplier of temperate zone agricultural goods: first, sheep and textiles woven from their wool; later crops for internal consumption, mainly potatoes and wheat. In the last 20 years, however, Chimborazo's agricultural production has declined steadily; today the area's main economic role is a provider of cheap labor to the growing urban areas and the oilfields of the eastern jungle. This decline in the agricultural sector of the area appears to have been the result of various factors, including successful competition for capital by more profitable sectors of the economy, stepped-up soil exhaustion and erosion as a result of over-use, and rising labor costs as a result of agrarian reform laws.

Throughout much of the province in the last 30 years, the cultivation of tubers and wheat has given way to dairy production. This switch, together with agrarian reform legislation, has meant both a decrease in agricultural sector jobs and less access to land for the province's indigenous campesinos. Haciendas have taken over lands previously used by their indigenous workers for domestic production and converted them to pasture. Dairy production is much less labor-intensive than the production of cereals and tubers which it replaced.

Forty-four percent of Chimborazo's population in 1980 is indigenous, giving it the highest percentage of indigenous population of all highland provinces.[7] In the past 20 years, increasing numbers of Indians, most of whom are campesinos, have migrated out of the area, both seasonally and permanently. They have been simultaneously forced off the land by agrarian reform, dairy transformation, and attracted by the higher wages in the cities, the coastal plantations, and the oilfields. However Chimborazo remains today one of the strongest seats of indigenous population, language and culture in the highlands.

This paper will argue the importance of indigenous ethnic identity in influencing economic development in the region. The contemporary agrarian structure of Chimborazo, affected as it has been by the macro-level processes of capitalist penetration and national policies, has also been shaped by the actions of indigenous campesinos in their struggles against proletarianization and ethnic assimilation. The following is a short overview of the history of inter-ethnic relations in the region since the Conquest.

Inter-ethnic Relations in Chimborazo

At the time of the Conquest, in 1532, the area around Riobamba was inhabited by the ethnic group, the Puruhá. The Puruhá were a fiercely independent and not easily subjugated group; the Incas needed to enlist the aid of the neighboring Cañaris before they were able to defeat them, and the area had been under Inca rule only 50 years when the Spaniards arrived. In the early colonial period the Riobamba area became one of the centers of the sheep-raising and textile industry in the Audencia de Quito. Coerced labor for this industry was provided by Indians working in the infamous *obrajes* (workshops).

Chimborazo distinguishes itself throughout Ecuadorian history as an important seat of Indian uprisings. Maynard (1965) cited 10 major indigenous uprisings there in the period 1764-1921 alone, and four of the ten 18th-century uprisings covered by Segundo Moreno took place in Chimborazo. Of all the various indigenous rebellions in Ecuador, the uprising in Riobamba in 1764 posed the most serious threat to the political control of the non-indigenous Spaniards and mestizos. In it, we see the extent to which the indigenous population of the area maintained socio-political networks and institutions that were still not under Spanish domination. Prior to the uprising, indigenous leaders from Chimborazo had been conferring with their counterparts in other areas of the Sierra. More than 10,000 Indians--men and women--took part, highly organized into batallions according to their communities; the open battle lasted several days. The goals of the uprising went beyond a protest of possible increased labor taxes; they included killing all Spanish, overthrowing the colonial government and replacing it with an indigenous one, for which two indigenous leaders, representatives of two different *ayllus*, (extended kin groups) had been chosen (Moreno 1978:46).

Towards the end of the 19th century, the indigenous population of Colta staged one more unsuccessful rebellion, this one triggered by the collection of the *diezmo*, a tax levied on the indigenous population. The community of Cacha, which had been the seat of the precolombian Puruhá rulers, became the focus of the uprising, which was headed by Fernando Daquilema, a descendant of the indigenous royal dynasty, the Duchicelas. Once again, in this uprising, Indians in Chimborazo attempted to secede from the republic and establish their own government, headed by an indigenous king and queen.

Incidents of inter-ethnic conflict have remained high in Chimborazo in the 20th century; in this century, the context of the struggle is usually that of indigenous campesinos against non-indigenous hacendado (hacienda-owner). Ecuador, like all countries closely integrated into the world market economy, was profoundly affected by the economic crisis of the 1930s. Falling cacao prices translated into a constriction of the internal market for agricultural products, with resulting massive social conflict in both city and countryside. Chimborazo's haciendas became the focus of pitched battles between indigenous workers and landowners, particularly on the haciendas of Pul and Galte in Guamote. Out of these struggles, which mobilized indigenous campesinos on a nationwide basis, and similar ones in Cayambe, was born the Federation of Ecuadorian Indians (FEI). The FEI was to take the lead, for several decades, in organizing indigenous campesinos in the Sierra.

The 1950s saw an expansion of Ecuador's economy related to the production of bananas for export, as well as an increase in urbanization, resulting in a growth in the urban middle-class market for dairy products. Hence, throughout Sierra haciendas, we find an intensification of the switch from agricultural to dairy production, with an accompanying expulsion of indigenous workers (*huasipungueros*). This process heightened conflicts between Indians and hacendados throughout the Sierra, including Chimborazo. These struggles were particularly marked in Guamote, and in Columbe, in the *cantón* (county) of Colta, and are one of the factors which militated for the passage of an agrarian reform law in 1964.

There are additional evidences of inter-ethnic conflict in Chimborazo in this period. Thus, government census-takers are physically attacked and driven out of rural areas. On the haciendas, strikes and land invasions are common. Government records show, for example, that in 1961, 30 haciendas in the Riobamba area, or 11% of the total, experienced labor conflicts serious enough to reach government offices. Writing in 1960, Hugo Burgos characterized the Riobamba area as a region of refuge, where a mestizo town dominates a rural indigenous countryside, and that characterization is valid today. The dominant ones, however, are far from secure in their domain. Chimborazo hacendados are rightfully fearful of their indigenous neighbors and workers, as witnessed to by the fact that many sleep with and travel with rifles or guns close at hand.

Contemporary Non-wage Remunerations on Chimborazo Haciendas

In the period 1980-82, 90% percent of the haciendas in the study engaged in at least one non-wage form of labor, and the mean number of such practices per hacienda was three. These practices include: the granting of rights to pasture animals on hacienda lands to workers, found on 67% of the farms; providing lunch for workers, found on 34% of the farms; providing *chicha*, an alcoholic beverage, on 37% of the farms; allowing dairy workers a daily ration--usually a liter--of milk, found on 34% of the haciendas; allowing workers to gather firewood from the haciendas, found on 33% of the haciendas; allowing workers in the potato harvest gleaning privileges, found on 31% of the farms; and the practice of using *ayudas*, or occasional labor, in return for pasture, water, or firewood, on 11% of the farms. These practices are found in combination with payment of a cash wage, which ranged in 1982 from between 30 and 100 sucres per day. This is equivalent to between $.60 and $2.00 a day. The mean daily wage paid was 71 sucres. Non-wage remunerations are outlawed by the Agrarian Reform law, and there is a minimum wage in agriculture, which at that time was 80 sucres. Therefore, I suspect that 1) the actual incidence of non-wage relations is probably somewhat higher than reported above, and 2) the actual mean daily wage paid is probably somewhat lower then reported. Sharecropping, practiced on 12% of the haciendas sampled, is different from the above non-capitalist labor forms. While all the above-mentioned are relations between workers and owners, sharecropping is a relationship between owner and entrepreneur.

The sharecropper is almost always non-indigenous, often of the same social class as the owner, and must have at his disposal a considerable amount of cash.

Modernization theory would maintain that the continuation of the above practices is evidence of economic underdevelopment in the region. However, this contention is contradicted by the fact that strong markets for both land and labor, as well as agricultural products, have long existed in the area. Additionally, the same people who engage in non-capitalist relations in Chimborazo are thoroughly involved in capitalist relations elsewhere: the hacendados as importers and bankers, and the campesinos as wage laborers on plantations and in the cities. Articulation of modes of production and dependency theories would view the continued use of these labor forms as beneficial to capitalism. Two facts contradict this last interpretation, however: 1) Capitalist hacendados in the area have made consistent attempts to eliminate many of them, and 2) haciendas in other areas of the highlands with similar geographical and ecological characteristics have successfully made the transition to pure wage labor.

In order to test these theoretical assumptions, a factor analysis of the survey data was performed. If the modernization model was correct, non-wage forms of remuneration would be found uniformly on the most "backward" or "traditional" haciendas. If the articulation of modes of production model was accurate, they would be found instead on the most "capitalist" or "modern" ones.

The factor analysis showed two things: first, the haciendas in the sample cannot be ranked on a simple modern-traditional or capitalist--non-capitalist continuum. Rather, there were six distinct factors that underlay the patterns of variations in the organization of production of the haciendas in the survey. Thus, we can speak of six dimensions of variation among haciendas in the area. They are: dairy farming, modern dairy farming, large agricultural farms, modern agricultural ones, and two different types of farms with higher incidences of non-wage remunerations than these first four. One type is where a major economic activity seems to be the renting out of pastureland, or taking *mesadas*, and the second distinguishes itself largely by the practice of allowing gleaning privileges to workers.

Secondly, the factor analysis showed that capitalist and non-capitalist, modern and traditional practices are combined in a number of different ways. As illustration, a description of three haciendas follows (pseudonyms are used).

The first one is Greenfields, which, at 4,500 hectares, is one of the largest haciendas in the province. Its owner is a banker, well-placed in national politics. His operation, in terms of mechanization and dairy herd management, is one of the most capital-intensive in the province. Like many other haciendas, Greenfields has converted from agriculture to dairy farming over the last 30 years, in order to take advantage of developing markets for dairy products, and also to reduce its dependence on local labor. At the same time, probably because of the owner's political clout, it is exceptional in that it has also managed to maintain its territorial monopoly. However, it still requires seasonal workers, and in order to meet its seasonal labor needs, it continues preagrarian reform practices, availing itself of free labor made possible by its monopoly over land. For the land-poor Indians of Greenfields, access to the hacienda's resources is essential for survival, and they continue to pasture their animals on hacienda lands and collect firewood from the hacienda. If apprehended by hacienda workers they are required to work a set number of days without pay on the hacienda. This is actually a transformation, in the post-agrarian reform era, of the old ayuda system, whereby members of neighboring communities provided labor for a hacienda in exchange for pasture, water, and firewood. However, now it is being conducted within an illegal and highly antagonistic context, whereas earlier it was done legally and with less antagonism.

The second hacienda, Chacón, combines agriculture with cattle-raising. Starting in the 1960s, it sold off much of its former expanse to neighboring Indians, its former workers, and began an aggressive modernization campaign. In the 1970s the hacienda experienced a great deal of labor conflict; its indigenous work force, well-educated and in close contact with union organizers, was in a better-than-average position to pressure for compliance with agrarian reform legislation. The response of the hacienda was to eliminate all non-wage forms of remunerations to workers (since these leave an owner vulnerable to the provisions of the agrarian reform law), and to reduce its labor needs to a minimum. It uses milking machines, potato harvesters, and other labor-saving machines that are rare in the province, and hires only a small core of year-round skilled and unskilled workers.

However, in the late 1970s and early 1980s returns to capital for certain agricultural crops--especially onions--were outstripping those available from cattle raising. In order to take advantage of this favorable market while at the same time avoiding the pitfalls of dependence on a large work force, the owner farms his agricultural land through a sharecropper, who absorbs all the labor headaches and risks.

The third hacienda is Sumac Ashpa, located further away from Riobamba than the other two, in an isolated and agriculturally productive region of the canton. This hacienda, like Chacón, sold a large part of its holdings to former workers in the 1960s and, like Chacón, it combines agriculture with cattle-raising. Because of both its geographical isolation and historical factors, Hacienda Sumac Ashpa is more dependent on the good will of its indigenous neighbors than are many haciendas. This dependence has led it to grant these neighbors a series of concessions. While a certain degree of mechanization has taken place, the owner has opted for using local labor over machines in many instances. Workers are allowed gleaning privileges plus a ration of potatoes each day when working in the potato harvest; several pasture their animals on the hacienda, and *peones* (day laborers) are allowed a daily ration of firewood or straw from the hacienda. In addition, the owner engages in such "old-fashioned" practices as the granting of *suplidos*, or cash advances to workers, and also gives preference to local labor over machines in hacienda projects such as road construction. In addition to these benefits, workers at Sumac Ashpa also receive some of the highest cash wages in the region.

These three cases illustrate the ways in which non-capitalist and capitalist labor practices are combined on Chimborazo haciendas. These practices serve different functions in different situations; sharecropping, at both Sumac Ashpa and Chacón, enhances capitalists' profits, while at Chacón it has the added function of reducing the owner's vulnerability to campesino pressures for land. Similarly, in one situation, illegal non-capitalist practices--labor fines--lower the labor costs of a highly capitalist owner. In general, however, non-capitalist labor practices such as the granting of rights to pasture, gleaning, etc., are clearly advantageous to indigenous workers; they provide access to vital resources still monopolized in large part by haciendas.

Hacienda Sumac Ashpa is typical of one kind of hacienda in the area, where non-wage forms of remuneration are found together with the highest daily cash wages. The situations on these farms clearly indicate that high cash wages and non-cash remunerations are not antithetical to each other, each being associated with a different mode of production. Workers on those haciendas that combine high salaries with high numbers of non-wage remunerations are clearly in a better position than are workers on other haciendas. These haciendas tend to be the ones furthest away from the urban center of Riobamba, in remote areas with low population densities. Thus, we may surmise that the relatively better position of these workers in the labor market may contribute to a greater bargaining power, and hence to their higher rates of remuneration.

Discussion

How can we best account for the particular mixture of capitalist and non-capitalist practices on Chimborazo's haciendas that have been described above? In any examination of Chimborazo's history, it becomes clear that the issue of control over land has been and continues to be central. Throughout the centuries, haciendas gradually usurped the best agricultural lands, often in the attempt to secure indigenous labor, since the displaced Indians were offered subsistence plots on the haciendas in exchange for their labor. Indians, attempting to maintain their economic and cultural autonomy, moved to the more remote, less productive regions, but were forced, both by taxes imposed by church and state and by their growing dependence on the market, to work on the haciendas in order to meet their cash needs.

In the issue of land, the distinctions between analytically distinct categories become blurred; the spheres of economy and culture, of politics and religion, are inextricably intertwined. For Indians, although the economic role of land is crucial, its importance extends into other areas. Local places like mountaintops and springs are important spiritually and the earth itself is sacred. In addition to its spiritual importance, land also embodies the continuity of the ethnic group itself, as represented in the phrase, "land of our ancestors." Maintaining a rural land base separate from non-Indians is a way in which people maintain cultural as well as economic autonomy. In the words of A. Andrango, an indigenous leader:

> Poverty forces the Indian to become a *cholo* [Indian of national culture]. In contrast, let us suppose that the Indian has three or four hectares, or works his community's land. This means that now he has no need to migrate if he can work his own land. Now he will have work or money from his own

land, or from the communal land. Now, indeed, he will be able to buy his poncho, his white trousers, [indigenous dress] and will participate in his community with his own, indigenous traditions. That is to say, land helps him conserve his authenticity. (1983:51)

As other Sierra regions have experienced a growth in capitalist agriculture, their indigenous populations have undergone a process of cultural assimilation or "cholofication." This has not happened to anywhere near the same degree in Chimborazo. Throughout the province, Indians have engaged in several strategies to maintain their access to land and hence their cultural and economic independence. In some areas, using the agrarian reform laws, they have succeeded in breaking the hacienda's monopoly over land. In other areas, however, they have had to resort to other tactics--either illegal land invasion, risky because of the degree of repression which they occasion, or, a struggle to maintain non-cash remuneration, especially rights to grazing land, for their hacienda labor. In an economic environment of spiraling inflation, real wages in agriculture, meager even in those few cases where the legal minimum is observed, do not keep pace with inflation. The advantage of payment in kind becomes obvious. The majority of indigenous families in the province subsist through combining a variety of economic strategies, including wage labor, agriculture, craft production and trade. At the strictly economic level, non-cash payments can mean in some cases the difference between a family's ability to maintain a home base in their community of origin, on the one hand, and forced urban migration, on the other. Important historical factors also contribute to the maintenance of non-wage relations; indigenous communities recall the days before the coming of the haciendas, when the land belonged to their ancestors, and although they may grant hacendados tactical superiority, they never grant them the moral right of land ownership. Thus, they continue to insist that they have right of access to hacienda resources. Under the circumstances outlined above, this results in their insistence on the continuation in non-wage remunerations, which simultaneously represent concrete material assets and a symbolic concession in an ongoing ideological battle with non-indigenous land owners.

Factor analysis of the survey data revealed that those haciendas which scored highest in agricultural worker strength, where high wages and non-wages remunerations were combined, were those furthest from the urban center, Riobamba. Population densities decrease with distance from Riobamba, and, because of the difficult mountain terrain and lack of good roads, the cost of importing workers into the more remote areas via labor contractors increases significantly. Thus, agricultural labor in the most remote areas becomes relatively scarcer, and workers there are in a relatively better bargaining position than those closest to Riobamba. These more remote areas are also those with the highest percentages of indigenous population.

At this point then, we are able to offer an explanation for the co-existence of relatively "high" wages and non-wage remunerations. This combination is found where the hacienda's land monopoly has not yet been broken, and where some indigenous campesinos find themselves obliged to work for the hacienda. However, because of the relatively better labor market conditions, they have been able to obtain slightly better working conditions than their counterparts elsewhere.[9] They, like the Peruvian campesinos described by Martinez-Alier, have acted as "proletarians"--forming unions and demanding higher cash wages--at the same time that they have acted as "indigenous campesinos"--claiming traditional rights to hacienda resources and maintaining payments in kind.

Chimborazo's relatively unassimilated indigenous population has more successfully resisted total proletarianization than have the mestizo or cholo population of other areas of the Sierra. In so doing, they have influenced the rate and kind of economic change in the province's agricultural sector. Marx is oft-quoted as having said that people make history, but not under conditions of their own choosing. In Chimborazo, indigenous campesinos have "made history," although clearly not under conditions of their own choosing. While acknowledging, then, the accuracy of the second half of Marx's statement, it is hoped that the presentation of these findings will encourage us to pay closer attention to the role of local histories, and to the people who make them, in shaping economic development.

NOTES

1   The 1980-1982 fieldwork on which this article is based was supported by grants from the National Science Foundation, the Fulbright Commission, and the Wenner-Gren Foundation. Thanks

are due to Susan Gal, Randy Smith, Yanet Baldares, Charity Goodman, Yolanda Prieto, and Hanna Lessinger for their support and comments. However, all interpretations and mistakes remain my responsibility.

2   The term "globalist" is borrowed from Carol A. Smith's "Local History in Global Context"(1984).

3   E.P. Thompson's *The Making of the English Working Class* (1966) was one of the first works to demonstrate the important role of local-level actors in economic changes.

4   I first encountered this term in Carol Smith (1984).

5   For the purposes of this study, "hacienda" is defined as a rural property larger than 50 hectares in size.

6   The word "campesino," usually translated as "peasant," more accurately refers to the poor residents of rural areas, regardless of their relationship to the means of production.

7   A discussion of why the indigenous populations in different regions of Ecuador have experienced distinct patterns of cultural assimilation and/or maintenance of ethnic identity is a much larger topic than can be addressed here.

8   Chicha is an alcoholic beverage traditionally supplied by employers to agricultural workers in this area. It comes in varying degrees of toxicity and nutritional content.

9   This statement should not be construed to mean that indigenous workers command true political power. Agricultural unions are often local affairs, representing only the workers on one particular hacienda. Although indigenas have gained some representation in national-level labor organization, they are all but invisible in political parties and in the Ecuadorian state. The "power" discussed here refers more to a demographic or labor market position.

BIBLIOGRAPHY

Andrango, Alberto
   1983 Contra la Discriminación y la Pobreza. *In* La Cuestión Indígena en El Ecuador. Cuadernos de Nueva, no. 7 (June):50–52.

Archetti, Eduardo
  1981 Campesinado y Estructuras Agrarias en América Latina. Quito: CEPLAES.
Arcos, Carlos and Carlos Marchan
  1976 Apuntes para una Discusión Sobre los Cambios en la Estructura Agraria Serrana. Cuaderno del Departamento de Ciencias Políticas y Sociales. Quito: P.U.C.E.
Barsky, Oswaldo & G. Cosse
  1981 Tecnología y Cambio Social: las Haciendas Lecheras del Ecuador. Quito: FLACSO.
Burgos, Hugo
  1970 Relaciones Interétnicas en Riobamba. Mexico, D.F.: Instituto Indigenista Interamericano.
Frank, Andre Gunder
  1966 The Development of Underdevelopment. Monthly Review 18:17-31.
Handleman, Howard
  1980 Ecuadorian Agrarian Reform: The Politics of Limited Change. Hanover, N.J.: American Universities Field Service Report.
Kahn, Joel
  1980 Miningkabau Social Formations: Indonesian Peasants and the World Economy. Cambridge: Cambridge University Press.
Martínez-Alier, Juan
  1977 Haciendas, Plantations and Collective Farms. London: Frank Cass.
Maynard, Eileen
  1965 Indians in Misery. Ithaca, N.Y.: Cornell University Department of Anthropology.
Meillassoux, Claude
  1972 From Reproduction to Production. Economy & Society 1(1):93.
Moreno Yañez, Segundo
  1978 Sublevaciones Indígenas en la Real Audencia de Quito. Quito: P.U.C.E.
Mouzelis, Nicos
  1980 Modernization, Underdevelopment, Uneven Development: Prospects for a Theory of Third-world Formations. Journal of Peasant Studies 7:353-374.
Smith, Carol A.
  1984 Local History in Global Context: Social & Economic Transitions in Western Guatemala. Comparative Studies in Society and History, April 1984.

Thompson, E.P.
   1966 The Making of the English Working Class. New York:
      Vintage Books.
Wallerstein, Immanuel
   1974 The Modern World System. New York: Academic Press.
Wolf, Eric
   1982 Europe and the People Without History. Berkeley: Uni-
      versity of California.

THE WAITING PROLETARIAT:
A NEW INDUSTRIAL LABOR FORCE
IN RURAL MAQUILAS

Donna J. Keren

Introduction[1]

The cornerstone of development is the drive to move people off the land and into industrial wage labor. The ability to do this is a key measure of development success in capitalist, socialist and mixed economies. The outcome of this real process of transformation, that is to say, the conditions under which agricultural labor becomes integrated into industry, varies with concrete historical circumstances. The balance of power between capital and labor and the ability of the state to direct this industrial transformation determine the development path of a country. A cooperative garment *maquila*[2] project in Querétaro, Mexico provides a case study not only of the actors and aims in one development project, but of the problems and contradictions of increasing capital penetration in the countryside.

In 1982 and 1983 I visited several villages with maquilas in rural Querétaro. Over a period of just months I was witness to the rapid transformation of a group of peasant women into industrial workers. If there was a hidden agenda in this seemingly well-meant government-sponsored development project, it was the formation of a waiting proletariat. By this, I mean, the process of creating an available labor force vulnerable to the market in terms of wages, job opportunities and work conditions; a surplus population waiting for future capital investment to bring jobs into the industrial corridor that connects Querétaro with Mexico City.

What may be unique about Mexican development is the alliance of a revolutionary state, founded upon a strong commitment to creating jobs and improving living conditions, with a strong national and international capital sector. The Mexican political-economic system (under the government of the Institutionalized Revolutionary Party - PRI) is based upon a complex negotiation process originally conceived with the state representing peasants, workers and the popular or middle classes, as well as assuming the goals of capitalist development (Keren 1985b, Sanderson 1981). As industrialization has proceeded the establishment of "tripartite" institutions with representatives of the state, capital and labor have been used by the government to achieve political stability at the same time as they served to legitimate the processes of capital accumulation in the country (Silva 1983:v). Although it is essentially capitalist in practice, in line with its revolutionary ideology the state continues to advocate different ends than the private sector. Still, the system survived because of the ability of these tripartite agencies, commissions and projects "to analyze and resolve the problems that arise from the social relations of production and the process of capital accumulation" (Silva 1983:ix, my translation).

As the early phase of the maquila project shows, the state redefined the problems of development and redirected the actors, as well as created new economic and political "shock absorbers", such as the cooperatives, for the conditions and contradictions of class relations. Unfortunately the maquila project also demonstrates that rarely could or did the government actually reorient the conditions of capitalist development. That was not in its own interest.

I argue in this article that when Mexico entered the current period of severe economic crisis, the government's ability to negotiate and redefine the economic model eroded. The crisis changed the balance of power among the participants in the transformation process. At first capital only gained advantage in relation to labor and may even have lost some ground to the state. In the long run, however, capital may do better than the state in the negotiated stability of power (Keren 1985b). The crisis brought about a change in the government policy for dealing with the Querétaro maquilas. The agroindustry project rapidly lost its cooperative character as plans were adapted to the declining economy. In order to continue opening up rural industrial jobs the government conceded to the private sector the right to capitalize, supply, and in the end, effectively run the so-called worker cooperatives it had helped establish.

The state-sponsored agro-industrial cooperatives are the focal point for this discussion of the creation of an industrial proletariat. Most explanations of the transformation process point out that workers driven off the land provide cheap labor by depressing wages; that is, the mass of people leaving the land exceeds the number of available industrial jobs, thereby increasing the supply of laborers and decreasing the wages paid to them. My analysis of the Querétaro maquila project suggests that the study of capitalist control over production process and labor is equally vital to the understanding of the formation and conditions of the reserve army and active labor forces in industrial economies. Capital's control over the work process and industrial discipline are the tools used to extract actual labor from the "cheap" labor power that flows from the countryside. Nevertheless, the historical literature on economic development in Europe and the Americas is filled with descriptions of efforts to overcome overt and covert resistance to capitalist work discipline. Cheap labor power is not useful unless these workers can be made to give up their notions of self-directed work.

The first part of this article outlines the Mexican economic crisis and particularly the local conditions in the state of Querétaro. The next section describes the maquila cooperatives as I saw them during the last months of my fieldwork in December, 1982, January and February, 1983, and then October, 1983. I focus in on the revamped government policy in the Fall of 1983. The economic crisis altered the power relations between capital and labor and between the state and capital, a shift which promoted the trend toward exploitation and capitalist control of the workers. The decreasing leverage of the state allowed capital greater influence over production, credit and ideology. Finally, using Marx's concept of the reserve army of labor I analyze some of the ways control over the new proletarian labor force in these rural areas was being achieved and labor's ability to protect its own interests was being undermined.

The Crisis

The almost inescapable starting point for any research done in or on Mexico in 1982 or 1983 has to be the ever-deepening economic crisis, especially when the questions asked are: Who was working and what were they doing? The daily ups and downs and the long-term implications of the crisis became the idiom of my research during those months. Mexican and outsider alike, we were observers to the economy's collapse.

Following the 1977 discovery of massive oil reserves, the newest Mexican economic boom was based primarily on mortgaging potential oil revenues to secure loans from private banks, the World Bank and other international lenders. In the four years between 1977 and 1981, Mexico achieved a remarkable 8% annual growth rate (Riding 1985:148). Prosperity did not last. The 1981-1982 drop in oil prices directly reduced government revenues from the state-owned oil company by at least 10 billion dollars (U.S.)(*Wall Street Journal* April 21, 1982). Down the line the rest of the oil and loan dependent economy was contracting. A year later, in December, 1982, Mexico was 90 billion dollars in debt. There were grave doubts in all quarters about the country's ability to repay the outstanding debt. Meanwhile rising interest rates in the U.S. and other international markets limited Mexico's ability to borrow more or to refinance. With over 80% of the industrial plant dependent on imported capital goods and raw materials (*Proceso* 1982), dollars not being spent to repay the foreign debt, or being smuggled out of the country were needed to keep the weakened economy running. At the same time the peso was devalued by 600% and inflation soared over 100%. As the cost of living climbed workers' real wages and consumers' purchasing power declined. The economy was in turmoil. Everyone acknowledged that the Crisis, with a capital "C", was for real. Although moderate recovery has occurred in some periods since 1983, Mexico is not out of economic and political trouble yet.

In September, 1982, Mexican President José López Portillo engineered the political and economic coup of his administration: he nationalized the private banking sector and established generalized control of currency exchange rates. The nationalization was a move to reestablish the government's hegemony in the negotiated stability; the controls were a too late attempt to prevent capital flight. The currency controls, however, together with import restrictions, effectively closed Mexico's borders to needed industrial inputs and added to the dimensions of the crisis (Keren 1985b). Although slowdowns and lay-offs had characterized industry throughout 1982; by year-end Mexican manufacturing was practically at a standstill, operating at less than 40% of capacity. Union officials claimed that between half a million and a million workers had been laid off just during the third quarter of 1982 (*Wall Street Journal* August 27, 1982:1; *Proceso* 1982). For those still working, emergency cost of living increases and annual pay adjustments only made up a small percentage of their lost purchasing power.

Querétaro is a small, semi-industrialized state located 150 miles northwest of Mexico City in the central plateau region. Since the 1960s when its industrial take-off began, rapid industrial growth has been achieved at the expense of output and employment in the traditional agricultural and service sectors. In 1979 the area was designated a "growth pole" (*polo de atracción*) in federal development plans. Tax breaks, subsidies and other external incentives have helped attract substantial investment to the two metropolitan industrial zones, Querétaro and San Juan del Río, both in the southern half of the state. Between 1979 and 1982 industrial development increased 67% (PRI 1982:39) making Querétaro one of the fastest growing areas in the country (Muñoz 1986).

Durable goods, food processing and textiles, much of it for export, led the manufacturing sector. Industrial development is concentrated in a few companies with over 80% of the productive capital invested in less than 10% of the firms. These companies represent national and transnational interests. Querétaro provides a home to members of powerful national holding companies (VISA - Clemente Jacques or ICA - Industria del Hierro), new and established multinationals (Celanese, General Electric [sold in 1984 to Black & Decker], Purina, Kelloggs) and state-owned enterprises (Fertimex).

Many factories employ a floating worker population, called *eventuales*, to meet the seasonal work demands and to keep their permanent (and unionized) labor forces as small as possible. Even in the best of times, when jobs were available, competition for good jobs was stiff. In this worst of times, the eventuales or provisionals were let go as early as summer 1982, permanent workers followed soon after. According to industrial survey data collected during my fieldwork, I estimate that between August and Decem-

ber, 1982, 35 to 40% of the Querétaro industrial labor force was
laid off or fired.

Querétaro also faced an agricultural crisis in 1982. Although
located on the edge of the agriculturally rich Bajío region, the
state is primarily mountainous and arid. Most agricultural land is
poor and dependent upon rainfall so that, in general, subsistence
farming can make little use of mechanization, fertilizers or genetic
enrichment of crops or animals (Banrural 1980). Irrigation projects
provide water for large commercial farms, not smallholders.
Ejidal land holders and peasants then are pressured by the local
livestock industry either to graze cattle or to produce sorghum and
alfalfa for feed. Technical aid and seed and stock improvement
programs have been instituted with development or credit bank
backing. Given these programs' reliance on international funding
it is not surprising that they favor larger commercial operations
(Bartra 1982, Edelman 1980, Grindle 1982, Redclift 1983). Even
with support, however, commercial agriculture and stock raising
do not offer a viable alternative for development and employment
in the state (Banrural 1980, PRI 1982). Years of drought, crop
failure and migration have meant that land is continually withdrawn from active production. In addition, because most of the
arable land is located in the same region as the densest population
and industrialization; small holders are in competition for land
with the expanding cities and industrial parks (Chant 1984, Hoops
and Whiteford 1983).

When economic crisis and agricultural crisis coincide labor
really gets squeezed. It can neither leave the land, nor live on it.
In 1982 with almost half of the state's population still in rural
areas, the 60% rural unemployment and underemployment posed a
serious problem. The governor declared an agricultural emergency. Querétaro had not been self-sufficient in basic food production for many years, but in the sixth year of drought more
than half the corn crop was lost. In the driest mountain areas
most growers did not even plant (Camacho 1982).

In an attempt to generate rural employment, the state government encouraged small-scale development including reforestation,
agricultural collectives, fruit growing and road building (Camacho
1982). Men, who comprised the primary workforce for these activities, sometimes organized independently to exploit local marble
and limestone deposits. The agro-industry maquila cooperative
project was one attempt to provide rural industrial work for
women. Excluded from the extractive industries and most com-

mercial agricultural ventures, women had only a few options in non-agricultural work, such as home knitting machines. Women's "choice" of migration meant working in domestic service, food service or other urban irregular occupations or accepting the conditions of super-exploitation in domestic outwork in Ciudad Nezahualcoyotl and elsewhere (Alonso 1979, Arizpe 1975, 1978; Benería 1983, Young 1981).

In the sections that follow I will explore how the crisis coopted this local development project and led to increased exploitation of the workers. As economic conditions deteriorated throughout Mexico both the revenues of the state and the profits of capital declined. Austerity on the part of the government and cut backs by capital were changing the environment in which people worked and lived and shifting the terms of the transition from peasant to proletarian.

In the boom economy optimistic plans assumed that the state would have sufficient revenue to consider its own interests, to support infrastructure and job creation and, at the same time, to finance social programs which provided workers some share in the benefits of development. In the declining economy, there might still be enough surplus produced to respond to social issues and create jobs. In the crisis social welfare concerns were made superfluous, as even the preservation of employment was in doubt. The Mexican economy went from boom to bust very quickly. The government lost the ability to buffer the effects of development on the workers. In Querétaro it seems it also lost interest in doing so. The Querétaro maquila project began in a declining economy, but ended in a crisis. Its autonomous cooperative purpose coopted by an argument about the need for profits and jobs at any wages.

A Model Development Project or a Model for Development?

The idea for the state's rural maquila job program was not a new one in Mexico or elsewhere (de Barbieri 1981, Dixon 1978). The stated goal of the plans was to create alternative sources of local employment in "agro-industry" for women in rural communities. This would counter rural-urban migration as well as improve living standards and provide a cash income. Although "agro" usually implies a direct link with the peasant economy, such as egg raising, dairy production or handicrafts; garment assembly plants and non-agricultural operations are possible (de Barbieri 1981, García 1982). The Querétaro maquila job program was notable when proposed because the maquilas were supposed to be run as worker cooperatives affiliated with a state cooperative association. The women workers and the communities would have control over their own activities and success.

The story of the rural communities' participation in the government sponsored agro-industries stands out because of the intensified participation of private sector firms and the consequent distortion of the cooperative status. Even the most autonomous cooperative cannot, as Thornley (1981:173) points out, avoid the capitalist market. Although not capitalist in structure or aim, through middlemen they too contribute to capital accumulation (Thornley 1981:97, de la Peña 1982:33). In Querétaro it was the extension of capitalist control over the organization and day-to-day operation of individual factories that further undermined their autonomy. Paradoxically, although private capital allowed many of these workshops to continue operations, they survived not as cooperatives but essentially as sources of "sweated labor" producing surplus value for the capitalist sector. This case of rural proletarianization within the maquilas provides an important insight into the effects of the economic crisis on the entire labor force. The crisis made even these seemingly independent, small-scale, often isolated rural factories more vulnerable to the exigencies of Mexico's dependence on an oil economy, technology transfer, and foreign loans.

The project had had a brief former life. The Federal Rural Credit Bank (known as Banrural) had funded an earlier attempt to set up a rural maquila program in Querétaro (1979-1980). Initially the bank-sponsored workshops appeared as a model development project, but showy buildings and expensive imported industrial sewing machines[4] were the only fruits of extravagant spending. Labor resistance surfaced almost immediately. According to an excerpt from my 1982 interviews: "They [Banrural] never ran it for more than four consecutive weeks at a time, and finally left it abandoned for more than two years."

Development bank project failures in Mexico or elsewhere are hardly uncommon and generally are due not to shortages of funds, but to organizational problems and contradictory outcomes (de la Peña 1981, Edelman 1980, Galli 1981, Grindle 1982, Kearney 1980, Lorenzen 1981, Redclift 1983, Williams and Miller 1973). Under Banrural direction, city-based officials could neither tell what was needed for the project nor how to get it. Nor did they have the authority to carry out decisions. Without adequate worker training or an autonomous means of worker control, the maquilas ran into a vicious circle: the lack of skills or incentives to learn kept productivity levels low; wages, which were based on piece rates, were not competitive or even close to a subsistence wage; poor marketing and distribution systems meant they could not sell what they produced. Obviously there were problems with paying wages on time. As one villager commented later, "No wonder they had labor problems."

The Querétaro state labor department (Secretaría de Trabajo y Previsión Social or STPS) took over the maquila project mid-crisis in the Fall of 1982. The STPS initiative was a planning showpiece aimed at creating rural employment opportunities in an otherwise declining economy. It was more efficient because decision making was vested in the director, whom I will call Faustino Mata. The communities, mobilized through local *caciques*, provided land and labor. The government provided limited capital, but mostly reactivated the original Banrural credits and gained access to the existing buildings and warehoused equipment. Mata, a consummate politician, seemed to enjoy his powerful administrative role as middleman between the communities and the private sector. The most striking feature of the new plan, in fact, was the degree to which the private sector was embraced as a source of active managerial "partners", not simply viewed as outside investors with no particular interest in the daily operation.[5]

The state intervention directly supported the communities and the maquila cooperative program by providing or improving roads, water, drainage and electrification.[6] Mata himself saw to expediting permits and licenses, arranging for additional credits, transporting machinery between locations.[7] The STPS also paid electric and other over due bills and in some cases provided salary subsidies, guaranteed wages or price supports. The initial concern with social welfare was further demonstrated by the provision of state-hired social workers.[8]

Theoretically acting as broker for the co-ops, the STPS, through Faustino Mata, worked with the private sector to locate suppliers, secure contracts, develop marketing and distribution systems and provide on-the-job training. The government approached individual owners of commercial clothing assembly plants (*maquileros*), and invited them "to support" this project. The terms varied but, in general, investors were to provide raw materials, supervisors and trainers and market outlets. In return these men were able to influence the product, the piece rate, and the production process and even to request favors from the government.

One of the more readily accessible sites, Las Fuentes workshop was located in an area of commercial maquila concentration. The factory was a 1-story building of cinderblock and concrete, about 20 by 45 feet with windows set in both long sides. It housed 35 sewing machines. In the center of the floor the women worked in two rows; ten machines sat unused against the wall. At 10:30 a.m. it was still cold inside and the women sewed by natural light since overhead fluorescent fixtures were not being used. Production during the 40-48 hour work week was recorded on a sheet hung by each place.

This cooperative was located on communal land, and so required that all the women be members of the ejido community.[9] The workers, many of them single mothers[10], ranged in age from 18 or 19 to thirty. When recruitment began in October, 1982, local interest in the project ran high and ten women were selected from over 30 applicants. A month into operation, 25 women were in training but turnover was becoming a problem.

Faustino Mata had persuaded a successful maquilero to invest in Las Fuentes. The maquilero, whom I will call Señor Verdugo, provided the trainer and production supervisor (his sister, Señora Caridad), the cut garments to be assembled, and marketed the finished products. After recovering his costs, the women or their representative Mata made payments on outstanding loans. Then with state support, the workers received a subsidized wage, rather than piece rates.[11] This wage support system was to revert to piece work after the 16 week training period. There was no provision to assure that workers' earnings kept pace with cost of living increases or with the wage gains made by organized labor.

During their first month of training, the women had not produced a single finished piece. The goal was set at 1500 blouses a week--assembled, quality checked, pressed and packed. Their start-up project, a complicated women's knit top, possibly intended for an international market through the maquilero's connections, had the women working not only on different pieces but on different styles and machines simultaneously.

The social worker's protean job was a contradictory mandate to facilitate the women's efforts to establish the cooperatives, while at the same time to advocate their adaptation to the work discipline of factory life. Ideally she should have helped the workers "run their own businesses" by teaching about marketing, production and decision-making. Her relationship to the project director made her the eyes, ears, and occasionally long arm of the state inside the workshops. In addition to overseeing the working conditions, she also acted as mediator between the workers and Sr. Verdugo. However, her visits each week, by concentrating on the development of a suitable factory work ethic, were aimed more at teaching the women to take orders rather than to make decisions.

On my last visit to the maquila three months later I saw only 13 women working. Production had shifted completely to the assembly of men's shirt cuffs and sleeves. This work had been subcontracted from Sr. Verdugo's nearest commercial factory. The supervisor, Sra. Caridad, argued that at least these women had work until the workshop could resume cooperative production. It should be noted that in this case subcontracted work for the private sector continued to receive subsidies in the form of state support for wages and training.

Between 10 and 14 workshops participated in the project at various times. Still there were crucial differences in this small sample of factories. Some like Las Fuentes were easily reached and took advantage of previous ventures. Others, like San Antonio El Doctor, located at the end of a dirt track on top of a 9,000 foot mountain, were new sites attempting to create local employment in unlikely places. Some maquilas were established in indigenous communities, others among mestizos. Their wage and price systems ranged from subsidized wages to salaries or piece work rates. Some even had government guaranteed prices. They varied in how directly they depended upon the maquilero-investor or the state for product choice and marketing of shirts, jeans, worker uniforms or hospital gowns. Task fragmentation, skill levels and external control of the work process differed from one workshop to another and resulted in differences in the training required or provided. Higuerrillas and perhaps one other site achieved cooperative status with autonomous operating committees, but even these were in debt to one of the private investors. Yet, in spite of the variation, there was one unifying similarity, the workers in each garment workshop shared the proletarianizing experiences of exploitation and external control.

From Social Welfare to Profitability

When the maquila program was first introduced the STPS project stressed social welfare, concentrating on the quality of work life and particularly a positive view of the women's adaptation to work. Rural *bienestar* (welfare) was an important aspect of the governor's development plan, with an underlying premise of "rooting the peasant to his environment" (Camacho 1981). The idea of responding to a critical need for jobs by creating cooperatives should have promoted democratically owned and managed workshops. The advantages, as Jackall and Levin (1984:3-5) point out, are that cooperatives can create more jobs than traditional capitalist enterprises for the same capital investment and they can keep productivity up by requiring fewer supervisors, monitoring their own quality control and decreasing worker dissatisfaction.

As the effects of the national economic crisis filtered down to local level projects during 1983, a new approach gradually came into being and sabotaged the minor social welfare achievements made by the new co-ops. The redefined maquila policy, responding to a new ideology at the national level, put the emphasis on productivity and protecting the investment. Faustino Mata, who had gone on to other projects was succeeded in the STPS by a more business oriented director. The two full-time social workers were gone, replaced by an administrator with a degree in business. His role was to make sure that the plants "ran like businesses", operating efficiently and profitably.

Even a minor change in policy and/or administration can have disastrous effects on a cooperative project since the direction of change is most frequently toward more privatized operations (Jones and Schneider 1984:64, Littlefield 1978, Singlemann 1978, Wells and Climo 1984, Williams and Miller 1973). The Querétaro cooperative project, I believe, was no exception. Policy in this case changed when the government party's revolutionary ideology came into contradiction with profit.[12] Certainly cooperatives have to pay their overhead, repay loans and stay competitive in the market. The crisis, however, stripped away the mask of the cooperative structure to expose the exploitative, capitalistic character of these workshops (Nash and Hopkins 1976).

The relationship between the maquilero-investor and the co-op members went beyond doing good business. More often than not he managed supervision, set production quotas, controlled purchasing and distribution. He even established membership and owned or financed the means of production. As the maquilero increasingly appropriated the surplus and claimed control over production the women's status went from co-op member to proletarian worker. As Alonso et al. (1980) demonstrated for the process they refer to as "disguised proletarianization", high levels of self-exploitation among small-scale producers actually mean higher rates of surplus extraction. It is a useful concept for looking at the Querétaro agro-industries.

Singlemann, discussing Mexican agriculture, draws the distinction between cooperative or controlled collectivization. Jones and Schneider (1984:59) do the same for U.S. rural industry, distinguishing between autonomous cooperatives and controlled ones. In controlled collectives, Singlemann (1978:30) says, land may be owned or controlled by the peasants but utilization of the land, labor and credit resources comes under the control of outside agencies. Furthermore, production and marketing are managed by hired administrators. Under these conditions, the peasants effectively "sell" their labor power to a collective enterprise which is only nominally theirs. With the weight of dependence on outside supports and financial institutions, government agencies and investors rather than co-op members impose the operating conditions. De la Peña (1982:33) considers that in Mexico both agricultural and industrial cooperatives "have been the object of systematic attacks...for the most part operated not like cooperatives but like enterprises that use salaried labor." Fritz-Krockow (1986:796) concludes, "Mexican cooperativism is, to a large extent, an instrument of government policy to advance development programs...the members many times are seen as salaried workers of some state office" (my translation). In this light, the Querétaro workshops must be described as externally controlled enterprises aimed at proletarianization.

It is tempting to describe this tendency to seek profits as a pragmatic response to economic conditions, but only if we ignore the hidden agenda: the need to create and maintain an available industrial labor force in the area and to subject these communities to increasing dependence on the capitalist system often without providing very much local benefit. The Querétaro maquila cooperative project, in spite of the problems inherent in establishing programs in highly competitive sectors, such as the garment industry, selected precisely that sector to receive state support. The cost of not playing by the rules is borne out by the fact that over 50% of Mexico's garment and textile workers lost their jobs in 1982 (*Proceso* 1982) and that in October, 1985, Faustino Mata reported to me that almost every cooperative maquila, except Higuerrillas, eventually had been closed by the STPS.

The changed 1983 STPS policy toward the workshops went from advocating social welfare to demanding productivity. This aggravated the problems faced by the Querétaro agro-industry cooperatives. In fact, with their economic and technological dependencies intact, the work was increasingly vulnerable to the crisis. In each so-called cooperative the attention paid to social issues, work conditions, and community welfare was meeting strong opposition. With the workshops now in operation, the government was no longer concerned with developing the work ethic or even with counseling "have patience it'll get better". Now the administration only wanted to know: how many pieces per week were produced? Was the operation showing a profit? Did the women accept their work conditions? If these requisites of work discipline were not satisfied the workshop was closed and the equipment relocated.

In the end the women workers absorbed the shock waves of the crisis. Their wages were imperiled, not the maquilero's profits. For example, the total dependence on imported equipment in all the plants magnified the consequences of a broken sewing machine. In one maquila women who had to work on broken machines earned one-half to one-third less than their usual wages, while waiting for imported repair parts which might never arrive because of import restrictions and currency controls. In another maquila the women sat idle amidst hundreds of unfinished garments waiting for one operator to complete an essential step on the sole overlock stitching machine. Many project sites manufactured workers' uniforms, yet even this presumed accessible and stable market was shrinking as industrial unemployment soared to 40%. As the crisis deepened the government was able to tighten its control over labor in the countryside as well as concede a free hand to private sector operations to do the same (de la Peña 1981:259, Grindle 1982, Wells and Climo 1984:165). The Querétaro maquila project may actually be the model for capitalist development in the region. Development in which, as Arías and Bazán (1980) suggest for Morelos, Mexico, the relations between capital, the state and the local population facilitate the creation of a growing proletariat waiting for the factories to employ them.

Capital Accumulation and the Control of the Labor Force

We can explain the creation of a waiting proletariat in rural Querétaro by examining the issue of control of the labor force.

The maquila development program was created and the women recruited to industrial work as part of the process of capital accumulation Marx described in Volume I of *Capital*. Marx's analysis of the creation of the industrial reserve army of labor in the process of capital accumulation established the nature of the relationship between capital and labor and focused on the mechanisms of control: "the increasing concentration of the means of production *and the [increasing] command over labor*" (Marx 1967:625, my emphasis). Capital accumulation, however, is not simply command over more and cheaper labor. To make a profit in a competitive environment capital accumulation also requires more command, that is, control of labor power achieved through control of the labor process. Labor recruitment, remuneration, the conditions of work and the worker himself must all come under capitalist control. By understanding that control is "all means for the development of production [which] transform themselves into means of domination over and exploitation of the producers" (Marx 1967: 645), we can see the various "cheap labor" arguments in a better light.

The tendency has been to emphasize the sheer numbers and availability of more workers, the reserve army of labor. There is no question that as industry develops masses of peasants move off the land and seek urban, industrial work. Nor is there a doubt that the increasing size of the reserve army exerts a downward pressure on wages and leads to increased exploitation. Nevertheless, if the equation--more reserve army members equals greater pressure on wages--were all we took away from this discussion, we would be confined to quantitative arguments about how many people make up "an inexhaustible reservoir of disposable labor power" (Marx 1967:643)? Or how much surplus value must be extracted to make labor cheap? What we still must explain is how capital extracts actual labor from the workers in these factories. How does capital exercise what Zimbalist (1979:xvi) calls "the levers of capitalist control in the workplace?"

The method of capital accumulation is the extraction of surplus value. That means producing more work per worker as well as creating a larger pool of workers to exploit. The price of "cheap labor" is determined ultimately by the market. Employers can pay lower wages by deskilling workers, or by movement to less developed regions and depeasantization, but they must also find a disciplined work force which will labor under the conditions needed to maintain high surplus values and low wages.

Employers need a labor force that can be controlled and kept stable, one where ideology has been coopted and worker resistance to work discipline has been undermined.

Cooperatives can be especially useful in this process of control and are frequently encouraged by the state in order to "to set up a bureaucratic structure through which the central government could increase its control of the countryside, and perhaps at the same time ensure that the excess population of agriculture or mining is drained off for the purposes of the national society" (Nash and Hopkins 1976:14). The women working in the Querétaro maquila project have been provided with, but do not own or control, the buildings, businesses, training, wage levels, contracts or markets. The terms of their entry into industrial labor were capitalist not cooperative relations of production. These maquilas offered the chimera of autonomy and the reality of being wage earners living in villages already embedded in a dependent capitalist economy. The women employed in the rural factories were industrial workers, proletarians not peasants. They were economically active; yet, as the work-shops were closed down one after another, they had few places to go to be active.

There was constant mystification of capital-labor relations in the running of the rural maquilas. The direct control by the maquilero was hidden behind the rhetoric of the cooperative organization and the government wage subsidies, price supports and incentives. An example I call "The Case of the Fired Workers" illustrates the attempts to manipulate ideology even early in the project.

When the social worker reported to the project director in December, 1982, that the "supervisor" had "fired" (*despedido*) four women, Faustino Mata turned red in the face and yelled, "You do NOT say fired! That is an owner-worker relationship and here there is NO owner. This is a cooperative." He continued, more calmly, "She could have said that she 'had to let them go' emphasizing that the women just did not have the desire to work or that it was not working out. But under no circumstances was anyone to ever say 'fired'."

Later that day Mata took the supervisor aside and reminded her that it was improper for her to fire anyone. She was only present as a trainer. He repeated his message to the maquilero, "You're only the investor, not the owner." Interestingly, at no time did anyone consider reinstating the four women. Whether or not they had work in the supposed worker cooperative was not the issue. The questions for the government representative and the capital investor were who was controlling the workers and what terms were used to express their decisions.

Despite some very real differences in the work conditions favoring the so-called cooperatives over the nearby commercial maquila operations, the workers in the government sponsored co-ops never really controlled the product, rates or conditions of production, nor the technology. Neither could they organize to express grievances or bring about change. Their discontent was met with the threat of equipment removal or closure of the cooperative.

The closing of another maquila demonstrates the result when some of the women in this labor force resisted the transfer to the maquilero of control over the production process, the change in the old social relations of production and the external pressure to work for low wages in increasingly capitalist defined conditions. San Pablo was a small maquila with a history of low-paid outwork at weekly wages averaging 400 pesos. Since incorporation into the government program, production had shifted to factory uniforms, but average earnings still were less than 800 pesos per week. Meeting with Faustino Mata in January, 1983, the women voiced discontent with their work conditions, lack of input into decisions, and low piece rate earnings imposed by a product they had not chosen. Mata only urged patience. When the new project director shut down San Pablo after only seven months and moved the equipment to another location, he said that "the workers had abandoned it". At the same time he had to admit that the women workers and the community were hostile as the STPS truck carted the sewing machines away.

I doubt that San Pablo was a failure in the business sense, sacrificed after failed attempts to make it operate profitably. As Williams and Miller (1973) suggest, development projects should be able to carry some unprofitable operations. Further, when Jones and Schneider (1984:78-81) recalculated the accounts for depression era co-ops in the U.S., they demonstrated that when the social benefits are included the cooperatives were not unprofitable despite uneven performance. Looked at this way the San Pablo maquila was a failure in the control sense. It was closed because the government and the maquilero could not control the workers.[13]

The control of credit by the government and increasingly by the maquilero was creating a new "debt peonage" in the countryside[14] (Edelman 1980:46-7, Brass 1984). In addition to the inherited Banrural loans still to be repaid, new debt was encouraged by the state and private investors. For example, in order to expand operations and remain competitive the Higuerrillas co-op board, one of the older and larger plants, had accepted a loan offer from Sr. Verdugo. As repayment he would deduct an extra 20,000 pesos each week from the factory's average gross of 70,000 pesos. As a result of this debt relationship, the women already linked to the government and the maquilero for access to equipment, supplies and distribution, were further separated from actual ownership of their cooperative. The leverage offered by the differential availability and disbursement of credit is a powerful tool in policy implementation as Kearney (1980:120) has noted. Others have documented how the extension of supervised credits in large or small scale development programs create technological dependency, further the government's authority in the region and increase the mechanisms of control over the peasants (Brass 1984:379, Galli 1981, Lorenzen 1981:92). The manipulation of the debt structure in Querétaro was an additional factor undermining the cooperative organization--the workers' power to negotiate wages, benefits, work conditions--and like other examples of debt bondage restricting labor mobility.

Conclusion

The alliance of private capital with the Querétaro state government in the planning, funding, running and future of these garment assembly "cooperatives" is helping define the position of labor in the long-term development of the whole regional economy. Capital accumulation in the Querétaro region will continue to bring highly capitalized industrial ventures with imported technology and direct or indirect dependence on transnational corporations. I believe we must identify capital penetration and proletarianization in the rural maquilas as a necessary prior step. Before a population can be exploited fully by capital it must first be created as a labor force with both active and reserve labor segments. This labor force is then constantly transformed, through greater or lesser absorption of labor, into either a relative surplus population or into an active proletariat (Arías and Bazán 1980:16-17, Cook 1984, Singlemann 1978).

The industrial reserve army of labor, however, is not just any group of people on the land or in the cities. What Marx

(1967:632) called that "mass of human material always ready for exploitation" is a labor force defined in an historical process which constantly changes its conditions. Faced with the limited availability of good agricultural land, the spread of non-subsistence agricultural and livestock production, the state of agricultural emergency, and the urban bound migrants seeking the fewer and fewer jobs, the Querétaro maquila development project was supposed to create rural jobs. That meant introducing industry and creating an industrial labor force where none existed. When this new labor force was exposed to the pressures of capitalist accumulation on a world scale, the balance of power in the local capital-state-labor alliance and the logic of local self-sufficiency gave way to the twin demands of capitalist control and profitability. Within one year maquilas had been closed. The women of San Pablo had returned to home-work, making dolls' dresses on treadle operated machines. The state's investment in infrastructure and jobs failed to create cooperatives as planned, but appears to have created a waiting proletariat.

Finally, if there is any question as to how these few hundred women in Querétaro provide an insight into the process of proletarianization, we need only look at a map of Mexico. Mexico's industrialization strategy since the mid-1970s has focused on decentralization. The choice of Querétaro as a growth pole takes advantage of its prime location linking the Bajio region with the Valley of Mexico along the Pan-American highway through the densely populated central region. Like a magnet it has drawn investment up the industrial corridor from the heavily developed Federal District (Muñoz 1986). The rural areas affected by the maquila project are located within 10 to 60 kilometers of this highway corridor. As industries and businesses continue to relocate here, these rural regions will be a primary source of future workers. Capital is making a very long-term investment in this area. In fact in November, 1986, the government announced new decentralization incentives for industrial investment in eight regions classified as "high national priority", including Pedro Escobedo and El Márques in Querétaro (*Comercio Exterior* 1987). The direct ties established between the rural communities and the privately-capitalized, government-sponsored agro-industrial maquilas exposed these women to the international division of labor and production, and created an available, essentially dependent, controlled and controllable labor force waiting for a future of industrial development.

NOTES

1   The implications of this rural development project were first discussed in the supportive environment of the New York Women's Anthropology Conference. Presentation of the data at the Association for Women in Development meetings (Keren 1985a) sharpened my focus. My writing and analytical efforts were helped by the insights and support of Larian Angelo, Susan Gabbard, Eleanor Leacock, Joan Mencher, June Nash, Barbara Schroder, Eric Wolf and the CMA readers, Christine Gailey, David Hakken and Fran Rothstein. I hope they find they made a difference. The flaws remain wholly my own.

2   In the manufacturing sector *maquilas* or *maquiladoras* are assembly plants or workshops, ranging in size from a few employees to several hundred. They can be locally owned, subsidiaries of large national or transnational (TNC) companies or wholly owned by the TNCs. Production of this type characterizes both the electric/electronic and apparel industries. Two excellent studies of large maquiladora operations are by Fernandez Kelly (1984) and Alonso (1979).

3   The maquila research was conducted as part of a larger study on the creation of the state's industrial labor force, supported in part by a Wenner Gren Foundation Grant in Aid.

4   Querétaro is the site of Singer Mexico, SA, the nation's largest manufacturer of sewing machines. But even here, no domestically manufactured industrial sewing machines were made. Mexico's entire output was for home use, the majority not electric but treadle operated. Therefore, not only the specialized machines such as overlocks, but also straight stitchers had to be imported. Most were made by Singer, Brother or Necchi.

5   Although funding from the private sector was not unusual, Williams and Miller (1973) point out that the lender was generally a disinterested party who was not involved in the operation. On the other hand, as Novelo (1976) points out, the direct involvement in cooperative and artisanal production was usually a government prerogative.

6   Electrification is crucial to the state's rural development plans. Of 1,117 rural localities in Querétaro only 434 are electrified, covering only 69% of the rural population (PRI 1982:48). Although

the villages included in this project had been beneficiaries of earlier electrification campaigns, most still required additional inputs
before they could support the demands of full-time use industrial
machines. The San Pablo site, with only 10-12 machines, blew the
power twice during the few hours of my visit.

7   Without foreign exchange and import permits, especially after
the nationalization of the bank, replacement equipment could only
be obtained by "pirating" from one location in the state to another.

8   Social workers with a minimum mandate of literacy training
were frequently attached to development projects (Edelman 1980).
One of the Querétaro social workers had just completed a 1-year
stint with an egg raising co-op.

9   The requirement that cooperative members be ejido members
(or wives, daughters, widows thereof) created a captive labor force
tied to the land. Problems faced in areas such as CIVAC in
Cuernavaca (Arías and Bazán 1980), where rural industrial opportunities brought migrant peasants from many other areas while
local peasants moved away, were eliminated. In the Sierra Norte
de Puebla (Edelman 1980) the government plan included slowing
down the rate of rural to urban migration by tying certain sectors
of the peasantry to their land. The project in Puebla used debt to
tie the peasants to the land as peasants and/or agricultural
workers, whereas in rural Querétaro the program used debt and
other mechanisms to bind rural proletarians to the land.

10   Querétaro, especially in the rural areas, had one of the country's highest birth rates, over 4.6% annually (*Diario de Querétaro*,
January, 1982), and one of the highest rates of single motherhood.
More than seven women in 100 have a child before they are 19
years old.

11   Because Las Fuentes was located in the commercial maquila
zone, wages were subsidized to make the salary competitive
enough to discourage worker pirating by private owners. At the
time of my 1982 survey the salary was approximately 220
pesos/day or about 80% of the current rural minimum wage. Successful pieceworkers could make between 1,900 and 2,500
pesos/week, exceptional ones were said to take in 4,000
pesos/week.

12   It must be remembered that the central purpose of the
Mexican Revolution and the PRI has been the creation of a modern, industrial, capitalist nation state (Keren 1985b, Sanderson

1981, Silva 1983). Mexican development priorities will always protect those interests. For a discussion of President López Portillo's concessions to business interests (the Alliance for Production, wage freezes, the New Agrarian Reform Law) see Grindle 1982, NACLA 1978:38.

13 See Scott (1974) for an excellent historical study of workers' resistance to the progressive loss of control over the means of production, the labor process, and the old social relations of production and reproduction in 19th century France.

14 Tim Parrish suggested this term to me and described an earlier Banrural agricultural-livestock development program (1976) in Querétaro in which repayment of the loan mattered less than creating a cycle of borrowing: increasing production--increasing borrowing--increasing indebtedness.

BIBLIOGRAPHY

Alonso, Jorge et al.
    1980   Lucha Urbana y Acumulación de Capital. Mexico, D.F.: Edic. de la Casa Chata.
Alonso, José A.
    1979   The Domestic Seamstresses of Nezahualcoyotl. A Case Study of Feminine Overexploitation in a Marginal Urban Area. Unpublished Ph.D. thesis, New York University.
Arías, Patricia and Lucia Bazán
    1980 CIVAC: Un Proceso de Industrialización en Una Zona Campesina. Mexico, DF: Cuadernos de la Casa Chata/CIS-INAH.
Arizpe, Lourdes
    1975   Indígenas en la Cd. de México. El Caso de las Marías. Mexico, DF: Sep/Setentas.
    1978   Migración, Etnicismo y Cambio Económico. Mexico, DF: Colegio de Mexico.
Banrural
    1980   Diagnóstico del Sector Agropecuario y Forestal del Estado de Querétaro. Qro., Mex.: Banco de Crédito Rural del Centro, S.A.
Bartra, Roger
    1982   Capitalism and the Peasantry in Mexico. Latin American Perspectives IX(1):36-47.
Benería, Lourdes
    1983   Domestic Piece Work, Subcontracting and Gender Relations: A Case Study from Mexico City. Paper presented at NY Women's Anthropology Conference.

Brass, Tom
1984   Coffee and Rural Proletarianization. Journal of Latin American Studies 16(1):143-152.

Camacho Guzmán, Governor Rafael
1981   II Informe de Gobierno. Qro., Mexico.
1982   III Informe de Gobierno. Qro., Mexico.

Chant, Sylvia
1984   Household Labour and Self-Help Housing in Querétaro, Mexico. Boletín de Estudios Latinoamericanos y Del Caribe 37:45-68.

Comercio Exterior
1987   National Affairs. January, 37(1):120.

Cook, Scott
1984   Peasant Economy, Rural Industry and Capitalist Development in the Oaxaca Valley, Mexico. Journal of Peasant Studies 11(4):3-40.

de Barbieri, Ma. Teresita
1981   Dos Experiencias de Creación de Empleo para Mujeres Campesinas. Pátzcuaro, Michoacán: Seminario Tripartito Regional para América Latina sobre el Desarrollo Rural y la Mujer, ILO.

de la Peña, Guillermo
1981   A Legacy of Promises. Agricultural Politics and Ritual in the Morelos Highlands of Mexico. Austin: University of Texas Press.

de la Peña, Sergio
1982   Proletarian power and state monopoly capitalism in Mexico. Latin American Perspectives IX(1):20-35.

Diario de Querétaro
1982   January 12:8-b.

Dixon, Ruth
1978   Rural Women at Work: Strategies for Development in South Asia. Baltimore, MD: The Johns Hopkins University Press.

Edelman, Mark
1980   Agricultural Modernization in Smallholding Areas of Mexico: A Case Study in the Sierra Norte de Puebla. Latin American Perspectives VII(4):29-49.

Fernandez Kelly, Ma. Patricia
1984   For We Are Sold: I and My People. Albany, NY: SUNY Press.

Fritz-Krockow, Bernardo
1986   Evaluación del cooperativismo mexicano. Comercio Exterior 36(9):789-796.

Galli, Rosemary
    1981   Colombia: Rural Development as Social and Economic
        Control. *In* The Political Economy of Rural Development.
        R. Galli, ed. Pp. 27-90. Albany, NY: SUNY Press.
García Rocha, Octavio
    1982   La Inversión Extranjera en la Agro-Industria No-
        Alimentaria. *In* Transnacionales, Agricultura y
        Alimentación. R. Echeverría, ed. Pp. 253-271. Mexico,
        DF: Edit. Nueva Imagen.
Grindle, M.S.
    1982   Prospects for Integrated Rural Development: Evidence
        from Mexico and Colombia. Studies in Comparative Inter-
        national Development XVII(3-4):124-149.
Hoops, T. and Whiteford, S.
    1983   Transcending Rural-Urban Boundaries. *In* Population
        Growth and Urbanization in Latin America. J. Hunter, R.
        Thomas and S. Whiteford, eds. Pp. 261-280. Cambridge,
        MA: Schenkman Publ.
Jackall, R. and H.M. Levin
    1984   Work in America and the Cooperative Movement. *In*
        Worker Cooperatives in America. Jackall and Levin, eds.
        Pp. 3-15. Berkeley, CA: University of California Press.
Jones, D. C. and D. J. Schneider
    1984   Self-Help Cooperatives: Government Administered
        Cooperatives During the Depression. *In* Worker Coopera-
        tives in America. Jackall and Levin, eds. Pp. 57-84.
        Berkeley, CA: University of California Press.
Kearney, Michael
    1980   Agribusiness and the Demise or the Rise of the
        Peasantry. Latin American Perspectives VII(4):115-121.
Keren, Donna J.
    1985a   Creating a New Rural Labor Force: From Social Wel-
        fare to Productivity--Women in Mexican Agro-Industry.
        In Women Creating Wealth. R. Gallin and A. Spring, eds.
        Pp. 29-34. Wash. DC: Association for Women in Develop-
        ment.
    1985b   Negotiating Control: Culture and Hegemony in Mexico
        After the Nationalization of the Private Banking Industry.
        Paper presented at annual meeting of the American Eth-
        nological Society, Toronto, Canada, May 9-12, 1985.
Littlefield, Alice
    1978   Exploitation and the Expansion of Capitalism: the Case
        of the Hammock Industry in Yucatan. American Eth-
        nologist 5(3):495-508.
    1979   The Expansion of Capitalist Relations of Production in
        Mexican Crafts. Journal of Peasant Studies 6(4):471-488.

Lorenzen, Hannes
1981   Integrated Rural Development in Papaloapan, Mexico. *In* The Political Economy of Rural Development. R. Galli, ed. Pp. 91-110. Albany, NY: SUNY Press.

Marx, Karl
1967   Capital, Volume I. New York:New World/International Publishers.

Muñoz, Humberto
1986   Urban Challenge in Latin America. Paper presented at the Bildner Center for Western Hemisphere Studies, CUNY Graduate Center, NYC. April 15, 1986.

NACLA
1978   Mexico: Labor Showdown. NACLA Report, May-June, Pp. 38-40.

Nash, J. and N. S. Hopkins
1976   Anthropological Approaches to the Study of Cooperatives, Collectives, and Self-Management. *In* Popular Participation in Social Change. J. Nash, J. Dandler and N. Hopkins, eds. Pp. 1-32. The Hague: Mouton.

Novelo, Victoria
1976   Artesanias y Capitalismo en México. Mexico, DF: CIS-INAH.

PRI
1982   Querétaro (Report to Miguel de la Madrid). Mexico, DF: Coordinación General de Documentación y Análisis, Partido Revolucionario Institucional.

Proceso
1982   September 27, (Mexico), 308:86.

Ramírez, Carlos
1982   *Proceso*, December 27, (Mexico), 327:11-5.

Redclift, Michael
1983   Production Programs for Small Farmers: Plan Puebla as Myth and Reality. Economic Development and Cultural Change 31(3):551-570.

Riding, Alan
1985   Distant Neighbors. New York: Alfred A. Knopf.

Sanderson, Stephen E.
1981   Agrarian Populism and the Mexican State: The Struggle for Land in Sonora. Berkeley, CA: University of California Press.

Scott, J.W.
1974   The Glassworkers of Carmaux. Cambridge, MA: Harvard University Press.

Silva Ruiz, Gilberto
  1983   La Negociación de la Estabilidad Política: Instituciones
         Tripartitas 1971-1982. Querétaro, Mex.: Universidad
         Autónoma de Querétaro.
Singelmann, Peter
  1978   Rural Collectivization and Dependent Capitalism: The
         Mexican Collective Ejido. Latin American Perspectives
         V(3):38-61.
Thornley, J.M.
  1981   Worker's Cooperatives. Jobs and Dreams. London:
         Heinemann.
Wall Street Journal
  1982   April 21 and August 27:a-1.
Wells, M. and J. Climo
  1984   Parallel Process in the World System. Journal of De-
         velopment Studies 20(2):151-170.
Williams, S. and J. Miller
  1973   Credit Systems for Small Scale Farmers. Austin, TX.:
         Graduate School of Business, University of Texas.
Young, Kate
  1981   Trabajo a Domicilio y Decentralización de la Produc-
         ción. Pátzcuaro, Mich.: Seminario Tripartito Regional para
         América Latina sobre el Desarrollo Rural y la Mujer, ILO.
Zimbalist, A., ed.
  1979   Case Studies on the Labor Process. New York: Month-
         ly Review Press.

MARKETERS AS PRODUCERS: THE LABOR PROCESS AND PROLETARIANIZATION OF PERUVIAN MARKETWOMEN

Florence Babb

The lack of anthropological attention given to the distinctly productive role of marketers and street vendors in underdeveloped economies comes as little surprise in a scholarly tradition that separates sharply the processes of production and exchange in society. Somewhat more surprising is the continued neglect of this area of study at a time when Marxist theory and research are gaining strength in the field of anthropology. The primary concern of this paper is to suggest that a return to Marxism's emphasis on the total production process in society presents the most promising direction for research on small-scale traders, a growing commercial sector in many third world areas. A second concern is to examine petty commerce in the context of various modes of production in capitalist social formations. This discussion is informed by Marxist efforts to explain articulating modes of production in terms of the changing requirements of capital accumulation.

Research among Peruvian marketwomen supports the view of small-scale traders as productive workers in societies experiencing uneven, and dependent, capitalist development. Yet close investigation of the marketers' work and social relations reveals that many are undergoing a transition from the relative autonomy of petty commodity traders to the subordination of proletarianized sellers. We see the gradual decline of a surviving non-capitalist mode of production as some sellers experience the erosion of their independence and subordination to the wage form. Incorporation within the dominant capitalist mode is thus accompanied by class formation among Peru's marketers. The changing labor process of marketwomen in Peru serves as an example of socioeconomic differentiation within the "informal" sector of an underdeveloped country. The marketers' response to proletarianization also suggests that the political potential of poor women traders warrants greater attention.[1]

Labor Process of Workers in Petty Commerce

Market studies have generally followed the liberal economic tradition and focused rather narrowly on the sphere of exchange,[2] but there are some significant developments in the study of marketing informed by Marxism. Problematic to most research on marketing is the failure to view as a unified process the production of goods for exchange, their passage from producer to marketer, and the realization of the exchange value of these goods as they pass from marketer to consumer. Only by understanding this as a total process is the marketer's livelihood seen to depend fundamentally upon the production of goods, and is marketing seen as the final step in the process which realizes the goods' value. Without such an analysis, most research has attributed marketers' subsistence to their ability to maximize profits, taking as given the goods they have for sale; i.e., value is mistakenly viewed as originating in the exchange process based on price determination, rather than in the labor process.

The need to take production as a starting point in the integrated process linking production to distribution, exchange, and consumption was set forth by Marx (1970:193-194), who pointed to the superficiality of trying to study distribution apart from the entire process (Marx 1970:201-202). Research on exchange systems, according to this view, must be placed in the contexts of the modes of production in which they are found (e.g., Dupré and Rey 1973). At a time when petty traders are frequently viewed as contributing to the immiseration of third world populations, it is all the more important to identify the role marketers play in dependent capitalist economies. Indeed, in societies with little capital, marketers keep down the cost of distribution of goods and services, and thus are vital (Mintz 1956, 1964, 1971, 1974).

In the recent scholarship on marketing, Cook's (1976, 1982) work stands out in its insistence upon analyzing the whole production process. He writes, "As an intermediate phase in the economic process, marketing depends upon production to generate and sustain it, just as it, in turn, facilitates and sustains utilization" (1976:139). Cook's research in Oaxaca, Mexico, on peasant-artisans producing and selling metates necessarily examined the production of metates as the starting point, and viewed the marketplace as a way station in the flow of products. Following Marx, Cook discusses the difference between producers whose objective in selling their products is to obtain needed goods and services, and marketers whose objective is to convert a quantity of money into a larger quantity of money through the mediation of the goods and services they sell (1976:157-160). The first transaction may be expressed as $C-M-C$ (C referring to Commodity and M, to Money), and the second may be expressed as $M-C-M'$. This distinction, while theoretically fundamental, is in practice complex, since the roles of producers and sellers so often overlap. Thus, Cook comments on the value added to the product by sellers acting as finishers of metates, extending the production phase into the marketplace (1976:165-166).

It is not enough to situate marketing *in* the production process: we must also recognize the distinctly productive aspect *of the work of marketers*. The expression $M-C-M'$, referring to the circuit made by money in the hands of traders set on extracting a profit (or surplus value) from the sale of commodities, may be too simple a formulation to describe the work of small marketers in contemporary third world economies. As expressed by Marx (1967a:155), this is "the general formula of capital," and accounts for the accumulation of capital by merchants who merely circulate commodities produced by others. However, many third world traders do more than circulate goods for sale. These traders process or transform the goods so that their value is enhanced before they are sold. Consequently, the "surplus value" realized through the sale of these transformed commodities may be better understood as compensation for work performed by marketers themselves. A more accurate formulation of the transaction might be $M-C-C'-M'$.

Thus, while marketers may work primarily in a distributive capacity, their role generally contains a processing, or productive, component. Sometimes this is plainly evident, as in the case of producer-sellers (e.g. Cook 1976, 1982; Chiñas 1975, Gerry 1978).

At other times, marketers are chiefly involved in locating, buying, transporting, and reselling goods. However it may be argued that this too is socially necessary, or productive, work (Mandel 1970:191-192). Frequently, marketers do perform work on their products, transforming raw materials or unfinished articles into ready-to-consume items through their own labor. Marketers' work in general is a complex combination of activities, many of them adding value to what is sold.

Marx himself might have viewed these small-scale marketers as resembling petty commodity producers more than petty capitalists. Where marketers are engaged in productive activity, adding value to the goods they sell, the marketers behave in many respects like the simple, or petty, commodity producers he described. Although first conceptualized by Marx (1967a:761-762) as a transitional stage, the petty commodity production form has been found flourishing, rather than diminishing, in a number of third world areas (e.g., Gerry 1978, 1979; Scott 1979, Long and Richardson 1978). Petty, or simple, commodity production represents a subordinate mode of production, characterized by an incomplete separation of labor from the means of production, coexisting with the dominant capitalist mode. The persistence of petty manufacture and trade in the cities, like the persistence of subsistence agriculture in the rural sector, is attributed to the distorted process of third world development. The urban poor, many of them migrants from rural areas, have little alternative but to enter such marginal occupations as petty manufacture and trading.

Petty commodity production analysis offers insights into why small-scale independent producers and sellers rarely accumulate capital, and may manage barely to reproduce themselves. Under certain conditions individuals may seize opportunities for expansion, but external, structural constraints (access to resources, exploitation by large-scale enterprises) rather than internal, individual ones (entrepreneurship) are shown to curtail growth in small-scale enterprises (Schmitz 1982). Furthermore, in this form of analysis attention is focused on the essential work carried out by petty producers and traders, who serve to subsidize capitalism. A number of researchers have in fact suggested that simple commodity production analysis may be the best approach for examining the work of small-scale traders who are oriented toward meeting household needs rather than accumulating capital.

Cook and Diskin, for instance, describe the market economy in the valley of Oaxaca as a case of simple commodity production and circulation, distinguishing it from the dominant capitalist mode of production in Mexico; as such, the primary objective of marketers is to provision their families and not to expand their businesses, casting doubt on the image of marketers as petty entrepreneurs (1976:272-273). Similarly, Gerry discusses the petty commodity production in which small- scale traders and producers work in Senegal, and how the capitalist mode benefits from its existence. He writes that the concept of petty production refers to "those units of production which exist at the margin of the capitalist mode of production, but which are nevertheless integrated into and subordinate to it" (1978:1159).[3] Gerry calls attention to the domination-subordination relationship of petty production and the capitalist mode, and to the important work that petty producers and traders carry out in society while keeping down the costs of reproducing the labor force through their self-employment. Like Cook and Diskin, Gerry emphasizes the extreme unlikelihood that petty producers and sellers will evolve into entrepreneurs, i.e., "to harness the production process to and evolve relations of production commensurate with the accumulation of capital, rather than reproducing the same amount of capital with unchanging objective conditions of production" (1978:1154-1155). A number of other writers have likewise pointed out that traders in the third world countries they studied rarely accumulate capital (e.g., Bromley 1978, Forman and Riegelhaupt 1970, Moser 1980).

In sum, marketing, in order to be understood in proper context, must be located within the total production process in society. An area of employment which incorporates "marginal" groups and which responds to changing labor force requirements of capitalism, marketing has a specifically productive aspect--productive in that it is value-creating and in that it contributes to the accumulation of capital at the societal level. Small marketers may have slight hope of accumulating capital themselves, yet they benefit capitalism by keeping down the costs of distribution and, therefore, the cost of reproducing the labor force, in this way contributing to the growth of capital. Finally, to assess the place of small marketers in third world economies it may be useful to replace the notion of petty capitalism with the analysis of petty commodity production as a non-capitalist form within the capitalist social formation.

Marketers and Proletarianization

So far, in this paper, the autonomy of marketers in the production process has been assumed. Yet while many writers (e.g., Bromley 1978, Bromley and Gerry 1979) concerned with the increasing presence of third world workers in petty commerce have pointed to the persistence of the "traditional" sector under conditions of underdevelopment, others have emphasized the growing incorporation of rural people and urban migrants into capitalist relations of production in dependent third world economies (Bradby 1975, Cohen et al. 1979). The persistence and dissolution of non-capitalist modes of production as capitalism penetrates third world societies has preoccupied a number of writers during the last decade (Foster-Carter 1978).

It is well known that Marx (1967b:34) outlined the destructive effects of capitalism and predicted that it would lead to the disintegration of "all forms of commodity production which are based on the self-employment of producers, or merely on the sale of the excess product as commodities." In the post-war period of the twentieth century, Rostow (1962) also predicted that capitalism would take hold (or "take off") in societies around the globe—though his view and that of Marx share little beyond their evolutionary framework.

In contrast to the Western assumptions and political bias of Rostow and fellow travelers, writers like Baran (1957), Frank (1969), and Latin Americans in the "dependency" tradition formulated a critique of modernization theory. Most wrote within the Marxist framework, but argued that under the terms of contemporary dependent capitalism and underdevelopment, third world societies were unlikely to follow the stages of development experienced by the Western nations. Critical analysts of dependency (Oxaal et al. 1975, Deere 1976) began to consider the persistence of non-capitalist sectors within capitalist social formations, showing that the extraction of surplus from the former often contributes importantly to capital accumulation. For example, subsistence producers who periodically trade or engage in wage labor keep down labor costs by satisfying part of their own household needs. In areas of incomplete capital penetration, this ability of workers to reproduce themselves is essential.

As researchers undertook to investigate the growing population of urban poor found in the so-called informal economic sector of third world cities, the question again arose as to whether this group represented evidence of the resiliency of non-capitalist forms, or instead was transitional, soon to be absorbed into the formal economy (Bromley and Gerry 1979). A number of writers took note of the continuing importance of informal economic activities, which provide needed employment as well as cheap goods and services, and reduce labor costs to capital (Portes and Walton 1981, Safa 1982). Some were critical of the notion of dual economy underlying the concept of the informal sector, and turned instead to the concept of petty commodity production and trade discussed in the last section, to analyze this sector of the working population (Moser 1978).

Yet several studies indicate that despite the continued growth of the petty commodity sector, a simultaneous process of incorporating this sector into the dominant capitalist mode may be occurring. Some authors such as Bradby (1975) have examined the broad phenomenon of the destruction of economies based on use-value production, while others such as Scott (1979) have called into question the accuracy of describing specific groups of workers as "self-employed" or "independent." More cases are being discovered of disguised wage labor, sub-contracted work, and other forms of dependent employment among those formerly considered independent. Several researchers (Moser 1978, Gerry 1979) present findings that suggest that as the number of workers in petty production and commerce is expanding in dependent capitalist countries, proletarianization is also occurring.

In the Peruvian case study that follows, the degree to which marketwomen are independent petty commodity traders or are undergoing proletarianization is problematic. Also problematic is the degree to which gender may be playing a part in the proletarianization process. While some aspects of women's experience in rural proletarianization have been examined (Deere 1977, Deere and León de Leal 1981, Young 1978, Arizpe and Aranda 1981), research has not yet turned to consider the spread of capitalist relations among women in the urban informal sector. Third world towns and cities contain large numbers of women who may lead lives very different from those of their rural counterparts.

Peruvian Marketwomen:
Petty Commodity Traders or Proletarianized Workers?

During the present period of economic crisis in Peru, which dates back to the mid-1970s, an increasing number of rural and urban people have turned to small-scale commerce. Traditionally a female activity in Peru as in much of Latin America, petty commerce continues to attract women predominantly. With unemployment soaring and the cost of living rising, small-scale marketing of food and other goods is a principal occupation, however uncertain the livelihood it provides, for women in Peru. Along with domestic service, marketing and street vending see the rapid entry of women who engage in "commercialized housework."[4] In contrast to domestic service, petty commerce frequently offers women the advantage of flexible working hours and the opportunity to take children along as they work (Bunster and Chaney 1985).

Research was carried out during three periods between 1977 and 1984 in the Andean city of Huaraz, capital of the department of Ancash in north central Peru. This provincial city of 45,000 Quechua-Spanish speaking people serves as the administrative and commercial center for the valley known as the Callejón de Huaylas. The city's small elite finds employment in government offices, in the local hospital and schools, and as owners of local hotels, restaurants, and shops. The larger working-class and poor population generally finds it necessary to engage in multiple economic activities at the household level. Many families have very small plots of land on which to grow food for their own consumption, but this must be supplemented by income generated beyond the household. Men may work periodically as day laborers on others' fields, as carpenters, or masons. Industry is almost nonexistent in Huaraz, with just a few men finding work at a soda bottling plant, a fishery, or in small enterprises making adobe bricks or chairs. Women's options are even more limited, with a few working as seamstresses or as employees in local stores, but a greater number finding work in domestic service or small-scale commerce. Of these last, some sell a variety of items from the front rooms of their homes and more enter the city's four marketplaces and its downtown streets as sellers of food and a variety of merchandise.

Worsening economic conditions over the last decade-- exacerbated by austerity measures mandated by the International Monetary Fund--have propelled more women into commerce in Huaraz. The number of sellers rose from approximately 1,200 in 1977, to 1,600 in 1982, and of these almost 80% are women. Men in commerce, though a minority, generally command somewhat larger enterprises; they may have access to capital from other ventures and sometimes have greater mobility to travel to production sites and thereby cut costs. Women marketers commonly make only a marginal livelihood, earning as little as US$.50 daily-- whether as periodic sellers who come from the surrounding valley, or full-time sellers from the city--despite their often long hours and hard work.

Undifferentiated accounts of commercial intermediaries in Peru fail to recognize the particular features conditioning the work lives of small retailers.[5] Although Huaraz marketwomen, like marketers elsewhere, are integrated in the capitalist economy, their relationship to it is rarely that of entrepreneurs or petty capitalists and few of them fit the stereotype of the exploiting intermediary. After doing field research in Huaraz in 1977, I concluded that the marketers could best be conceptualized within the framework of petty commodity production and trade (Babb 1981). Only a few take to the markets the product of their own fields or manufacture. Yet marketers as a group add value to the goods they buy from producers and wholesalers, thereby extending the production process into the marketplace. The work contributed by marketers before their goods are ready for sale ranges from a fairly simple cleaning of fruits and vegetables to the preparation of complete meals for on-the-spot consumption or the confection of clothing and craft items. To this work must be added the time-absorbing process of buying up supplies, then transporting and preserving them until the time they are sold.

It is essential to see the direct connection between the production and distribution of goods in this unified process. Though the production may begin in other hands, retailers are "finishers" inasmuch as they complete the preparation of goods and make them available to consumers. Many Huaraz marketwomen are busy as they sell, readying more items for sale. The work of others is less visible since it takes place at home before they leave for the market. For example, sellers of poultry buy live chickens which they must attend to at home, and sellers of flour take grains to local mills, before they are ready for sale. Vendors of tamales go through the steps to prepare these snack foods in their kitchens, then bundle them on their backs for sale in the streets.

In contrast to a far smaller number of large wholesalers, chiefly men, whose profits are high, the earnings of small retailers are typically very low. Under the recent military government (1968-80), basic food prices were controlled at the regional and national levels in order to hold down the cost of food to urban consumers. Since 1980, controls have been lifted from all but a few food items, but marketers' earnings remain low. This seems due to the expanding number of sellers in Peru, and their willingness to work for very little reward. Given their lack of alternatives, many are satisfied to have small amounts of food left over to take home at the end of the day--or enough money to buy some--and indeed measure their success this way.

During return visits to Huaraz in 1982 and 1984, I found that it is truly the exceptional marketwoman whose business has expanded in recent years. Those who have done so have frequently managed it only with the help of a husband or brother who could advance some capital. While reinterviewing a number of women I knew from my first visit, I was not surprised to discover that in many cases their level of business was contracting. The majority described the hardships they had experienced, and this was all too often obvious from their declining health and impoverished appearance. Increasingly, within this context of immiseration, their market incomes needed to be supplemented by additional family resources. In other words, it seemed that as petty commodity traders these marketwomen were often unable even to reproduce their present conditions.

On further investigation, I found evidence to suggest that the autonomy of these workers in petty commerce may be undergoing a process of erosion. Already in 1977, I questioned whether small retailers could accurately be defined as independent, within the terms of the petty commodity production model. It appeared to me that their subordinate relation to wholesalers, on whom they were generally dependent for the extension of credit, was enough to cast doubt on the view of petty traders as autonomous. Furthermore, differentiation was evident among small retailers, with some sellers employing others to work for them. Examples include the food stall operator who hires an elderly woman as assistant on a regular basis, and the seller of ground garlic and chili peppers who occasionally hires another woman to peel garlic for her on a piecework basis. It should be noted that although in both these examples marketers employ wage labor, only in the first does this contribute to a process of capital accumulation.

During my later visits, I found more reason to question the independence of workers in petty commerce. Not only had the total number of marketers and street vendors in the city increased substantially, but my interviews suggested that there were more dependent sellers--waged employees and commission-sellers--

present now. Particularly striking was the expanded number of street vendors who sold ice cream, candy, prepared drinks and the like from carts by day and by night; a large number, if not the majority, of these sellers are wage workers, hired by absent employers (some of whom hire up to a half dozen sellers). In addition to this group, seamstresses and other artisans are sometimes employed by marketers as outworkers; often these workers are hidden from view, since they are supplied with materials to work at home on items which will later be sold by their employers. And then there are commission-sellers, some of whom travel to Lima to buy goods on contract, direct from factories. They return to sell in Huaraz until it is time to pay off debts and replenish their stock. In all cases, we find the subordination of some groups to others who represent larger commercial interests that have seized the opportunity to expand under economic conditions that constrain most marketers.

My impression that in some measure marketers, especially the small-scale female sellers, are losing control over their work process was corroborated by marketers themselves. Even those who retain a degree of autonomy over their work agreed that marketing is increasingly controlled by more powerful interests. Many see themselves as subordinated to large wholesalers through the institution of credit which renders them dependent. They say, for example, "We are just slaves of the wholesalers." Others perceive that larger capitalist interests, such as the D'Onofrio company which supplies small ice cream vendors throughout Peru, are making inroads in Huaraz and undercutting the business of local producer-sellers. Although this study carried out over an 8-year period is not sufficient to document a process of subordination to the wage form, or proletarianization among marketers, the evidence lends support to the view that this is occurring.

What can be said at this point regarding the gender and class status of Peruvian marketwomen? Like women in most third world countries, these marketers suffer the consequences of both economic underdevelopment and a subordinate sexual status. While many women entering marketing value the "independence" it will offer, they frequently find themselves in the lowest ranks of commerce where they earn miserable incomes, despite their efforts to move ahead through hard work. Moreover, they continue to balance work in the marketplace with all the household responsibilities women generally shoulder, meaning that they experience a "double day." Whatever changes may be occurring in their work as marketers, this gender inequality persists.

The class identification of marketwomen appears to be changing in more pronounced ways. Formerly showing more of the characteristics of petty commodity traders in control of their work process--not having experienced a separation of labor from the means of production--many Huaraz marketwomen are now subordinated to larger interests as commission-sellers, outworkers, or hourly employees of other marketers. Moreover, since many marketers operate without capital and are dependent on credit from wholesalers, they might be considered "disguised" commission-sellers, turning over to the wholesalers the earnings on their goods minus the margin they retain as a "commission." In cases such as these, we may see that small marketers are losing autonomy, are frequently proletarianized, and form part of an exploited working class.

Viewed in broader perspective, marketers as a group may be described as exploited as a consequence of their relation to the regional and national levels in Peru. Their surplus labor is extracted at the regional level through the payment of a variety of market fees which comprise the bulk of city and provincial revenues, as well as through official price controls. Nationally, unequal terms of trade between the agricultural and industrial sectors serve to subsidize manufacturing. Thus basic food prices are controlled in the interest of urban middle-class consumers, while the prices of factory-produced goods needed by rural as well as urban consumers are unregulated and often high. For these reasons, and not for lack of ability or motivation on the part of marketers, their commerce rarely expands and more often contracts at times of crisis.

We see then that while some marketers in Huaraz have retained control over their work, others are experiencing proletarianization. If the class position of many marketers appears ambiguous during this period of transition, this has not prevented marketers themselves from identifying with workers' issues. Despite the economic differentiation of Huaraz marketers, as a group they express a surprising degree of solidarity and a number of them are members of the half dozen market unions in the city.[6] Though many women do not join the unions "for lack of time or interest," "because they try to manage their problems alone," or "because their husbands do not approve," marketwomen form the ranks of union membership and play a forceful role. Within the unions, typically under male leadership, women marketers have often been especially outspoken on such issues as rising market fees, the harsh treatment of street vendors by officials, and the increasing restrictions on all marketers enforced by the municipal government. Many have been highly critical of the national government's efforts to make scapegoats of them for steeply rising food prices[7] over which they have little control. When faced with locally repressive measures, some Huaraz women have threatened to call a marketers' strike. In the face of economic hardship, union women have gone beyond the limited reformism of their labor federations. Their active defense may be attributed to their incipient class identification as well as a degree of female solidarity. "Without us," marketwomen say, "Huaraz couldn't survive."

Looking at Huaraz marketers' work at close range, we can also appreciate better the role of marketers in the national economy. First, we may see that at a time of high unemployment in Peru, these workers have found resourceful ways to make a living. Second, though they operate on a small-scale, petty traders supply consumers with needed goods, often at lower prices than larger enterprises. This serves to keep down the cost of the reproduction of the labor force, a clear advantage for the dependent capitalist economy. Such an analysis makes it possible to interpret the government's campaign against marketers as an effort to use them as scapegoats and thereby to divert attention from real economic problems, rather than actually to curtail their activity.[8]

Conclusions

Our efforts to conceptualize the work and social relations of marketwomen at the local level in Peru must ultimately be linked to a broad analysis of petty commodity production and distribution within third world economies. The Marxist perspective has advanced us toward this goal by redirecting our attention to the details of the labor process and to changing relations of production in society.

This paper began with the premise that marketwomen have an integral role in third world capitalist development, however uneven the process of this development may be. In order to consider the class standing and mode of production characteristic of these marketers, the question was framed in terms of the linkage of non-capitalist and capitalist sectors, or modes of production, within dominant capitalist social formations. It was suggested that petty commodity production analysis may serve us well in examining small-scale marketers and street vendors under conditions of underdevelopment.

Non-capitalist sectors may be ignored, or even encouraged to survive, for the contribution they make to capital accumulation at the national level. The goods and services offered cheaply by non-capitalist sectors offset the high cost of living to the poor and allow capital to hold down wage levels. Moreover, the employment they provide offsets high unemployment in the capitalist sector. On the other hand, we have seen that in a number of countries workers in petty commerce appear to be undergoing proletarianization as capital undermines non-capitalist relations in both rural and urban areas. Analysts of articulating modes of production have disagreed, with some pointing to the persistence of non-capitalist forms and others calling attention to the spread of capitalist relations. In fact, we find tendencies toward both the conservation and the erosion of non-capitalist forms as a consequence of uneven development.

At a time when Peru's dependent capitalist economy is facing deeper troubles, there is evidence of a transition as independent producers and sellers lose ground to larger commercial interests. More research will be necessary to explore persistence and change in Peru's underdeveloped economy and to assess changing class relations. But whether "independent" petty commodity traders or incipient commercial proletarians, the majority of marketers in Peru are poor and female, and in this respect there is no striking contrast among them. To the extent that proletarianization is occurring, it may be a long, slow process. After all, capitalism was introduced in the Andean region at the time of European contact and its penetration has been only gradual. The real significance of the process for Peruvians may lie in whether changing modes of production and changing class relations--in a sector made up principally of "marginalized" women workers--will result in new forms of consciousness and political mobilization.

NOTES

1 Field research was made possible in part through funding from the SUNY Research Council and the University of Iowa and in large measure through the cooperation and friendship of marketers

in Huaraz, Peru. A small portion of the material presented here was published in *Cultural Survival*, Summer 1984. I am grateful to Christine Gailey, David Hakken, John P. McCarthy, and especially to Hanna Lessinger, for their comments on earlier versions.

2   During the 1950s, concepts from classical economic theory were employed by such "formalists" as Tax (1953) and Katzin (1959, 1960) in their studies of peasant marketers; this formalist thinking continued to characterize some work, e.g., Dewey (1962), Belshaw (1965), Davis (1973), and Beals (1975). However, a challenge to the universal applicability of formal economic theory had emerged from the "substantivists" Polanyi (1957), Bohannan and Dalton (1962), and others who called for a cross-cultural definition of "economic" which would include non-market as well as market forms of distribution and exchange. Most substantivists, in fact, do not really challenge the underlying beliefs of the formalists, but simply restrict their own use of liberal economic theory to those societies they judge to be integrated in market economies.

3   Gerry locates petty commodity producers and traders in "units" or "forms" of production within the capitalist mode. Other writers, including myself, describe coexisting petty commodity and capitalist modes in articulation within dominant capitalist social formations. Despite this difference in the terminology, the analyses are in most ways comparable.

4   However, see Babb (1985) for a discussion of some shortcomings of an analysis that relies on viewing women's paid work as an extension of their household roles, or "reproductive" work.

5   José Matos Mar, former director of the Institute for Peruvian Studies, has held the commercial sector responsible for rising prices (*El Diario de Marka*, June 21, 1982:13), and argued that the informal sector is overwhelming the formal sector (*Andean Report*, April 11, 1986:6). This view, which is popular in Peru, fails to recognize the expansion of petty marketers as a consequence rather than a cause of the economic crisis.

6   The two principal unions each had several hundred members. The larger of these was the Union of Market Workers, founded in 1965 and later affiliated with the CTRP (Confederation of Workers of the Peruvian Revolution), a labor organization sponsored by the Peruvian government as an alternative to party-affiliated labor unions. The other union, founded a few years later, was the Union of Retailers and Sellers, affiliated with the

CGTP (General Confederation of Peruvian Workers), the labor federation connected with the Communist Party in Peru.

7   That food prices have risen sharply may seem to contradict the above remark that prices are controlled in the interest of urban consumers. However, while official prices have gone up, the government has sought to keep them at a *tolerable* level to appease the urban middle class.

8   At this writing, it is too early to assess any new directions taken by the government of President Alan García. Yet it is noteworthy that in his inaugural address in July, 1985, García championed poor street vendors, among others. Furthermore, he has reinstated price controls and introduced a new agrarian policy designed to favor rural food producers (*Andean Group Report*, February 28, 1986, p. 6).

BIBLIOGRAPHY

Andean Group Report
    1986   Apra Unveils Its Agrarian Policy. Latin America Regional Reports (London), February 28, 1986:6.
Arizpe, Lourdes and Josefina Aranda
    1981   The "Comparative Advantages" of Women's Disadvantages: Women Workers in the Strawberry Export Agribusiness in Mexico. Signs 7(2):453-473.
Babb, Florence E.
    1981   Women and Marketing in Huaraz, Peru: The Political Economy of Petty Commerce. Ph.D. dissertation, State University of New York at Buffalo. Ann Arbor: University Microfilms.
    1985   Producers and Reproducers: Andean Marketwomen in the Economy. *In* Women and Change in Latin America. June Nash and Helen Safa, eds. Pp. 53-64. South Hadley, MA: Bergin and Garvey Publishers.
Baran, Paul
    1957   The Political Economy of Growth. New York: Monthly Review Press.
Beals, Ralph L.
    1975   The Peasant Marketing System of Oaxaca, Mexico. Berkeley: University of California Press.
Belshaw, Cyril S.
    1965   Traditional Exchange and Modern Markets. Englewood Cliffs, NJ: Prentice-Hall.

Bohannan, Paul J. and George Dalton, eds.
 1962 Markets in Africa. Evanston, IL: Northwestern University Press.
Bradby, Barbara
 1975 The Destruction of Natural Economy. Economy and Society 4(2):127-161.
Bromley, Raymond J., ed.
 1978 The Urban Informal Sector: Why Is It Worth Discussing? World Development. Special Issue, Vol. 6, No. 9/10.
Bromley, Ray and Chris Gerry, eds.
 1979 Casual Work and Poverty in Third World Cities. New York: John Wiley and Sons.
Bunster, Ximena and Elsa M. Chaney
 1985 Sellers and Servants: Working Women in Lima, Peru. New York: Praeger.
Chiñas, Beverly L.
 1975 Mujeres de San Juan: La Mujer Zapoteca del Istmo. Mexico: Sep/Setentas.
Cohen, Robin, Peter C.W. Gutkind, and Phyllis Brazier, eds.
 1979 Peasants and Proletarians. New York: Monthly Review Press.
Cook, Scott
 1976 The "Market" as Location and Transaction: Dimensions of Marketing in a Zapotec Stoneworking Industry. *In* Markets in Oaxaca. Scott Cook and Martin Diskin, eds. Pp. 139-168. Austin: University of Texas Press.
 1982 Zapotec Stoneworkers: The Dynamics of Rural Simple Commodity Production in Modern Mexican Capitalism. Washington, D.C.: University Press of America.
Cook, Scott and Martin Diskin
 1976 A Concluding Critical Look at Issues of Theory and Method in Oaxaca Market Studies. *In* Markets in Oaxaca. Scott Cook and Martin Diskin, eds. Pp. 247-280. Austin: University of Texas Press.
Davis, William G.
 1973 Social Relations in a Philippine Market. Berkeley: University of California Press.
Deere, Carmen Diana
 1976 Rural Women's Subsistence Production in the Capitalist Periphery. Review of Radical Political Economics 8(1): 9-17.
 1977 Changing Social Relations of Production and Peruvian Peasant Women's Work. Latin American Perspectives 12-13:48-69.

Deere, Carmen Diana and Magdalena León de Leal
  1981 Peasant Production, Proletarianization, and the Sexual
      Division of Labor in the Andes. Signs 7(2):338-360.
Dewey, Alice
  1962 Peasant Marketing in Java. New York: Free Press.
Dupré, Georges and Pierre-Philippe Rey
  1973 Reflections on the Pertinence of a Theory of the
      History of Exchange. Economy and Society 2(2):131-163.
Forman, Shepard and Joyce F. Reigelhaupt
  1970 Market Place and Marketing System: Toward a Theory
      of Peasant Economic Integration. Comparative Studies in
      Society and History 12:188-212.
Foster-Carter, Aidan
  1978 Can We Articulate 'Articulation'? *In* The New Econom-
      ic Anthropology. John Clammer, ed. Pp. 210-249. New
      York: St. Martin's.
Frank, Andre Gunder
  1969 Latin America: Underdevelopment or Revolution?
      New York: Monthly Review Press.
Gerry, Chris
  1978 Petty Production and Capitalist Production in Dakar:
      The Crisis of the Self-Employed. World Development
      6(9/10):1147-1160.
  1979 Small-Scale Manufacturing and Repairs in Dakar: A
      Survey of Market Relations Within the Urban Economy.
      In Casual Work and Poverty in Third World Cities. Ray
      Bromley and Chris Gerry, eds. Pp. 229-250. New York:
      John Wiley and Sons.
Katzin, Margaret F.
  1959 The Jamaican Country Higgler. Social and Economic
      Studies 8:421-435.
  1960 The Business of Higglering in Jamaica. Social and
      Economic Studies 9:297-331.
Long, Norman and Paul Richardson
  1978 Informal Sector, Petty Commodity Production, and the
      Social Relations of Small-Scale Enterprise. *In* The New
      Economic Anthropology. John Clammer, ed. Pp. 176-209.
      New York: St. Martin's.
Mandel, Ernest
  1970 Marxist Economic Theory, Volume 1. New York:
      Monthly Review Press.
Marx, Karl
  1967a Capital, Volume 1. New York: International Pub-
      lishers.
  1967b Capital, Volume 2. New York: International Pub-
      lishers.

Marx, Karl (cont'd)
  1970 A Contribution to the Critique of Political Economy. New York: International Publishers.
Mintz, Sidney
  1956 The Role of the Middleman in the Internal Distribution System of a Caribbean Peasant Economy. Human Organization 15:18-23.
  1964 The Employment of Capital by Market Women in Haiti. *In* Capital, Saving and Credit in Peasant Societies. Raymond Firth and B.S. Yamey, eds. Pp. 256-286. Chicago: Aldine.
  1971 Men, Women, and Trade. Comparative Studies in Society and History 13:247-269.
  1974 Caribbean Transformations. Chicago: Aldine.
Moser, Caroline
  1978 Informal Sector or Petty Commodity Production: Dualism or Dependence in Urban Development? World Development 6(9/10):1041-1064.
  1980 Why the Poor Remain Poor: The Experience of Bogotá Market Traders in the 1970s. Journal of Interamerican Studies and World Affairs 22(3):365-387.
Oxaal, Ivar, Tony Barnett and David Booth, eds.
  1975 Beyond the Sociology of Development. London: Routledge and Kegan Paul.
Polanyi, Karl
  1957 The Economy as an Instituted Process. *In* Trade and Markets in the Early Empires. Karl Polanyi, Conrad Arensberg, and Harry Pearson, eds. Pp. 243-270. Glencoe, IL: Free Press.
Portes, Alejandro and John Walton
  1981 Labor, Class, and the International System. New York: Academic Press.
Rostow, Walt W.
  1962 The Stages of Economic Growth, A Non-Communist Manifesto. Cambridge: Cambridge University Press.
Safa, Helen I.
  1982 Towards a Political Economy of Urbanization in Third World Countries. Delhi, India: Oxford University Press.
Schmitz, Hubert
  1982 Growth Constraints on Small-Scale Manufacturing in Developing Countries: A Critical Review, World Development 10(6):429-450.
Scott, Alison MacEwen
  1979 Who Are the Self-Employed? *In* Casual Work and Poverty in Third World Cities. Ray Bromley and Chris Gerry, eds. Pp. 105-129. New York: John Wiley and Sons.

Tax, Sol
    1953 Penny Capitalism: A Guatemalan Indian Economy.
    Smithsonian Institution, Institute of Social Anthropology,
    No.16. Washington, D.C.: U.S. Government Printing Office.
Young, Kate
    1978 Modes of Appropriation and the Sexual Division of
    Labour: A Case Study from Oaxaca, Mexico. *In* Feminism
    and Materialism: Women and Modes of Production.
    Annette Kuhn and AnnMarie Wolpe, eds. Pp. 124-154.
    London: Routledge and Kegan Paul.

Newspapers
Andean Report, Latin American Newsletters, London, England.
El Diario de Marka, Lima, Peru.

GANGS, GRASSROOTS POLITICS,
AND THE CRISIS OF
DEPENDENT CAPITALISM IN JAMAICA

Faye V. Harrison

The 1980 demise of Jamaica's democratic socialist People's National Party (PNP) administration and the current failure of the Jamaica Labor Party (JLP) government's alternative to generate economic growth and stability force political analysts interested in radical change in Jamaica and the Caribbean region to rethink their positions. They must now identify and closely examine those varying conditions that constrain and create possibilities for sustained popular mobilization and structural transformation.

Research on political processes in third world cities has shown that the urban poor, through their grassroots movements and other forms of political expression, play increasingly important roles in the struggle for social change (Castells 1982, Portes and Walton 1976, Singer 1982). Social scientists and political activists alike have often raised questions about the political character and potential of the growing numbers of unemployed and underemployed persons in peripheral capitalist cities (Fagen 1983:21, Worsley 1972). This population, variably labelled lumpen- or sub-proletariat, marginals, and informal sector labor, has possibly been more subject to stereotyping and misrepresentation than any other sector of dependent capitalist societies.

The lack of fundamental change in the third world is sometimes attributed to deficiency on the part of the urban poor. According to varying arguments, this group is rendered politically conservative, apolitical, or inhibited by such factors as its peasant or rural origins (Bonilla 1962); its heavy participation in ephemeral, organizationally fragmented, small-scale economic activities and its present-day-survival value orientation (Roberts 1978:135). While these factors point to the immediate conditions and sociocultural forms of the poor, there are also other variables that stem largely from external structures and controls. These supralocal constraints include the containment of disquiet and political rebellion by police repression, government and political party patronage-clientelism (Stone 1980, Laguerre 1982, Harrison 1982), and hegemonic processes operative through mass media, schools, and churches which validate a ruling-class ideology advocating notions of the social/political inferiority of the undereducated mass (Austin 1984).

Rather than immediately asking why structures of domination persist, or why the urban poor are politically disabled, more scholars are beginning to approach grassroots political practice processually, situationally and dialectically (cf. Lessinger 1985, Susser 1982, Vélez-Ibañez 1983, Worsley 1984:187). They have begun to focus on the variant and multifaceted forms and phases of political expression. As Susser notes, workers and the poor do not always have the opportunity for mobilizing power (1982:7). These analysts, therefore, look for the modes of struggle available under historically-specific conditions, which change over time. They accept as a basic premise that the path to empowerment and structural transformation is usually indirect and full of contradictions, ambiguities, and reversals (Portes and Walton 1976:110).

With such an approach it becomes possible to appreciate the significant role of "small victories" in the broader scheme of political struggle and change. Grassroots praxis sometimes engenders significant micro-cultural change. As Vélez-Ibañez says, we must look at conditions which permit the coalescence of cohorts of men and women that project "their sense of social autonomy by defying the power of the state" and its "rituals of marginality...that crosscut sector and class cleavages" (1983:241). Such occurrences, though restricted to particular localities and neighborhood movements, may have important implications for developments in political consciousness and organization.

My purpose here is to show the multidimensional and often ambiguous character of political processes in slum neighborhoods in Kingston, Jamaica. I do this by analyzing certain sociopolitical patterns in a particular locality, which I shall call Oceanview.[1] The individual and collective behaviors of Oceanview actors are seen in the context of a specific historical period, c.1967–1985, during which political and economic changes at both the national and international levels engendered salient shifts in local-level political expressions and configurations. These shifts in grassroots politics, particularly in the field of gang relations, represent responses to the pressures, constraints, and interventions attendant upon Jamaica's status in the world system, specifically in "Uncle Sam's backyard."

The ensuing analysis suggests that the violent political rivalry, colloquially called "tribalism," generally associated with Kingston's street gangs, is not a necessary or natural outcome of gang formation. It is a result of gangs constituted amidst rampant political clientelism, wide class disparities, and turbulent, disruptive economic change partially induced from outside. In other words, the criminal, mercenary, and reactionary aspects of gang behavior so often underscored should be viewed as characteristics stemming from specific sets of historical circumstances rather than as intrinsic features.

The Oceanview case demonstrates that before the late 1960s gangs were largely innocuous and fairly constructive units of local organization. They provided a basis for association, cooperation, and exchange among male adolescents and adults under 30-35 years of age. With major changes in the downtown economy, the expansion of the marijuana or "ganja" trade, the introduction of guns, and the consolidation of a partisan economic niche, the social field which gangs comprised became increasingly vulnerable to criminalization and clientelist politicization. These processes over time became deeply entrenched in local political life.

Locality politics is in great measure constituted by gangs and their relationships with other local interest networks, with government, and with political party machines; yet the complex and ambiguous dynamics of gang power are rarely seriously examined beyond a cursory acknowledgment of its mercenary opportunism, criminality, and political corruption (Stone 1973, 1980). The following discussion, therefore, represents an attempt to offset this simplistic view.

The major phases that mark Oceanview's political life during the 1967-85 period can be described as follows. In the late 1960s and early 1970s, intense inter-gang rivalry became institutionalized and eventually assumed a partisan character. This state of affairs persisted throughout most of the 1970s and, in fact, intensified. In 1978 there was a marked shift away from the inter-party and inter-gang rivalry which too often characterizes patronage-clientelist politics. Instead an extra-partisan alliance, namely a Peace Movement, emerged to challenge the conventional pattern of party and government intervention. During late 1979 and 1980, an election year, conditions promoting broad-based solidarity and consciousness among the formally unemployed and marginally employed eroded and were subverted by gang fighting, or "tribal war," of unprecedented proportions. By 1983, after nearly three years of JLP rule, the conventional polarization of political party forces had given way to intense internecine fighting among ruling party clients/henchmen. Since late 1984 the local scene has been marked by the rise of a largely non-partisan solidarity among those most alienated from the government and party system, including traditional rivals.

My analysis of the above shifts highlights the dynamic and fluid character of local politics in urban Jamaica. Moreover, by approaching grassroots political action in situational and processual terms, I attempt to illuminate patterns of micro-cultural change. Such instances may be prerequisites for the development of broad-based consciousness and struggle which can eventually bring about fundamental, macro-structural change.

Oceanview: A Profile

Oceanview is a waterfront slum inhabited by approximately 6,500 people. Some 75% of the neighborhood's working-age population is formally unemployed, supporting itself and its dependents largely through informal economic activities ranging from chicken raising to "selling a lickle [little]," the petty marketing of foodstuffs or manufactured goods. People also engage in a number of illegalities, principally the marketing of ganja. Oceanview's economic situation is compounded by a high level of dependency since it has large numbers of children and senior citizens (Department of Statistics 1970). According to a 1975 survey, the mean annual income was $450 or J$819 (Urban Upgrading n.d.). Income from the informal economy is not sufficient for survival and must be combined with that from intermittent wage-work, often only available in the public sector.[2] Opportunities for wage-work are, therefore, strongly politicized, accessible only through party/government connections and sponsorship, and primarily available to party supporters and clients.[3]

The most strategic of the neighborhood's political fields are those directly aligned with the state: constituency politics, mediated by local party associations--JLP "branches" and PNP "groups"; urban redevelopment politics, mediated by government programs concerned with housing and social welfare; and street corner gang hierarchies, based to a considerable extent on illegally-gained resources and gun power. It is this last field which will be emphasized here. The risks and dangers involved in partisan rivalry lead many people in Oceanview to retreat from "polytricks"--party politics. Consequently, much sociopolitical action occurs in non-partisan domains such as Parent-Teacher Associations (PTAs), churches, and kin and peer networks. These so-called non-political bases of local action represent adaptive responses to the painful and often life-threatening excesses of "tribalism" and patronage politics. Oceanview residents define for themselves a variety of non-partisan social fields in which to pursue local goals and special interests; hence, they behave and act politically (Swartz 1969) despite their formal political invisibility. Local political activities tend to be pragmatic, economistic, ephemeral, and fragmented. Political positions in the various fields are usually in flux. Such flexibility and ambiguity permit the locality as a locus of power to come to terms with a contradictory and harsh socioeconomic and political environment (Leeds 1973:23).

Tribalism and the Post-War Expansion, 1967-72

Before the late 1960s, Oceanview's political landscape was relatively unmarked by volatile partisan rivalry and gang conflicts. These became institutionalized partly in response to disruptions in the local economy produced by the country's economic boom.

Jamaica entered its post-colonial phase (1962) during a period of rapid economic growth which began in the 1950s and lasted through the 1960s. While the national bourgeoisie and the middle class benefitted from the expansion propelled largely by United States investment in the bauxite/alumina industry, the peasantry, agroproletariat, and the least skilled and secure in the urban work force suffered a doubled rate of unemployment and received a smaller share in the national income (National Planning Agency 1978:6, Girvan and Bernal 1982:37).

In this context of widening disparities and class polarization, a limited form of income distribution through patronage allocation served as a means of placating sections of the impoverished majority. It also conferred some measure of legitimacy on the state,

administered by a petty bourgeoisie rooted in domestic and foreign capitalist interests. In post- or neo-colonial Jamaica, the
political directorate has relied on clientelism to consolidate power
and authority (Stone 1980) over an impoverished electorate whose
interests are not being met by Jamaica's form of peripheral capitalism. The two major political parties, the PNP and JLP, are
highly centralized and elitist. They restrict rank and file participation to electoral campaigns and voting, and during terms of office to patronage allocation and "enforcement," which often involves coercive tactics (Stone 1980:97). Along with marked economic disparities, contradictions between *de jure* democracy and
the *de facto* disenfranchisement of the mass of Jamaicans generate
considerable disaffection which the state cannot always contain.

Prior to the post-war decline and relocation of the port and
commercial districts (Clarke 1971:238), a great deal of Oceanview's
population had found both formal and informal work opportunities in the nearby downtown. The economic disruption was
offset somewhat by government-provided jobs. However, labor
recruitment, done largely through political party associations and
top-ranking gangs, did not allay the widespread disaffection surrounding retrenched employment. In fact, local divisions and disparities intensified due to the differential allocation of jobs.

Another change affecting Oceanview's political relations was
Jamaica's increased importance in the international ganja trade
during the mid- to late 1960s (Lacey 1977:159). With the decline
in legitimate income-making opportunities, Oceanview's involvement in the illegitimate sector, especially the ganja trade, grew.
Accompanying this expansion was an increased availability and use
of guns, because ganja exported to the U.S. was exchanged for
cash and arms (Lacey 1977). By the late 1960s the means by
which gangs as well as formal political brokers and bosses ac-
quired power and access to sources of income and capitalization
had changed dramatically. The entrenchment of gun use escalated
local conflicts and prompted persistent tribal war.

One such long-term conflict erupted between Oceanview's
two major gang hierarchies, Ethiopia and Israel, in 1967. Before
this juncture, shifting alliances, realignments, and sporadic
skirmishes between street gangs rarely had serious impact on the
neighborhood's political and economic life. The immediate context for this war was a changing local economy, wherein traditional niches eroded and gave way to new ones in which party affiliation was increasingly determinant.

After 1972 when the PNP won office, the war assumed un-
equivocally partisan dimensions. Israel became encapsulated in the
PNP machine and was given control over numerous contracts for
municipal sector work, such as road maintenance. Ethiopia had
ties to the JLP opposition, but these were at best sporadic and
tenuous. Nonetheless, while not closely linked to JLP brokers and
patrons, Ethiopia was clearly an intractable oppositional force with
which the local PNP constituency had to contend.

Tribalism, the Recession, and Destabilization, 1973-77

During the middle and late 1970s, tribal divisions deepened in
the midst of a national crisis which destabilized both the economy
and the political and national security system. This crisis, abetted
by national as well as international opposition, had its origins in
1972-76 during the PNP's first term of office.

Widespread political protest, set off by the social inequalities
Jamaica's economic boom engendered, culminated in the PNP's
1972 succession to executive office. The Manley administration
instituted various reforms designed to redistribute income and
secure greater national control over the dependent island economy
(Girvan and Bernal 1982). Largely in response to the effects of
the international recession, in 1974-75 the government initiated a
series of radical moves toward "Jamaicanization." It imposed a
production levy on the bauxite companies; it pressed to acquire a
51% share in the mines; it helped form the International Bauxite
Association; and it announced its commitment to democratic
socialism and anti-imperialist struggle throughout the world.

The PNP's turn to the left prompted adverse reactions from
foreign capital (particularly the bauxite companies), the U.S.
government, and Jamaica's national bourgeoisie. The JLP, backed
by the U.S., designed and implemented a massive destablization
campaign to undermine PNP legitimacy and oust it from office
(Keith and Girling 1978:29). Foreign and domestic investment
diminished drastically. Bauxite companies cut back production
and, consequently, reduced the government's revenues and displaced workers. By highlighting anti-North American sentiments,
the U.S. press discouraged tourism and thereby undermined
Jamaica's second largest foreign exchange earner. Local entrepreneurs in large numbers closed down businesses and sought refuge
in North America. By March, 1976, international commercial

banks ceased making loans. Jamaica's economy was brought to a near collapse.

On the political front, the JLP launched a large-scale "anti-communist" campaign in late 1974, two years before scheduled elections. By early 1976 political and criminal violence had reached unprecedented levels. In reaction, the government declared a state of emergency in June. In December elections were held, and although the PNP won by a landslide, the government had to maintain acute vigilance against ongoing destabilization efforts over the next four years.

In 1977 the government's shortage of foreign exchange forced it to turn to the International Monetary Fund (IMF) (Girvan and Bernal 1982:39). The restrictive IMF policies (currency devaluation, removal of price controls, and restraints on wage increases) exacerbated the economic slump as well as the political climate, and were a major catalyst for the PNP electoral loss in October, 1980 (Girvan and Bernal 1982:43, African Mirror 1978:44).

Whereas the PNP administration made strides in democratizing an elitist polity through numerous progressive reforms, it, nonetheless, zealously continued a tradition of political patronage. The accompanying tribal violence and victimization also lived on (Ambursley 1983:87). In localities like Oceanview, those embedded in ruling party networks--the "socialists"--benefitted from whatever the government had to offer the poor. However, those outside these networks--opposition party supporters, called "labourites," and the unaffiliated alike--were denied benefits and in some cases even their constitutional rights. This kind of differential access served to discredit democratic socialism in the disillusioned eyes of many at the grassroots.

Political relations in Oceanview during this period of PNP decline grew increasingly polarized and volatile. The unemployment rate rose, and jobs and job contracts grew more and more the object of violent local political contests. Increasingly, the only source of wage-work was the government-controlled sector, which had rapidly expanded to allow the state to manage key areas of the national economy.

The economic collapse also precipitated an expansion of informal and illegal economic activities. Ganja marketing remained one of the most rampant forms of hustling, and the black market and its attendant crimes hypertrophied as goods became scarce or unobtainable on the formal market. The foreign exchange deficit severely constrained the importation of a wide range of consumer and capital goods; consequently, these commodities became available only through illegal means.

Barred from more than occasional token jobs with a local urban redevelopment construction scheme in its immediate territory, the gang called Ethiopia specialized in illegal activities and managed to gain a competitive edge in that domain. Israel, on the other hand, monopolized local access to municipal government patronage, but as these resources waned, rivalry grew with Ethiopia over niches in the ganja trade and the black market.

Diminishing patronage, the increased politicization of contracting wage-work opportunities, contentions over turf in the illegal sphere, and, as we shall see, the government's drastic repressive security measures, all contributed to the volatility which made life in Oceanview a continuous nightmare and threatened to destroy Jamaica's social order.

The Peace Movement, 1978

At the very depths of the 1970s crisis, a city-wide Peace Movement emerged, formed by rival gang leaders aligned with the two major political parties.[4] One of the most significant events in Jamaican politics during the 1970s, the Peace Movement was an unprecedented manifestation of popular democracy. It permitted Kingston's so-called lumpen elements to articulate their collective interests and demands. Through it the urban poor attempted to elevate their political consciousness and to develop more coherent and sustained patterns of mobilization outside the conventional machinery of the 2-party system.

"The Peace," as it came to be known, was catalyzed largely by the Green Bay Massacre of January 5, 1978, a tragic point in Jamaican urban politics. With the help of plainclothes military intelligence agents, the army apparently lured 14 men from Central Kingston into an ambush at the Green Bay firing range 14 miles outside Kingston.[5] Five senior members of one of the neighborhood's major gangs were killed. The remaining nine men managed to escape and tell of their experience. Later the security forces claimed that the Central Kingston gang was caught while engaged in target practice and that the soldiers shot back in self-defense. However, the arms the gunmen supposedly used were never found.

Several days later, major rival gangs called a halt to their fighting. Within days most gangs in the metropolitan area had accepted the truce and rallied their forces around a demand for "Equal Rights and Justice"--which meant in this context peace, jobs, and better living conditions. The truce sought to prevent the police and national security forces from committing further atrocities against alleged criminals as well as to stabilize relations between PNP- and JLP-affiliated gangs. Realizing that the "contract politics" which sparked violence between rival party clients only gave security forces a pretext to attack and led ghetto[6] youths and young men to their deaths, the peace-makers asserted their political autonomy by defying clientelist cooptation and brutal repression. The movement's discourse (as evidenced in media coverage and in local-level discussions) indicated that ghetto peace activists themselves recognized how the political patronage system benefitted individual brokers while maintaining the marginalization and victimization of the popular masses (see Vélez-Ibáñez 1983). By challenging both patronage-clientelism and repression, the Peace Movement threatened the very efficacy of the state apparatus.

The truce was operationalized by a 2-tiered committee structure that formed and implemented various grassroots programs designed to create jobs and to occupy otherwise unemployed youths with constructive community projects (Stephens and Stephens 1986:236-237). These peace programs allocated work on a non-partisan basis, a clear departure from the conventional mode of recruitment. The 2-tiered administration allowed both gang and other ghetto leaders and representatives of established institutions like the Jamaica Council of Churches, the Private Sector Organization of Jamaica, the major political parties, and the government to participate in the movement. The local-level activists belonged to a Peace Council, and the supralocal representatives comprised an Advisory Committee.

Oceanview's Peace

The 1978 truce and the movement which supported it created a climate in which Oceanview residents could again leave the refuge of their fenced-in "yards" (co-residential compounds), put down their weapons, and walk down lanes and alleys without the constant fear of death or injury. For the first time in years it became possible for ghetto people--so-called labourites, socialists, and neutralists alike--to believe they could unite to find solutions to their common "sufferation" (suffering).

The immediate effect was that local networks of kinspeople and peers extended and strengthened. Relatives and former friends who had severed contact with those involved in gang activities re-established communication and interaction. Middle-aged and old people, forced to stop attending evening lodge meetings and religious services by the war, now resumed their various organizational activities. They were much less afraid of having to travel through gang territories and former war zones.

Even gang members found it possible to interact with their former enemies--albeit quite cautiously. A number of Ethiopians and Israelites who had been school-mates or friends before the war managed to revive their relationships and to reduce some of their ambivalence toward each other. During the height of the Peace, Ethiopians and Israelites could be seen frequenting the same bars, gambling together, and playing on the same football (soccer) field. Disputes which arose in these situations were usually resolved informally without resort to violence.

The truce also made possible the formation or renewal of extra-local networks based on kinship, church membership, and youth club activities. Although intra- and extra-local cohorts were still largely bound by common party sympathies, there were more cases of individuals who successfully managed to interact across tribal and neighborhood boundaries without contending with accusations of betrayal or physical reprisals.

Demise of the Peace

Oceanview was more fortunate than many ghettoes in that some remnant of the truce (namely, the absence of fighting) was sustained for close to two years, until the latter months of 1979. However, the momentum of the formally organized city-wide movement was lost well within a year, undermined by both internal and external dynamics. Conflicts between the Peace Council and the Advisory Committee emerged over funds and illegal arms (Stephens and Stephens 1986:236-237). Ghetto leaders, whose initiatives had provided the impetus for the movement and whose constituents were to be the direct beneficiaries, wanted control over the Community Peace Fund and the grassroots programs. Their credibility was lost when proceeds from an April One Love Peace Concert were mishandled. Their stature as responsible, legitimate leaders was even further diminished by their adamant refusal to relinquish their arms in return for government amnesty.

They feared victimization by national security forces and the police, who were conspicuously absent from the peace efforts. Such fears were in fact realized when one of the key architects of the movement, Claudie Massop, was assassinated by the police in 1979.

The slow pace of local improvements meanwhile eroded the movement's popular base of support. The Community Peace Fund was too small to support the scale of enterprise and activities required to improve the lives of a chronically unemployed constituency. Hence, the peace projects turned out to be short-term palliatives which initially raised expectations and hopes and then triggered frustrations.

Beyond the above contradictions, constraints also emanated from the volatile relations between the Peace Movement and the police. Moreover, the movement had to contend with covert partisan opposition to potentially subversive political realignments, with the JLP-led, U.S.-supported government destabilization campaign, and with IMF-aggravated economic conditions.

Although the PNP and JLP were officially supportive of the movement, the two parties walked a difficult tightrope since their unofficial agenda was to maintain or to reclaim authority over their ghetto constituencies. To this end, they supported the truce while at the same time maneuvering to circumscribe the peace efforts and to keep them within the scope of the parties' and government's goals and interests. To preclude jeopardizing the party structure or either party's respective position in the contest for control of the state, the movement had to be curbed. It could only be allowed to progress so far in its attempts to develop horizontal or class-based solidarity as an alternative to the competitive, divisive vertical alignments characteristic of the clientelist political system.

While vulnerable to attacks from both major parties, the movement was especially susceptible to the massive force of the JLP opposition. The movement's critical focus on the state system rather than on the PNP administration per se ran against the grain of the destabilization campaign. The campaign's objective was to oust the PNP and replace it with a party sympathetic to U.S. foreign policy and economic interests. Furthermore, the movement's attempt to enforce peaceful relations between gangs and to form a broad-based alliance among lumpen elements controverted the opposition bloc's tactic of fomenting and exploiting partisan cleavages.

War-Time Campaign, Late 1979-1980

After late 1978 when the peace programs could not sustain adequate financial backing--because of the nation's grave economic situation and the mishandling of movement funds--one of the few remaining sources of material resources for those outside the government's pool of client-workers was the JLP machine. This was generously supported by the U.S. By 1980, in the context of a 35% national unemployment rate, rising crime, shortages of basic commodities, sharp price increases, and constant currency devaluations, large numbers of ghetto adolescents and men-- desperate for "a money," "a wok" (work), or a gun for protection-- had become vulnerable to the persuasion and more immediate gratification offered by labourite brokers and bosses. The general disrespect for and distrust of police and "wicked" politicians widely articulated by ghetto peace activists and followers were reinterpreted and translated into a blind hostility directed toward the PNP, whose alleged corruption, mismanagement, repression, and communist leanings had "mash up de cuntry."

Although Ethiopia, particularly its top-ranking or "vanguard" cluster, had managed to avoid becoming directly entangled in JLP brokerage networks during much of the latter 1970s, by 1980 its relations with Israel were enveloped by the hysteria of party rivalry. Ethiopia's former autonomy from the opposition party stemmed in considerable measure from its relative success in forming a resource base derived from illegal activities. At the same time, it maintained a durable relationship with the resourceful headmistress of Blessed Sacrament School, who provided intermittent welfare benefits and continuously discouraged Ethiopians from becoming involved with JLP politics and from, consequently, escalating local conflicts.

Toward the latter part of 1979, the gang's ability to resist partisan pressures waned. Several influential seniors had emigrated, and an influx of arms, channelled initially through a secondary-level gang with ties to JLP branch activists, upset the power balance within the hierarchy. The gang faction with labourite connections prevailed, and Ethiopia's fight against its traditional rival became a part of the larger contest between the JLP and the PNP, between U.S. government and corporate interests and the recalcitrant PNP.

When the PNP government announced general elections in 1980 to determine the country's economic path, the electoral

campaign took political violence and terror to unprecedented proportions. A former JLP "enforcer" or gunman, recounting his experiences during 1980, claimed that many youths in their teens
and early twenties, himself included, were lured into the ranks of
political bodyguards by the bait of the temporary "good life." The
prospect of accompanying "big men" politicians to posh
restaurants, hotels, and other "uptown" settings, of having fancy
foods and drink, of being able to wear stylish clothes, and of
sporting guns mesmerized many ghetto youths. The informant
went on to claim that henchmen commonly were drugged furtively
via their food. Some of the excessively violent and inhumane behavior exhibited during the campaign can perhaps be ascribed to
this kind of manipulation. In the war of 1980 over 700 people
lost their lives in either the fighting or the crossfire of an irra-
tionally violent campaign for "deliverance."

The Unfulfilled Promise of Deliverance, 1981-85

The "deliverance" Edward Seaga and the JLP promised
Jamaicans was to have developed out of an economic recovery
supported by the IMF and the Reagan administration's Caribbean
Basin Initiative (CBI). Jamaica was to become a model democracy
and free enterprise haven in a region where, during the past
decade, socialist insurrection and other alternatives to dependent
capitalist development have whetted the imaginations, visions, and
praxis of social forces in Grenada, Nicaragua, El Salvador, and in
Jamaica itself.

The CBI provides duty-free trade provisions such as softened
tariffs and quotas for a period of 12 years and special tax concessions to U.S. corporations investing in the area (Girling 1983, Department of State 1984). Yet, despite massive support from the
U.S. government and international institutions, the Jamaican economy has deteriorated over the past few years. The prospects for
the predicted boom are not bright. The redeployment of international capital has not favored Jamaica, which has a relatively well-
organized and expensive formal labor force. Moreover,
"Reaganomics" militates against recovery in that high interest rates
and reduced North American contributions to the IMF and World
Bank serve to annul the special concessions the CBI makes (Ambursley 1983:100).[7]

While in the first year or two of the JLP administration the
massive influx of loans and aid engendered optimism, by late 1983

few hints of a growth dynamic remained (Jamaican Weekly Gleaner 1985a, 1985c). The balance of payments deficit grew. Whereas in 1980 the deficit was around J$200 million, in 1984 it had grown to J$600 million (Jamaican Daily Gleaner 1984). The country's debt repayments now exceed the flow of loan funds.

Following stringent IMF directives, the government has denationalized public-owned businesses, drastically cut back in public employment, lifted price regulations and food subsidies, imposed restraints on wages, and devalued the currency several times. These austerity measures have made living conditions more severe than at the height of the crisis the former PNP administration confronted. The Jamaican people's expectations and hopes of being delivered from volatile economic recession have been met by the frightening prospects of "Haitianization" (Headley 1985:39).

The deterioration of the economy has been accompanied by an erosion of democracy. Since late 1983 there has been no official parliamentary opposition (Jamaican Weekly Gleaner 1983a, 1983b; Headley 1985:40). When the government failed IMF performance tests in 1983, it responded to a PNP challenge by calling early elections. The PNP boycotted the elections partly because the electoral lists were not current (Jamaican Daily Gleaner 1984). Approximately 20% of the eligible voters (primarily young adults) were not included on the list, while 10% of those listed were reputed to be dead. The elections were considered bogus by nonpartisan groups like the Jamaica Council of Churches as well as by PNP proponents. As a consequence, parliament has 60 JLP representatives and eight "independents" appointed by the Governor General on the Prime Minister's recommendation. They serve as a pseudo-opposition (Jamaican Weekly Gleaner 1983a). Later in 1984, the PNP lost its foothold in the Kingston metropolitan government, the Kingston-St. Andrew Corporation (KSAC) (Jamaican Weekly Gleaner 1984c). The government subsequently disbanded the reputedly mismanaged KSAC and transferred its functions to central or national government ministries.[8]

State militarization has also grown to be a problem. Evidence suggests that the government has increased its capacity to repress the power of intractable gunmen--whose numbers have grown since the massive influx of arms during the late 1970s and in 1980. It is also able to repress labor militancy by increasing the importation of heavy arms (Jamaican Weekly Gleaner, 1984b). Security forces have become increasingly visible, and Seaga has begun to speak in terms of enforcing discipline, that is, of putting teeth into labor and criminal laws so that the state can act more punitively against the forces of disorder (Headley 1985:39, 40).

Opinion polls, the pattern of strike actions (particularly the 22Dday general strike against gas price increases in January, 1985), and the PNP's rise in popularity demonstrate that the populace overwhelmingly lacks faith in the government's IMF/CBI policies for national development. Unlike a decade ago, the current upsurge in oppositional consciousness, discourse, and mobilization all across Jamaica has not produced a risk of civil war. Whereas in the 1970s the government confronted a massive onslaught orchestrated by North American and domestic bourgeois interests, the present opposition bloc is primarily national in scope. It relies more on labor militancy, mass rallies, and boycotts than on the use of terror. The JLP with its heavy backing from the U.S. government retains the edge in the sphere of physical coercion.

JLP Factionalism at the Local Level

Since late 1983, the intense rivalry between JLP and PNP supporters that marked Oceanview's political landscape after the demise of the Peace has subsided. What has risen instead is acute factionalism within the JLP ranks: gangs vying against each other; gangs competing against JLP associations--all competitively mobilizing their forces to obtain dwindling patronage during a period of IMF-enforced austerity. The flow of heavy arms, which inundated many ghettoes during the destabilization campaign, is partly responsible for this turn of events. Illegitimate, unauthorized gun power, monopolized mainly by JLP henchmen, increasingly operates independent of party and government control (Jamaican Weekly Gleaner 1984a). This, combined with contracting patronage resources, has multiplied internecine conflict, dividing and polarizing JLP supporters. The JLP's inability to discipline its gunmen effectively has undermined its authority.

In May, 1984 a 2-day feud occurred in Rema, a major JLP stronghold. Two gang factions fought it out until seven persons were killed and many more injured. During the fall of 1983, there had been a similar eruption in Oceanview. The Ethiopian gang hierarchy, once a fairly cohesive formation of allied street networks, fissioned. The corner gang with the closest, most direct ties to the JLP, in this case to the office of a member of parliament (MP), was as a consequence the most heavily armed. It attacked members of another corner network on the grounds that the latter were actually socialists. Before 1980 the latter cluster had been the highest ranked gang in Ethiopian territory, and its leadership was reputed to be independent of the JLP machine.

In late 1983 and 1984, the newly emergent vanguard or top-ranking gang attempted to consolidate its position in the partisan niche by discrediting or eliminating its major competitor, still widely respected by most Ethiopians. Accusations and threats abounded, and gun fighting occurred in broad daylight, injuring some of the intended targets and killing an innocent person on the street. As a result of this war, many JLP sympathizers became alienated from both the vanguard gang and from the ruling party's administration.

Non-Partisan Mobilization, Anti-Government Protest and Local Solidarity

In 1984 Blessed Sacrament School's headmistress, Sister Elizabeth, gathered support from local people to spearhead a campaign to build a job training center and bakery adjacent to the school. Under the aegis of a major service club, J$2.1 million was raised to build the center, which opened in the fall of 1984. This project was deliberately designed to be a non-partisan effort. The constituency's MP and councillors (aldermen) were not invited to become involved in any way.[9] In a locality where a large%age of the population is disillusioned with the government as well as with both major parties, the project would have been open to question and suspicion had it been associated with partisan interests.

Throughout the 1970s in the midst of political polarization, there had been organized attempts to build a non-partisan basis for local action and development. The principal locus of this impetus had been Blessed Sacrament School, situated on the edge of Ethiopian territory. For approximately two decades, under the administration of Sister Elizabeth, the school had provided a number of social services to local people according to need rather than political identity. The school's PTA was one of the neighborhood's most active voluntary associations, tackling larger community issues as well as school problems.

Sister Elizabeth's class and institutional status permitted her access to a wide spectrum of political and economic benefits and favors. Having both relatives and friends strategically placed in the private sector and government, and able to galvanize moral and material support from Catholics, she managed to channel into Oceanview resources otherwise unavailable to poor slum inhabitants, especially those lacking ruling party connections and sponsorship.

Sister Elizabeth had won the respect of most of the locality's population, gangs included. According to local oral tradition, she was known to have walked the streets during gun battles and successfully demanded that the fighting stop. In the mid-1970s, before the emergence of the Peace, she worked with others in the neighborhood to organize and enforce a local truce that lasted a full year--a long time by Oceanview standards. Her especially close relationship with Ethiopia is partly responsible for the former vanguard's relative autonomy from party clientelism during a considerable period before the tribal nightmare of 1979-80.

Over the years, therefore, Blessed Sacrament School's many activities--the PTA, the medical and dental clinic, the distribution center for scarce goods like rice and soap--built and sustained a base of local support across gang and party lines. The apparent success of the school's most recent and ambitious project, the training center, served to reinforce local people's hope that a peaceful, unified basis could be found to develop opportunities which would improve living conditions and life chances.

The Blessed Sacrament project and the prevailing national mood, as evidenced by the January, 1985 general strike, contributed to a promising change in Oceanview's political climate. Beyond a small number of JLP stalwarts (whose numbers have been reduced by emigration), there is[10] growing dissatisfaction with the government. Oceanview inhabitants now seem to share a common basic outlook toward the JLP administration and the painful austerity its policies have imposed. During the general strike, both Ethiopians and Israelites, labourites and socialists took to the streets, expressing solidarity in protest against unbearable local and national conditions. While for some participation in mass protests such as the general strike represents support for the opposition PNP, for many others, such protest actions are largely independent of party loyalty or affiliation. In fact, Oceanview's PNP groups had been dormant before the strike. Moreover, much of the population in neighborhoods like Oceanview is skeptical of the ability of either major party, as presently constituted, to genuinely represent the interests of poor people (Jamaican Weekly Gleaner 1985b).

Currently, hard times and "sufferation" are equally borne by Oceanview's majority. As one resident put it, without significant differences between Ethiopians and Israelites, between labourites and socialists, there is more unity in the area now than there has been in a long time. The increased influence of non-partisan sociopolitical fields such as that dominated by the Blessed Sacrament School, and the simultaneous narrowing of party and gang schisms are significant patterns. They can be viewed as adaptive processes which enable Oceanview to mobilize the totality of its severely limited resources for economic survival. Moreover, in the face of the increasing authoritarianization of Jamaican society, they may create a sense of collective defense, autonomy, and empowerment (see Vélez-Ibañez 1983:246).

Microcultural Change and Prospects for Structural Transformation

The above case would be merely a story of political violence and party clientelism in their various permutations and configurations were it not for two phases in Oceanview's recent history: the Peace in 1978-79 and the recent climate of embryonic unity in 1984-85. In both these instances, extra- or non-partisan relations, alliances, and social fields offset cleavages based on party loyalty and/or gang membership. And in both phases, the clientelist character of Jamaica's democratic system is challenged by the withdrawal of considerable grassroots support from the major political parties and the government. Such a radical realignment defies the efficacy of the state, and is a precondition for the formation of class-based cohorts and more inclusive mobilization. This process could have an historic and potentially transformative impact on national and local political life.

But the Peace Movement failed, and the recent evidence of non-clientelist mobilization and solidarity is, at this early stage, only a hopeful possibility. Can these departures from the normal state of affairs signify something of consequence?

The fact that the Peace Movement, as a mobilization from the very bottom, emerged at all suggests the willingness and the ability, however limited, of the urban poor to form a broad-based alliance articulating common interests and demands. The movement demonstrates that the most progressive sections of the lumpen can in fact progress beyond mercenary action and struggles over patronage to a rudimentary stage of class consciousness and class formation (Stone 1980:45). The failure of the movement to sustain its momentum and to actualize its ambitious goals is not due to endemic flaws in Kingston's most alienated poor. Instead, the demise of the Peace and the return to tribal warfare must be understood in the context of the economic and political instability wrought by the forces of North American intervention. The Peace Movement, along with state policies of democratic socialism, was subverted, and U.S. dominance in Jamaica and the Caribbean Basin was upheld.

Although the direction and pace of structural change in Jamaica are certainly constrained by international conditions, the latter are not omnipotent. Despite prevalent and often overpowering limitations, the totality of Jamaica's political life--its many formal institutions as well as a multiplicity of informal fields-- offers possibilities, opportunities, and maneuvering spaces for promoting social transformation. Local-level patterns such as Oceanview's Peace and the neighborhood's recent response to austere national conditions elucidate some of the means those who bear the brunt of political and economic underdevelopment have for resisting oppression and bringing into their collective lives some degree of autonomy and empowerment.

NOTES

1   The fieldwork on which this study is based was conducted from September, 1978 through August, 1979 and later during the summer of 1984. Funding was provided by a Fulbright-Hays Predoctoral Fellowship and a summer faculty grant from the University of Louisville's Committee on Academic Excellence. Stanford University, the Wenner-Gren Foundation for Anthropological Research, and the Dorothy Danforth Compton Fellowship Program supported my data analysis. Fieldwork would not have been viable without the cooperation and support I received from informants, among them senior and junior members of Oceanview's two major gang hierarchies, police officers, PNP and JLP activists, community organizers for government-sponsored urban redevelopment and social welfare agencies, and members of the Blessed Sacrament PTA. Correspondence and telephone conversations with friends and informants were important sources of data when travel to Jamaica was impossible. Comments on an earlier draft from David Hakken, Johanna Lessinger, and Merrill Singer were helpful and greatly appreciated.

2   This combination of income strategies is often achieved within households if not by individuals.

3   Even small businesses were on the margins of solvency. Small proprietors and own-account tradesmen are often compelled to seek supplementary income from state/party contracts.

4   Thanks are due to Elliott Leib and Jake Homiak, who have done research on the Rastafari movement, for reminding me that Rastafarians, particularly the Twelve Tribes of Israel sect, encouraged rival gang leaders to join forces and organize a truce. See White (1983:299-300).

5   There are varying explanations of the Green Bay affair. According to PNP supporters, the Central Kingston gang was involved in the JLP's destabilization campaign. The police claim that the gang was involved in serious criminal offenses. White claims that the gang was reputed to be an intractable gang of PNP clients (1983:299).

6   The term "ghetto" is used in Jamaica to denote low-income neighborhoods--slums and shantytowns.

7   Girling (1983) points out that the CBI is also flawed in that it excludes many labor-intensive industries such as textiles, footwear, and leather goods from its concessions. Rum and sugar are still subject to quotas. Moreover, the lack of markets is not the crux of the balance of payments deficit problem. The real problem lies in the low prices received for export commodities.

8   As a result of local government elections held in July, 1986, the PNP restored its control over the KSAC (Jamaican Weekly Gleaner 1986).

9   Although this project was initiated and organized by a non-partisan group of activists, the benefactors--among them service club members, major Jamaican businesses, banks, and the United States Agency for International Development--were not necessarily non-partisan in their loyalties and agendas. Furthermore, such a private, non-governmental program is compatible with current national policies which limit government support of social services and encourage private initiative in development.

10   The "ethnographic present" here is 1985; however, the general climate described for the 1984-85 period remains largely intact two years later.

BIBLIOGRAPHY

African Mirror
      1978   Jamaica's Dilemma: Is it Manley's Fault? (October):39-
      46.
Ambursley, Fitzroy
      1983 Jamaica: From Michael Manley to Edward Seaga. *In*
      Crisis in the Caribbean. Fitzroy Amburseley and Robin
      Cohen, eds. Pp. 72-104. Kingston: Heinemann.
Austin, Diane J.
      1984 Urban Life in Kingston, Jamaica: The Culture and
      Class Ideology of Two Neighborhoods. New York: Gordon
      and Breach Science Publishers.
Bonilla, Frank
      1962 The Favelas of Rio: The Rundown Barrio in the City.
      Dissent 9:383-386.
Castells, Manuel
      1982 Squatters and Politics in Latin America: A Comparative
      Analysis of Urban Social Movements in Chile, Peru, and
      Mexico. *In* Towards a Political Economy of Urbanization
      in Third World Countries. Helen Safa, ed. Pp. 249-282.
      Delhi: Oxford University Press.
Clarke, Colin
      1971 This Changing World: The Development and
      Redevelopment of the Waterfront in Kingston, Jamaica.
      Geography 56(252):237-240.
Department of State, U.S.
      1984 Gist: Caribbean Basin Initiative (January).
Department of Statistics, Jamaica
      1970 Demographic Atlas of Urban Areas: The Kingston
      Metropolitan Area, Vol. 6, Part 1. Kingston, Jamaica:
      Division of Census and Surveys, Commonwealth Caribbean
      Population Census.
Fagen, Richard
      1983 Theories of Development: The Question of Class
      Struggle. Monthly Review 35(4):13-24.
Girling, Robert
      1983 Pulling the Aid Plug. South (January):63.
Girvan, Norman and Richard Bernal
      1982 The IMF and the Foreclosure of Development Options:
      The Case of Jamaica. Monthly Review 33(9):34-48.

Harrison, Faye V.
    1982 Semiproletarianization and the Structure of Socioeconomic and Political Relations in a Jamaican Slum. Ph.D. dissertation, Anthropology Department, Stanford University.

Headley, Bernard D.
    1985 Mr. Seaga's Jamaica: An Inside Look. Monthly Review 37(4):35-42.

Jamaican Daily Gleaner
    1984 PNP Questions State's Ability to Cope with Economic Strains. (July 3).

Jamaican Weekly Gleaner
    1983a JLP Returned to Power. (December 5):1.
    1983b Church Council Calls For New Elections. (December 12):1.
    1984a Nation Within a Nation. John Hearne column. (May 28):13.
    1984b Economic Hardships. Carl Stone column. (December 22):11.
    1984c KSAC Council Dissolved. (October 22):1.
    1985a Alcoa Closing. (February 11):1.
    1985b The PNP's Problem. Stone column. (October 7):11.
    1985c Mr. Seaga's Government. Stone column. (November 11):11.
    1986 PNP Sweeps Local Government Polls. (August 4):1,3.

Keith, Sherry and Robert Girling
    1978 Caribbean Conflict: Jamaica and the United States. NACLA Report on the Americas 12(3):3-36.

Lacey, Terry
    1977 Violence and Politics in Jamaica, 1960-70. Manchester: Manchester University Press.

Laguerre, Michel
    1982 Urban Life in the Caribbean: A Study of a Haitian Urban Community. Cambridge, MA: Schenkman Publishing Company.

Leeds, Anthony
    1973 Locality Power in Relation to Supralocal Power Institutions. *In* Urban Anthropology: Cross-cultural Studies of Urbanization. Aidan Southall, ed. Pp. 15-42. New York: Oxford University Press.

Lessinger, Johanna
    1985 Nobody Here to Yell at Me: Political Activism Among Petty Retail Traders in an Indian City. *In* Markets and Marketing. Stuart Plattner, ed. Pp. 309-331. Lanham, MD: University Press of America.

National Planning Agency
1978   Five Year Development Plan, 1978-82. Ministry of Finance and Planning. Kingston, Jamaica.

Portes, Alejandro and John Walton
1976   Urban Latin America: The Political Condition From Above and Below. Austin: University of Texas Press.

Roberts, Bryan
1978   Cities of Peasants: The Political Economy of Urbanization in the Third World. Beverly Hills: Sage Publications.

Singer, Paul
1982   Neighborhood Movements in Sao Paulo. *In* Towards a Political Economy of Urbanization in Third World Countries. Helen Safa, ed. Pp. 283-303. Delhi: Oxford University Press.

Stephens, Evelyne Huber and John D. Stephens
1986   Democratic Socialism in Jamaica: The Political Movement and Social Transformation in Dependent Capitalism. Princeton: University Press.

Stone, Carl
1973   Class, Race, and Political Behavior in Urban Jamaica. Mona: Institute of Social and Economic Research. University of the West Indies, Jamaica.
1980   Democracy and Clientelism in Jamaica. New Brunswick, NJ: Transaction Books.

Susser, Ida
1982   Norman Street: Poverty and Politics in an Urban Neighborhood. New York: Oxford University Press.

Swartz, Marc
1968   Introduction. *In* Local-Level Politics: Social and Cultural Perspectives. Pp. 1-51. Chicago: Aldine Publishing Company.

Urban Upgrading
n.d.   Introduction to Urban Upgrading. Kingston, Jamaica: Ministry of Local Government.

Vélez-Ibañez, Carlos G.
1983   Rituals of Marginality: Politics, Process, and Culture Change in Urban Central Mexico, 1969-74. Berkeley: University of California Press.

White, Timothy
1983   Catch a Fire: The Life of Bob Marley. New York: Holt, Rinehart and Winston.

Worsley, Peter
    1972   Frantz Fanon and the Lumpenproletariat. *In* The
    Socialist Register. Ralph Miliband and John Savile, eds.
    Pp. 193-230. London: The Merlin Press.
    1984   The Three Worlds: Culture and World Development.
    Chicago: University of Chicago Press.

MANAGEMENT BY PARTICIPATION:
THE DIVISION OF LABOR, IDEOLOGY AND
CONTRADICTION IN A U.S. FIRM

Nina Glick Schiller

Over the past decade, Marxist students of the labor process have recognized that the organization of the labor process can vary within the capitalist mode of production (Friedman 1977, Burawoy 1985). Believing that the working class becomes a revolutionary class as a result of its experience at the point of production, a number of these scholars have scrutinized variations in the labor process to determine which form of labor process organization has the greatest potential to produce a revolutionary consciousness within the work force (Wren 1982, Herman 1982). Several writers have argued that the particular organization of the labor process which management experts call "management by participation" (Morrow 1975) has "revolutionary potential" (Gorz 1976, Espinosa and Zimbalist 1978). Workers come to control certain aspects of the productive process and, it is argued, through this experience begin to organize to control all of society.

This paper is a case study of the use of such management by participation within the market research division of a multinational corporation. "Management by participation" is a form of organizing the work process which, in theory, allows workers to participate in decision-making by according them an overview of the productive process, teaching them skills and allocating them responsibilities which, in other forms of the labor process, are the prerogative of management.

I will use the present case study to examine the degree to which management by participation allowed a particular group of workers to obtain temporary control of the labor process. I will argue that this same technique of management by participation eventually generated contradictions between the workers and managers. As a result of these contradictions changes did occur in workers' consciousness. However, management by participation created no fundamental differences in the locus of control over the work process. The capitalist class continued to control the overall labor process. And while workers came to understand this reality and to resist this control, their experiences did not lead them to any overall understanding of the capitalist system or of the need to overthrow it.

As a case study, this paper can not refute those who argue for the revolutionary potential of management by participation. Nor can any case study disprove the contention that the workers develop revolutionary goals from their experiences at work. However, a fine-tuned anthropological analysis of a particular application of management by participation can call these theories into question. Such questioning opens discussion, once again, of Lenin's contention that a revolutionary party is needed to divert the working class away from the spontaneous trade union consciousness which it develops at the point of production and toward opposition to capitalism and preparation for revolution (Lenin 1964, Avakian 1984).

History of the Labor Process

Some historians have argued that even before the introduction of the vast technical changes which came to mark capitalist industries, fundamental changes took place in the organization of work (Noble 1977, Marglin 1976). Each worker came to perform only part of the larger task; no longer did a worker have the knowledge and skill to produce an entire product. With the development of machines each worker's knowledge of the entire process was reduced even further.

Along with the development of the capitalist labor process came the separation of control of production from the other aspects of production. As workers came to sell their labor power to the capitalist, they lost not only their knowledge of the entire labor process but also their control over it. Owning neither their labor power, nor the products of their labor, workers lost interest in the productive process. It was left to the capitalist to try to wrest as much productive labor as possible from the worker whose productive capacity had been purchased. Moreover, with the in-

creased division of the labor process into individual tasks performed by different unskilled workers, the need for the coordina-
tion of production grew. Individual unskilled workers now lacked
the overview of the productive process necessary to regulate and
integrate their individual tasks.

It is not surprising, therefore, to discover that much of the
history of the emerging capitalist labor process is the history of
the development of formal systems of management (Friedman
1977, Edwards 1979). These systems of control serve not only to
compel the worker to produce, but also provide ideological
justification for the structuring of the capitalist labor process and
the position of the workers within it.

The most famous management system was developed in the
early 20th century by Fredrick Taylor whose "Taylor system" of
"scientific management" sought to rationalize production and justify the establishment of professional managers. Taylor advocated
an extreme division of labor in which each task was reduced to its
simplest components. While few work places actually implemented
all aspects of the Taylor system, the ideological aspects of the system were widely utilized. Mastery over the worker was now
legitimized in the name of science. Work rules and the pressure to
produce as rapidly as possible, always part of the capitalist labor
process, were now justified in terms of the necessities arising
from the "science" of production, rather than the economic interests of the capitalists.

Although the Taylor system has come to symbolize the capitalist labor process, it is not the only system of capitalist management. Variation in the system of capitalist control reflects the interaction of a number of factors: the nature of different industries as capitalism itself changes and diversifies; the scale of
different work places; and the history of each industry and each
work place.   This history includes the extent and nature of the
workers' struggle against capitalist control, the degree of monopoly
within each industry, and the role of the industry in the national
or world economy (Edwards 1979).

By the beginning of the 20th century, both Taylorism and
"Fordism" (Gartman 1979) had in large plants replaced the personal, familistic ties between worker and capitalist which had been
a hallmark of earlier, smaller industrial firms. Under Fordism the
mechanical demands of the assembly line itself seem to regulate
production, rather than the interests of the capitalist. However, as
large scale corporations developed, their tendency toward the mo-

nopolization of industry was accompanied by a process of bureaucratization, in which a set of regulations came to impose discipline while allowing workers certain privileges within the system. In this form the rules and regulations became the control system itself. Managerial control was justified in the name of rationality, while workers were induced to identify with the system which seemed to grant them certain rights.

Management by participation is the most recent managerial system to emerge. While experiments in worker participation enjoyed some popularity in the 1950s (Pantick 1978), it was not until the 1970s that management by participation became the latest word in innovative management (Myers 1970, Industry Week 1981). These techniques became especially popular in the primary sector of U.S. industry when corporations, faced with fierce competition from European and Japanese firms, found they were unable to elicit loyalty, productivity, and attention to quality from North American workers.

For example, Alfred Morrow, a leading management consultant in the 1970s, has described the limitation he sees in trying to control the work force by means of a Taylor-like system. To quote Morrow:

> A worker who feels he is being turned into a robot, that he stands powerless before the clangorous automatic system, with no hope of changing his drudgery and loss of self-esteem, finds psychic withdrawal the only temporary escape against his growing fury. His morale is low and his productivity minimal (1975:36).

The solution to these limitations, according to management experts such as Morrow, is to make work a more meaningful experience. The techniques of management by participation attempt to tap the productive capacity of workers by acknowledging openly and then manipulating their abilities and capacities for innovation. At the same time these techniques induce workers to identify with their jobs. Under this system the labor process is rearranged to eliminate some of the minute divisions of labor which Taylorism had established between various related tasks. Such an arrangement is often labeled "job enlargement" or a "work team" approach to production. In addition, some of the divisions between production, supervision and planning are eliminated. These changes are often presented to workers as "job enrichment."

In management journals, these changes are more bluntly labeled "planning by the pawns" (Phare 1980).

Marxist Analysis of the Labor Process

Marx, exploring the interpenetration of ideological, political and economic relationships within the capitalist labor process notes, that embedded in the capitalist mode of production are ideological mechanisms which obscure the exploitative nature of the capitalist class. He was primarily interested in the role of the wage labor system in concealing the capitalist appropriation of value produced by the working class (Marx 1972).

Marx was also aware that the capitalist labor process itself served to legitimate and perpetuate capitalist control. He wrote that "it is a result of the division of labour in manufactures, that the labourer is brought face to face with the intellectual potencies of the material process of production, as the property of another, and as a ruling power" (1972, vol I:361). Workers experience feelings of powerlessness and subordination as a result of the division of labor at the point of production. Marx focused on the division of labor because he believed that the general direction of capitalist development was toward the destruction of skilled labor and the creation of the working class as "detail laborers."

Almost a century after Marx wrote *Capital*, Harry Braverman in *Labor and Monopoly Capital* continued and developed Marx's discussion of the labor process. Braverman, as did Marx before him, acknowledged other possible ways of controlling the labor process. However he saw the division of labor at the point of production as the primary means by which capitalism comes to control the worker. Braverman focused on the Taylor system as the quintessential division of labor in the capitalist work place. Through the Taylor system, control of the work process is wrested from the working class and placed in the hands of a strata of capitalist managers. Workers, stripped of their skill and knowledge of the work process, become "an objective element in a productive process now conducted by management"(1974:172).

Marxists who have built critically on Braverman's seminal analysis have emphasized various shortcomings in his approach. Burawoy, for example, argues that Braverman's description of workers as "objective elements in the labor process" tends to negate their active participation in the ideological system. Burawoy prefers to examine how the structure of the labor process itself induces workers to consent to their own subordination and control (1979). He demonstrates "*how the day to day adaptations of workers create their own ideological effects that become focal ele-*

ments in the operation of capitalist control" (italics in the original
1978:273).

Other theorists have criticized both Braverman and Burawoy
for painting the working class as quiescent. These writers stress
that working-class resistance has shaped the structure of the class
and capital's necessity to develop systems of control (Peck 1982,
Aronowitz 1978, Ehrenreich and Ehrenreich 1976). By describing
the multiple forms of worker resistance, such "resistance theorists"
want to do more than provide a factual corrective for Braverman.
Their focus on worker resistance contains a political agenda: they
are searching for revolutionary struggle against capitalism and they
believe that it will emerge out of working-class resistance at the
point of production.

Those Marxist who have welcomed the introduction of management by participation represent a variant of resistance theory.
Zimbalist, for example, argues that

> There is ample evidence that, once given a taste of the control
> of their work, workers go after more. If this occurs, the capi-
> talists control over the program is lost and their control over
> the entire production process becomes threatened (Espinosa
> and Zimbalist 1978:21).

Those, including Zimbalist, who have made such statements
have tempered their enthusiasm by noting that certain conditions
must exist before the "taste of control" becomes a threat to capitalism. For example, Herman tells us that

> depending upon the cultural context, ideological orientation,
> and organizational capacities of the workers, the taste of
> autonomy and participation may lead to an escalation of
> demands which could ultimately threaten the reproduction of
> social relations of domination within the firm and in capitalist
> society as a whole (1982:18).

Fortunately Marxist scholarship has also developed a more
useful perspective on the changing forms of the organization of
production and capital than the narrow vision of point of production studies. This alternative perspective places worker resistance,
and changes in the form of the labor process, within the context
of global development of capitalism. Edwards (1979), for example, demonstrates that the internal contradictions of each system
are themselves structured by the cyclical crises of capitalism. He
provides us with a glimpse of how each different organization of

the labor process conditions the work force ideologically in ways which legitimize the system of control to which the workers are currently subjected. Each way of organizing the work process contains contradictions which lead to worker resistance and force capitalism to develop other systems of control. Similarly, Friedman recognizes that

> because labor power is alienated under the capitalist mode of production, each strategy in its ultimate vision, is based on a contradiction.... The contradiction may be suppressed, or disguised, or bypassed, but its continued existence will regenerate tensions which will again threaten good order unless actively suppressed once more (1977:7).

Lotta links the reorganization of capital to global processes of imperialism which can result from and lead to world war, and can generate revolutionary conjunctures (1984).

Worker Rebellion Among Market Researchers

Consumer Products Incorporated (CPI), a toiletries and food manufacturer which used a system of management by participation both in its factories and offices, is the subject of this case study, in which I will examine the use of these techniques among the 30 full time office workers who were employed as interviewers in the company's Market Research Division (MRD) in 1980-81. The study was conducted while I worked as a part-time interviewer for CPI. The name of the corporation has been changed to protect the anonymity of my co-workers who continue to work there. The goal of the Market Research Division (MRD) was to obtain information about consumer attitudes and practices through telephone interviews carried out in a large central office called "the field"; in special circumstances, interviewers flew to cities throughout the country to work on research projects.

While this interviewing was a low-level entry job, the prosperity of CPI was linked to the accuracy and productivity of its interviewers. CPI has established a strong competitive position on the basis of its product development and marketing. Decisions involving the investment of millions of dollars are made on the basis of market research data. If interviews are not conducted properly, if questionnaires are not filled in accurately, and if the sampling procedures and rules for conducting interviews are not followed systematically, the accuracy and usefulness of the data are compromised. To ensure accurate data, CPI maintained its own in-house staff of interviewers. This costly undertaking meant constant pressure to make sure that the productivity of the unit was high.

The MRD interviewing staff were expected to work rapidly and to produce accurate data during a complex interviewing process which left many decisions to interviewer discretion. When conducting telephone interviews, MRD staff read from sheets of a text, and recorded the responses on IBM cards. While texts and the rules of procedure were standardized, a respondent's answers, of course, were not. Interviewers had to decide, depending on the answers given, which of the 80 pages of rules to follow, what to record, and what to probe further. Under the pressure of producing a large number of interviews, interviewers could abandon standardized research procedures, or fake answers, or even whole interviews. Unlike assembly line production where the pace of work is tied to the pace of the machines, interviewers could, and did, vary the pace of the interviewing process. They could dial and interview rapidly, or work in a leisurely fashion, chatting amiably with each respondent after the interview, and gossiping with co-workers between interviews. The dilemma of CPI management was that it was forced to give workers a large measure of autonomy in carrying out the work, while trying to maintain high rates of productivity.

The classic managerial technique to insure that workers perform their tasks accurately and fast is close supervision of the work process. It is not surprising that interviewers at CPI were closely supervised. However CPI did not rest content with close supervision. Instead the company also used techniques of management by participation to try to insure that interviewers, by identifying with the company, would perform accurately and productively.

Developing an Identification with the Job

All full-time CPI interviewers were told in memos from management that they were "developmental," meaning that they participated in job enlargement, job enrichment and worker management committees. Job enrichment consisted of training and participation in numerous different tasks including the task of supervising other workers. After two weeks at initial training and approximately six months of interviewing, interviewers were trained to perform other tasks, such as overseeing the sampling procedures, checking completed questionnaires, and listening to fellow workers to check the accuracy of their interviews. By performing these tasks, interviewers were given the opportunity to help coordinate and supervise the interviewing process.

This organization of the work process served both to reduce the division of labor between the workers and to obscure the division of labor between manager and worker. All of the tasks done by interviewers, including interviewing, also were performed by supervisors at least part of the time. On any particular study, a field supervisor, (the lowest rank of management), might be interviewing, while a worker might be coordinating the study.

The second component of development was a form of job enrichment. All full-time interviewers were given training in the methods, purpose, and outlook of market research. This training served to give the field staff an overview of the work process, enabling them to see how crucial the production of accurate interviews was to the entire enterprise of product development and marketing.

This training began during the first day on the job. It was incorporated into the two weeks of orientation during which interviewers were trained in the interview process. The training manual which introduced the newcomer to the process of interviewing had an entire section devoted to the "science" of market research. This section included articles on the history of product development at CPI, guidelines for proper sampling and questionnaire design, and the "management considerations of a consumer-oriented business." This training manual told new interviewers that "the market researcher can agree with the Australian Medical Research Doctor Duke-Elder who said; 'Research is worthwhile because of the finding of new things, of being alive, of being a spearhead in the world progress, and is always great fun.'"

Note that in this passage the pleasures and work of medical research carried out by physicians are equated with market research. The theme--that market research is a science and the interviewers are professionals engaged in a scientific undertaking-- was echoed by both CPI experts and managers in all of their training sessions.

This training of the interviewer as a market research professional continued with classes on other aspects of market research.

These presentations, attended by all full-time staff, were made during working hours; all interviewing stopped while everyone went to class. The sessions were run by MRD managers with presentations given by CPI experts.

In its recruitment of interviewers, CPI selected individuals who would be receptive to such professional development. All interviewers were either college graduates or students who were majoring in marketing. Most of those with college degrees also had M.A. degrees, most frequently in English or education. Ninety percent of the 30 interviewers were women; most saw the job as a means of obtaining paid training in a profession. This goal seemed attainable; the field supervisors and all but the top MRD directors were women who had begun as interviewers.

The language of research science which was introduced during the training sessions was maintained in the course of supervision of the work process. The pace of the work, the need to produce rapidly, the need to work overtime, and the necessity for frequent monitoring of the interviewer were all explained and justified by managers in terms of the requirements of the research design.

Interviewers accepted this rationale, and spoke to each other in these terms. Even when contradictions began to develop between workers and managers, workers at first voiced their disagreements both to management and privately to each other in terms of the goal of insuring that the research was accurate, rather than in terms of their own needs.

Committees composed of both workers and managers were the third component of development. The task of these committees was to discuss pressing work place issues. These committees further reduced the division of labor between workers and managers, and gave the workers an overview of the work process. These committees were never described as joint management-labor committees, a term which carries the implication that two different points of view are being represented.

During the period of my research there were two such committees which met regularly. The first was called the Modernization Committee. Modernization was the CPI euphemism for the computerization of the interviewing process. Computer consultants had been called in to write programs so that the computer would control aspects of the interview process over which the interviewer had previously exercised discretion, such as dialing and the pacing of the questions. The Modernization Committee worked with the consultants to decide questions of format and procedure.

The Modernization Committee, in turn, called and chaired meetings, attended by the entire field staff including the research director and the personnel director, to discuss the decisions which were being made. At one such meeting a field supervisor, delivering a report on behalf of the Modernization Committee said, "We can set up a system together which serves our needs.... No one is telling us what to do. It is your system."

The second committee, the Production Committee, produced a list of suggestions about how interviewers could speed up the pace of work. "Fill in your dialing slip while the phone is ringing" read one item on the list.

"I Love My Job"

The breaking down of the division of labor among workers, and between workers and managers, the meeting together of workers and managers on committees, the blurring of the lines of corporate hierarchy, and the ideology which stressed that workers were being trained as professional researchers all had an impact on the activities and consciousness of the interviewers.

On a day-to-day basis, workers identified with their work. They talked and acted as if it were in their interest to work themselves into exhaustion. When there was pressure to complete a study by a certain date, full-time workers would dial constantly for hours on end. Even before the Production Committee issued its report, most interviewers had, on their own initiative, found ways of speeding up production. On several occasions, I observed a worker who had been put in charge of a particular study voluntarily and without consultation with a supervisor stay beyond his or her quitting time to get in some extra calls.

Moreover, full time workers displayed concern about the accuracy of the research procedures they were employing. They paid attention to the details necessary to insure that the data was of the best quality. When a problem arose about how to interpret the rules, how to probe a question, or how to record a response, workers spontaneously consulted with each other. There were long discussions about the nuances of the rules of interviewing, discussions joined by people who were not even directly involved in that study.

In many ways CPI's Market Research Division seemed to have achieved the goals of work place harmony promised by the advocates of management by participation. Interviewers worked a difficult schedule of five days and three evenings a week, and their lives were disrupted by trips to unglamorous cities for more long hours of work. While workers might complain about a particular interview, or gripe about a rude respondent, as long as CPI continued the techniques of management by participation, they never said that they didn't like their jobs, or criticized the company. On the contrary, during dinner outings and coffee break when the conversation turned to previous jobs they had held, workers would tell horror stories about previous jobs. In contrast, when queried about their current jobs, they frequently responded, "I love my job".

Contradictions

But underneath the surface an observer could see latent contradictions. First of all, while interviewers came to identify with management; field supervisors (managers) also came to identify with the workers. They worked side by side on the same tasks and became personally close. During dinner breaks interviewers and field supervisors would sit together in the cafeteria or go out to eat together; after work they would go drinking together.

A second indication of the contradictions being produced could be found within the report of the Production Committee. While Part I of the report was filled with suggestions for speedup, there was also a Part II, filled with suggestions for reorganizing the work process to suit the needs of the workers. These suggestions ranged from rewarding productive workers with such things as cars, or extra holidays, to sending particularly obnoxious studies to outside market research firms. Trained to identify with the work of the Market Research Division, the MRD workers were beginning to try to manage the division. And this situation was produced directly by the management techniques in use.

A month after the Production Committee issued its report, upper levels of CPI management stepped in to make it clear who was really in control. The Director of Personnel attended the next Production Committee meeting. She announced, as a policy statement which was not to be discussed, that all full-time interviewers now would be required to work four nights a week instead of three. The same policy was to apply to field supervisors.

Even if interviewers had not started to make policy suggestions which differed from the interests of management, CPI managers might well have decided to tighten direct control over the MRD staff. Like many other U.S. corporations in 1981, CPI was facing what *Fortune* magazine described as a "crunch" reflected in a rapid drop in the value of CPI stock. To try to remedy the situation CPI launched a cost-cutting campaign, and this campaign seems to have impinged on the costly management techniques MRD was using to obtain peaceful labor relations. In its push for immediate increases in MRD department productivity, management did not wait for workers to decide for themselves to work more evening hours.

The direct intervention of management took both the interviewers and the field supervisors by surprise. Immediately after the announcement, they voiced objections. At first their objections were phrased in terms of the harm which the added evening hours would do to the sampling procedures. This was followed by several weeks of whispered conversations, and discussions between small groups on the work floor.

Finally, interviewers and field supervisors began to meet together secretly to organize resistance, using the very offices they had come to see as their own, to discuss their right to control their own time, and to plan a response to management. Two months after the personnel director's announcement the rebels confronted the MRD directors and declared that they would not work the additional night. They delivered an ultimatum: either management would rescind its decision or they would all find other jobs.

For the next two months, very little work was done in MRD. Although no one labeled these actions a slowdown, both interviewers and field supervisors worked as slowly as possible. Instead of working, people stood around in small groups for periods of 15 minutes to an hour, discussing their grievances against the company and their alienation from it. One interviewer initiated her own study of the educational level of the interviewers in order to strengthen the argument that they deserved better treatment. People compared notes about their efforts to obtain other jobs.

Almost all of the interviewers and field supervisors had began to look for other jobs. The general conclusion which they drew from their experience was that there was something wrong with the CPI management. Some people thought that the problem was with the Market Research Division and sought to transfer to another section of CPI. Others felt the problem was with the company as a whole and sought other employment. The one person who did draw a broader conclusion argued that she now realized that "all companies were the same", and "don't give a damn about the opinions of the workers." Her solution was, therefore, to stay right where she was but to stop "giving her all" for the company. She said that she realized now that the workers in the division needed some kind of protection. First, she felt they needed to know their rights so she contacted the American Civil Liberties Union. Then she felt they needed some kind of organization. However she had a hard time interesting her friends since they were bent on leaving either the division or the company.

At the end of these two months, the personnel director met with the interviewer and field supervisors to make another announcement. Only new, full-time workers, hired with the understanding that they would work four nights a week, would be required to work such hours regularly. Part-time workers might also be required to work four nights and the numbers of part-timers might be expanded.

The rebels realized immediately that they had won the battle but lost the war. The newer people would need supervision so all full time interviewers and supervisors would end up working four nights anyway. And this indeed proved to be the case. The formal resistance collapsed but the grumbling and slowdown continued. For the first time full-time workers and supervisors began to say that they hated their jobs. Meanwhile management began to experiment with new techniques with which to control the work force. They began to hire a large number of part time workers and greatly increased the amount of work they contracted out to small independent market research firms.

The techniques of management by participation not only had legitimated management's control of the work process; they also had generated contradictions to that control. The source of both the process of legitimization of management's control, and the generation of contradictions to that control was the reorganization of the work process brought about by management by participation.

Analysis

Management by participation is more than company propaganda; at CPI aspects of the work process actually were changed. Real changes were made in the division of labor, including significant changes in the division of knowledge about the work process. Interviewers were given more information about the entire process of market research than would otherwise have occurred under other capitalist management procedures. This many-faceted reduction in the division of labor led interviewers to identify with their jobs in a way that would not have been achieved by a bureaucratic system of management. As Edwards has pointed out, workers within a bureaucratic system who have worked to comply with an elaborate system of rules to obtain and maintain their position come to identify with their jobs, and feel that the jobs are theirs by right. This type of identification can make individuals feel loyal to a company rather than to fellow workers, but it may not impel them to work hard, since identification is with the position, not with the task itself (1977:130-152). Management by participation, by reducing the division of labor, results in a different type of identification with the company. Workers come to identify with the work itself. To a certain extent, the alienation of workers from their work, a fact which is at the heart of the division of labor under capitalism and central to most management schemes, seems to be overcome.

This reduction of worker alienation seems to occur in two ways. Allowing workers to choose how their productive capacity will be employed seems to overcome the alienation which workers experience when they sell their labor power. In the process of performing supervisory tasks, and sitting on committees which made choices about questions of productivity and the use of computers, CPI interviewers felt that their productive capacity was being restored to them. The result of this decrease in alienation was that the interviewers experienced a sense of empowerment.

This feeling of empowerment was strengthened by the simultaneous reduction of a second type of alienation -- the alienation of knowledge and skill from the worker. As Marx pointed out, when labor is divided between worker and manager, "the labourer is brought face to face with the intellectual potencies of the material process of production, as the product of another, as a ruling power"(1972:364). The techniques of management by participation, by de-emphasizing managerial control, breaks down this type of alienation. At CPI, the interviewers and supervisors shared knowledge of market research methods, both in formal training sessions, committee meetings and in informal conversations. This led to a bonding between workers and managers, eliminating the sense of being subordinated and powerless to the "ruling power" of management. Interviewers felt competent and willing to do work which they saw as their own.

Within this reduction of alienation, this identification of the worker with the work, and the resulting sense of empowerment, lie the contradictions of management by participation. The changes which this technique makes in the work process are real. But workers' sense that their productive capacity and control of the work process have been restored to them is false. Workers still sell their labor capacity to the capitalist. Therefore that capacity remains alienated from them, however much they might think otherwise.

But feeling empowered, workers at CPI acted as if they were in charge. As this case study shows the ideology generated by such changes in the division of labor becomes a material force. In CPI Market Research Division this meant that interviewers tried to plan for and control aspects of the work process which had not been allocated to them by management. When CPI managers stepped in to assert their power there was resistance. The lesson of who really controlled the work and whose interests it served, was quickly learned.

Once the false consciousness created by the techniques of management by participation was destroyed, the interviewers could see clearly that they had no interest in production, and they did as little work as possible. Management was legitimated neither by the reification of its knowledge as a ruling power, nor by the identification with the work and with management.

Two final points should be made. First, the internal contradictions generated within the work process by the use of management by participation were sharpened by the contradictions and crisis of capitalism worldwide. It was the current economic crisis which pushed CPI managers to demand the increased in productivity of longer evening hours. CPI could no longer afford the time and effort required to convince interviewers they were the ones who were making decisions about productivity. The internal contradiction of particular management systems must be placed in the context of the worldwide functioning of capitalism.

Secondly, the resistance of the interviewers, and the consequent rupture of false consciousness generated by management by participation, was not a radical rupture. Edwards and others have argued that "some control over work place decisions raises the demand for industrial democracy" and that "in Britain, France, Italy, and elsewhere, work place democracy appears well on the way to becoming a mass demand, and the revolutionary potential seems great"(1979:156).

At CPI there was nothing revolutionary in the consciousness of workers although they first tried to take control, and then rebelled against their lack of control and began to see their interests as different from those of CPI. Rather, CPI interviewers tried to take more control of the work process because they identified with the company and its managers, not because they stood opposed to the entire system of social production, private appropriation. Although interviewers ultimately went on to rebel against their lack of control at CPI and to reject the legitimacy of the management of a company with which they had previously identified, none reached any broader conclusions about their lack of control over the entire society.

Gorz has argued that the revolutionary potential of worker participation can not be judged in the abstract.

> As with any reform, the meaning of new non-despotic forms of work organization depends on the relation of forces presiding over their introduction.... When instituted from above, it is a reformist cooption by capital of workers' resistance; when imposed from beneath in a test of strength, it opens a breach in capital's system of domination (1976:60-61).

This case study of management by participation at CPI demonstrates that even when introduced "from above," management by participation causes contradictions in the domination of capital to arise. However, such "a breach in capital's system of domination" does not lead workers, even as they rebel, to comprehend the source of these contradictions or the solutions. Would the imposition of "non-despotic" forms of work organization in response to workers' demands make the rebellion any more revolutionary? While this study does not directly speak to the question, it demonstrates that it is possible for workers to struggle over control of the work place without developing a revolutionary consciousness. At the heart of the development of a revolutionary consciousness is the rejection of the legitimacy of the ruling class as a whole.

NOTES

Earlier versions of this paper were delivered at annual meetings of the American Anthropological Association in 1982 and 1983. I would like to thank Hanna Lessinger for her invaluable advice and editorial assistance and David Schiller, Nancy Bonvillain, Eva Friedlander, Betty Levin, Fran Rothstein and Ida Susser for all their helpful suggestions and encouragement.

BIBLIOGRAPHY

Aronowitz, Stanley
　1973　　False Promises: Shaping of American Working Class Consciousness. New York: McGraw Hill.
Avakian, Bob
　1984　Why We Are What Is To Be Doneists? Chicago: RCP Publications.
Braverman, Harry
　1974　　Labor and Monopoly Capital: The Degradation of Work In The Twentieth Century. New York: Monthly Review Press.
Burawoy, Michael
　　1978　Towards a Marxist Theory of the Labor Process: Braverman and Beyond. Politics and Society 8(3-4):261-299.
　　1979　Manufacturing Consent: Changes in the Labor Process Under Monopoly Capitalism. Chicago: University of Chicago Press.
　　1985　The Politics of Production: Factory Regimes Under Capitalism and Socialism. London: Verso.
Edwards, Richard
　　1979　Contested Terrain: The Transformation of the Workplace in the Twentieth Century. New York: Basic Books.
Ehrenreich, J. and B. Ehrenreich
　　1976　Work and Consciousness. Monthly Review 28(3):10-18.
Espinosa, Juan and Andrew Zimbalist.
　　1978　Democracy: Workers' Participation in Chilean Industry 1970-1973. New York: Academic Press.

Friedman, Anthony
  1977   Industry and Labor: Class Struggle at Work and Monopoly Capitalism. London: Macmillan.
Gartman, David
  1979   Origins of the Assembly Line and Capitalist Control of Work at Ford. *In* Case Studies on the Labor Process. Andrew Zimbalist, ed. Pp. 193-205. New York: Monthly Review Press.
Gorz, André
  1976   Tyranny of the Factory: Today and Tomorrow. *In* the Division of Labour: The Labour Process and Class Struggle in Modern Capitalism. André Gorz, ed. Pp. 55-61. Atlantic Highlands, New Jersey: Humanities Press.
Herman, Andrew
  1982   Conceptualizing Control: Domination and Hegemony in the Capitalist Labor Process. The Insurgent Sociologist 11(3):7-22.
Industry Week
  1981   Organizing for Productivity. February 9:53-55.
Lenin, V.I.
  1964   What is to be Done. Collected Works. 5:346-567. Moscow: Progress Publishers.
Lotta, Raymond
  1984 America in Decline, vol 1. Chicago: Banner.
Marglin, Stephen
  1976   What Do Bosses Do? The Origins and Functions of Hierarchy in Capitalist Production. *In* The Division of Labor. André Gorz, ed. Atlantic Highlands, New Jersey: Humanities Press.
Marx, Karl
  1972   Capital. New York: International Publishers.
Morrow
  1975   Management by Participation. *In* Management and Work in Society. Eugene Cass and Frederick Zimmer, eds. Pp. 33-47. New York: Van Nostrand.
Myers, M. Scott
  1970   Every Employee a Manager. New York: McGraw Hill.
Noble, David
  1977 America by Design: Science, Technology and the Rise of Corporate Capitalism. New York: Alfred A. Knopf.

Pantick, Leo
   1978 The Importance of Workers' Control for Revolutionary
       Change. Monthly Review 29(10):37-48.
Peck, Gary
   1982 The Labor Process According to Burawoy: Limits of a
       Nondialectical Approach to Capitalist Workplace Relations.
       The Insurgent Sociologist 11(3):81-90.
Phare, Alphonso
   1980 Planning People. Productivity Management Planning
       28(4):39.
Wren, Robert
   1982   Management and Work Humanization. The Insurgent
       Sociologist 11(3):23-38.

CORPORATE HEGEMONY AND INDUSTRIAL RESTRUCTURING IN A NEW ENGLAND INDUSTRIAL CITY

June Nash[1]

The failure of the U.S. working class to develop a distinctive proletarian political position is often attributed to false consciousness. This usually means that workers identify their interests with those of corporate owners and implies that a true consciousness would oppose these on the basis of antagonistic class relations. This implicitly economic determinist view is challenged when we consider the multiplicity of cultural factors that condition the relations between classes. When basic needs were not the issues of struggle, as was true until recently in the United States, a more complex model assessing both ideological persuasion and government intervention is needed.

With the development of monopoly capitalism, simple repressive control of the labor force gave way to more subtle forms combining force with persuasion. Gramsci's (1973) notion of hegemonic control develops the Marxist concept of class struggle by emphasizing cultural practices in the formation of consciousness.[2] He shows how during the interwar years corporations combined force with persuasion to incorporate workers in the institutional structures that they dominated. I differ from Gramsci in emphasizing that this was not simply the imposition of a dominant ideology on workers but, rather, a negotiated process in which labor has made the moves that ensured stable employment and high wage levels. Although opposed by corporations, these moves benefitted U.S. industrialization by providing a broad national market for consumption of goods and a basis for labor peace. But in the cooptation of these initiatives, corporate managers transformed them into economic drives devoid of political demands. This deprived the workers of an entry into decision-making in the corporation and in government.

Corporate capitalist hegemony is contained in a culture shared by all sectors of the society. This culture appeals to basic sentiments of familism, freedom, liberty and equality. In business, production, family, sports, and community affairs, the striving toward precision, technical know-how and one-upsmanship define the behavior that is exhibited, applauded and emulated. The culture in which corporate hegemony thrived is predicated on a family wage in a single-worker household. When women entered the work force, their employment was considered a temporary expedient to pay for luxuries like dining out or vacation travel. Ideas of equal opportunity and upward mobility offered important validations for corporate hegemony. And if mobility was often translated into horizontal geographical movement, that was blamed on individual failures. As long as one could assume equal opportunity, every individual was expected to maximize his or her potential. This was freedom, or what the United States had and what was lacking in the Soviet Union. Patriotism and willingness to fight for these ideals was recognized in preferential employment and was accorded ritual recognition on Memorial Day, the Fourth of July and Veteran's Day.

The construction and maintenance of this hegemony in the U.S. is based on inputs from labor and professionals as well as corporate managers. This was not always so. A socialist ethic and communal activities pervaded ethnic communities in the late 19th and early 20th centuries (Gutman 1976, Montgomery 1979). The period was marked by bitter labor struggles and even in times of peace, the lines were drawn sharply between owners and managers of the means of production and the workers dependent on them for jobs.

Welfare capitalism of the 1920s initiated the incorporation of workers on corporate terms. This was the period Gramsci analyzed in "Fordism and Americanism" (1973). Until War II, a working family's take-home wages could pay off a home mortgage in 30 years and buy a second-hand car, but there was little inter-generational mobility. Children were expected to be on their own by the time they graduated from high school, and not long after that they began their own families.

What changed this picture were the labor struggles of the 1930s and the institutionalized processes of income redistribution that labor leaders, together with some progressive representatives at state and national levels, succeeded in establishing. The Wagner Act legalized trade union organization, and the National Labor Relations Board (NLRB) provided the legal machinery to ensure its enactment. These changes affecting the work place were combined with opening up of educational opportunities in state-supported schools which allowed entry of working-class children into technical and managerial positions. Social Security legislation passed in 1935 lessened the dependency of the old on their adult children and ensured the right to live with dignity after retirement.

The fruits of the 1930s organizing were not realized until after the war, when strike waves spread from auto and steel to the electrical machinery industry. Nationally organized trade unions confronted nationally integrated industries for the first time. Veterans marched on the picket line in their uniforms. Patriotism was clearly identified with the unions. The 10-cent-an-hour average increase won by the strikers was not great, but the show of power startled management into devising new labor control mechanisms.

These gains made by labor reinforced workers' commitment to a system that opened up mobility for at least a sector of the work force and permitted entry of their children as professionals in the burgeoning service sector of industry and government. Organized labor became committed to the free enterprise market system to a greater extent than monopoly capitalist enterprises that avoid its operations in every way possible.

The current threat to corporate hegemony is brought about by the erosion of the preferred position of core industrial workers as multinational corporations seek cheap labor sites for production overseas. It also stems from the attack by Reaganomics on the wage and welfare support programs that ensured social stability. The inability of most organized sectors of labor to confront this new threat is a result of the failure to extend organization to the secondary work force and overseas.

How did the unions lose this initiative in the intervening decades from 1946 to the present? How were the political and economic goals of the men and women who organized the industrial unions channeled toward reinforcing monopoly capital and the centers of power in government and industry? How is the resulting corporate hegemony affected by the withdrawal of the contribution on the corporate side of the ledger--jobs and security?

I shall try to answer these questions by analyzing changes that are taking place in the industrial city of Pittsfield, Massachusetts. I chose the city to study the impact of industry on community and family because it was one of the earliest towns to industrialize and because it was among the early sites for the development of monopoly capital when General Electric Corporation (GE) bought out an electrical machinery manufacturing firm at the turn of the 20th century.

In the century of large-scale manufacturing that occurred in this city one can see the transformation of society with corporate hegemonic control. The population increased along with the expansion of production in the firm from 22,000 in 1890 when electrical machinery began to be produced to 60,000 in 1960 when power transformer production reached its peak. It has declined to 49,000 as the corporation has withdrawn production of medium-size and small transformers to the south and overseas, and is now disinvesting from electrical machinery and turning to the production of military electronic systems and research and development in plastics. The loss of population is consistent with the loss of blue collar production work and the shift to high-tech industry, a process that is happening throughout the U.S. Some of the technicians and engineers displaced when General Electric moved production sites elsewhere have started their own plastics production businesses. These are, for the most part, small-scale, non-union shops that pay little more than minimum wages. The few enterprises that have survived from the 19th century--in paper products and a braid factory--were not able to take up the slack as over 8,000 workers were laid off from the main GE plant.

Along with the shift to high-technology production, employing a greater proportion of professionals and technicians, has come the development of the tourist industry that used to cater to urbanites from New York and Boston but now responds to a resident population. A year-round theatrical company has taken up residence in an old movie palace, and singles bars are more popular than the sex-segregated blue collar bars of the past.

The announcement by General Electric spokesmen in November, 1986, that the company would shut down production in the Power Transformer Department and lay off up to a 1,000 workers in 1987 stunned the city despite many advance warnings. The responses of the unions and of state and federal representatives

reveal some of the premises on which hegemony was constructed
and the fissures that are developing as the corporate side of the
ledger--well-paid jobs with security and benefits--is being withdrawn.

HOW CORPORATE HEGEMONY WORKS

The basic rules of corporate hegemonic control that emerged
after World War II can be summarized as follows. First and para-
mount has been management's assumption of leadership over any
broadly supported initiatives that stem from the rank and file.
Second was the control over the local labor market to minimize
pressure on the wage structure. Third was the containment of
political activism within an ideology orchestrated by corporate
elites. Finally there is the appeal to patriotism and to the American way of doing things to validate these strategies. All required
a cultural management that reduces opposition and reinforces
managerial dominance over the work force in both the work place
and in the community. In Pittsfield, General Electric provided a
base for the improved standards of living that characterized the
American way of life. The company's slogan, "General Electric
brings good things to life," seemed to be realized in the growth
decades of the corporation up until the decade of the 1970s.

Cooptation of Union Initiatives

The corporate tactics of repressive labor control that marked
the early decades of corporate consolidation at the turn of the
20th century changed in the years of Gerard Swope's presidency
of General Electric. Unlike other executives of large corporations,
Swope did not oppose the Wagner Act or New Deal reforms
directly during the stormy years of the Depression when industrial
unions were being formed. Jim Matles (Matles and Higgins
1974:63), one of the leaders in the United Electrical Workers
Union (UE), sized up Swope's administrative skill, based on
paternalism:

> After the AFL craft organizations had been shattered by
> General Electric in the twenties, Swope set up Works Councils
> which were company unions. But the National Recovery Act
> of 1933, affirming the right of workers to form their own
> unions, compelled some changes in the General Electric policy
> of company unionism.

Although the Works Councils were effective in fighting trade union activity when it was illegal, the UE made tremendous strides in organizing shops following the 1934 National Labor Relations Board (NLRB) decision. Swope again tried to seize the initiative, publishing a labor code, GE Q105A, that set forth the corporation's policies on wages, hours, overtime, vacations, and employment conditions. That code anticipated many of the union's demands. Instead of fighting this, the UE incorporated these policies in their first proposed contract with GE, with the addition of grievance machinery.

Pittsfield workers were late in achieving an independent union contract, and depression conditions persisted in the community until just before World War II. Workers were never sure of how many hours they would work in a day or a week. Sam, a retired worker, described the conditions of work before the UE was recognized:

> If you came in to work in the morning in those years, even if you had work, if the boss told you to take the day off, you had to go home and not earn anything....During the Depression years I lost two years, six months and 12 days. I picked up odd jobs, I couldn't get on the WPA [Works Progress Administration, a federal work relief program]. When I got laid off, I had almost seven years service, and they kept guys that had one and two years. But you couldn't do anything about it. That was it. And then after the Depression when I went back to work, I got less money. I started at 55 cents an hour. And then you'd work, my God, you'd work for a year, and they'd never give you a raise. But if you asked them for a raise, you know what they'd give you? A penny an hour, and it would take you six months to get it.

Lacking seniority, older workers like Sam were at a disadvantage before independent unions were formed. In order to prevent the laid-off workers from leaving the area, the company set up a plan of charging everybody who was working a certain amount from their pay that went into a fund for those without work. Married men with dependent children were given priority when layoffs came. This meant that married women were laid off first, even when they were the main support for the family, followed by older men whose children were grown up. This affirmative family plan enabled the corporation to take advantage of the male workers in their prime years of production and to lay off older workers who had higher incomes and were in line for pensions. The pension plan, which GE prided itself on introducing to the electric industry, did not even meet basic subsistence needs of retired workers.   Sam knew people pensioned off in the 1920s who were getting 15 dollars a month.

With the victory of trade unions, individualistic authoritarianism in management was replaced by bureaucratic rules. Critics of the union movement often attack this development, but from the workers' perspective, it helped them rescue their self-respect since they did not have to curry the favor of the foremen or superintendents to hold a job or gain mobility. This was particularly important for women, who previously faced pressure to grant sexual favors in return for mobility or higher pay in the shop. One woman who started working in the GE in 1924 and who never favored unionism admitted that, "The union is good because the GE can't get away with a lot of the things that it did before, like preferences, you know.... With no union, when a time of layoff came, even if one has as much ability or more, if you were liked by your boss they would keep you, which they can't do today; with the union it's all based on service." Men also reported feeling released from personal favoritism by the new union regulations. A chief shop steward, now retired, reported that, when he returned to work at the GE in 1940 after a short break during which the union was established, he found a definite change in attitude. The boss was no longer king, and the workers had new rights in a setting where the dignity of the worker was recognized.

Despite decades of resistance to independent unions, when they became an established fact, the General Electric Company adopted the collective bargaining machinery, established by the unions, as its own. General Electric plants across the nation often promoted shop stewards to quasi-managerial labor relations positions. We interviewed one of these men whom I shall call Herb. He had risen from a stock boy's job to head of plant labor relations and finally became a regional representative for General Electric before his retirement. His mobility began shortly after he re-entered the company after World War II in the machinist training program. After two years he was made a foreman and then advanced to supervisor of standards and methods. In 1956 he became management's negotiator in union relations and from 1962 to 1968 he served as administrator of union relations. He was clearly a master of the technique of coopting initiatives from labor or government into managerial prerogatives. In discussing affirmative action he said:

> The greatest increase [in intra-firm mobility] has been in the last seven years as a result of a promotional program we negotiated with the unions. The main feature was that jobs were posted whereas formerly movement came through chance. In the promotional system introduced in 1974, opportunities were made available to everyone.

When I asked whether this promotional system was a result of equal opportunity legislation, he replied that it was, but that, while it was immediately a response to gender discrimination charges brought before the NLRB against five companies, including Sears, this "hastened a program that we had been working on earlier. It was well-recognized as a need that we had to have a formal promotional system."

Herb's skill as a mediator came from his own origins in a working-class family combined with the mobility offered within the corporation. His identification with the firm resulted from his immediate experience in it. He told us:

> GE is the company with the best opportunities and the best pay you can get.... Pittsfield has had better relations between management and workers than elsewhere. We don't have that picking up of sides. There is some militancy there when it should be, but on the whole, people realize that what's good for business is good for the people in it. They listen, try to understand before making decisions. That's why the relations department developed. We feel that it is to the union's advantage to understand that business needs mutual agreements beneficial to all concerned.

The man and his house, an immaculately kept Cape Cod cottage set in landscaped grounds in a prestigious residential neighborhood, embodied the industrial accord that enveloped all the participants in the industrial setting in a sense of personal progress. According to one of the union's former business agents, "That guy gave us a real insight into management." He, like the other business agents who followed him, all agree that the union and the corporation should work together to get contracts, since workers need jobs and the company needs workers. This was, and continues to be, the basic premise of management's social contract.

With the support of people like Herb, whenever the union introduced an issue that proved popular, the company picked it up. The alcohol rehabilitation treatment promoted by a former business agent of the International United Electrical Workers (IUE) offers a good example. The business agent found a place in Vermont offering a 6-week program. The GE resisted, preferring a cheaper 2-week program in Pittsfield. Finally the company agreed to the longer program but found their own in New Hampshire. The business agent accepted this decision philosophically, commenting that, "GE likes to say it's going to be *here* not *there*, 'cause they are paid to be managers and they have to prove themselves."

A recent example of management's talent for taking over popular issues initiated by the union came in the fall of 1983 when the business agent campaigned on a program to help reduce medical costs, particularly dentistry. The popularity of the issue led to the corporation co-sponsoring a Health Fair along with the union and other business and community groups. The medical director from corporate headquarters gave the main address, focusing on "the most frequent diseases" of the day: cardiovascular and respiratory problems. He claimed that the high incidence of these diseases was "more a matter of individual lifestyle." There was no mention of PCBs (polychlorinated biphenyls)[3] used in General Electrical manufacturing until banned in the 1970s and suspected to be causing the high incidence of cancer among older workers. The latest union drive, a campaign to assist in finding missing children, was gladly adopted by General Electrical management at a time when the layoffs were increasing dramatically and there was fear that the corporation might be planning to phase out all power transformer production.

Control over the Labor Market

During my first interview in General Electric, the community relations director of the company told me,

You've probably heard that the General Electric Company has kept other employers out of the area. Well, that is no longer true. We don't want to be the big fella on the block, and we have done everything we could to encourage other businesses to come in.

At the time of the interview, I had not in fact heard that charge, but in the following months, workers recounted incidents that corroborated such charges. A past president of the union local who had served on the Berkshire County Development Committee recounted his frustration in trying to get the committee to bring in new industry. He told me,

> I made those people aware of the fact that we needed a new industry in Pittsfield and that we should put up a building someplace that would house anywhere from 500 to 750 people.... But it went on deaf ears. But I always had a feeling that there was [sic] obstacles in Pittsfield, General Electric number one, it was the main employer, so number two was whoever was on the City Council and the mayors.

He recalled that in 1950 or 1951 when he was attending a district council meeting, several agents for a helicopter manufacturing company told him and the other union representatives that they had tried to buy a site in Pittsfield for testing their planes and producing some parts but that they had always been rebuffed by city officials. The business agent of the union local sent a release to the local newspaper concerning this, but there was just a small piece printed in the back pages. That was when the plant was employing 14,200 people. Since that time, employment has declined steadily. He said that a member of the development committee who owned a motel told him several years after he resigned in disgust, "We realized what was going on and that you were telling us the truth, but you must remember what one of our problems is: GE, number one. A lot of us do business with General Electric, and if we had pursued your thoughts, a lot of us would have been knocked off the list."

The union has collaborated with General Electric to gain contracts to keep up production. This was particularly true during the years when Power Transformer was the main production unit in town. The business agent of the union travelled with management teams to state and federal representatives on missions to gain contracts for the local plant. This collaboration reinforced corporate hegemony at the same time that it compromised labor's political position. On one occasion, the local union's delegates travelled to Washington to press their representatives to vote against some anti-labor legislation. They were not able to gain a meeting with their congressman before the session in which the legislation was voted on, and later they discovered that he had voted for it. When they objected, he told them that he had been advised that if he voted against it, the company would take out production on one of its contracts and put it in another plant. The union officials agreed that the congressman had done the right thing.

Containment of Political Initiatives of Workers

The fear which the united industrial union movement inspired in capitalists in the 1940s provoked two major corporate maneouvers in that period which persist into the 1980s. The first was to brand all politically active trade union leaders as Communists and thus to isolate them from the main body of organized labor. The second was to expand production in the South during the 1950s and 1970s and then, in the 1970s, to move overseas into countries with low wage policies where trade unions were banned.

The anti-communist campaign translated the patriotism of these workers, the sons and daughters of immigrants, into divisive fights within the union. A retired welder who was vice president of the UE Local told me about the split:

> The worst thing they ever did here was when they split up the union into the UE and the IUE in 1950. They played right in to the company's hands. They were fighting amongst each other--Communist, Communist--that was all you heard.

The difference between the two unions was, according to a former chief shop steward of the UE, that "the UE used to educate the members." He claimed that when the IUE (International Union of Electrical Workers) came in, the quality of the leaders went down. Whereas the UE used to have an organizer who came to every meeting to advise workers about national policies, the IUE eschewed national political issues. He concluded,

> I've always considered the I in IUE to mean imitation. And it's just a poor imitation. They kept the same constitution with one clause added which made it undemocratic. The one clause said if you are part of the Communist Party, or in any way support the policy of the Communist Party, you cannot hold office. The UE says that regardless of race, creed, political belief--any political belief--is welcome. And they're so far ahead with that.

A UE shop steward who was cut out of leadership in the IUE suggested some of the reasons behind the change at the time the IUE was being formed in 1950:

> Phillip Murray used to say that this red-baiting was the most evil thing possible and was being promoted by the reactionaries and so on. But finally he was sucked into this anti-communist thing. Pressure was put on him, especially on the point of respectability, that he was going to be an outcast in society. Here the guy was, making lots of money and playing golf with the big shots and he didn't want to be an outcast. So all of a sudden, he started red-baiting together with a good deal of the national union officers of the CIO.

He went on to talk about the atmosphere on the shop floor at the time. "Word would get around the shop that so-and-so was a Communist, that the UE leaders were Communist, and that the union organizer was almost certainly a Communist, and look what's happening to our boys in Korea, and that sort of thing."

Part of the technique was to identify anti-communism with a rejection of political ideologies of any kind. A Phillip Murray award for Americanism still hangs on the wall of the union hall, under the portrait of President Kennedy and next to the U.S. flag. The IUE was certified by the government, and in the local union, the UE was beaten four to one. The shop steward concluded that, "The big thing about the UE, and why guys like Truman and the architects of the cold war wanted to get rid of the left wing union, was because they would explain union principles, would explain how various political questions and actions were affecting them, would explain the international situation, would explain how the corporations were consolidating, working against the little people."

By the 1960s the divided unions came back together in coordinated bargaining sessions. GE's Lemuel Boulware (1969) developed a new strategy in collective bargaining to meet the reunified leadership. This was to research the work place, find out what the minimal demands of the rank and file were, and present a "firm, fair, and final" offer in the negotiations for a new contract. This effectively ruled out collective bargaining, making the union appear unnecessary. This tactic was not effectively challenged until the 1969 strike, but by then General Electric had developed a stronger tactic. The move of small and medium power transformers to the South that had begun in the 1950s was accelerated and in the 1970s it was combined with the move overseas. Within a decade the productive work force was cut from 10,000 to 7,000 and beginning about 1982 rumors were circulating that the division would be completely shut down. The company denied this, calling for improved productivity to keep the plant going at the same time that they were making massive layoffs.

The IUE Local was kept busy organizing bumping rights and claims after the decision was made to reduce Power Transformer. "We are beggers when we go in to negotiations," the business agent told me when I interviewed him in December, 1985, just after the corporation announced expected declines of 600 more jobs in Power Transformer. With the restriction of trade union action to the work place and the acceptance of market conditions as the legitimate basis for decisions, the unions have not broadened their action in the present decline of blue collar production.

AMERICANISM AND GENERAL ELECTRICALISM

The success of the cold war and the isolation of political unionism is embedded in a broader context, in which the benefits accruing from the presence of the corporation are accepted as the "American way of life". The top management of the local General Electric plant serves on the boards of community organizations along with union leaders. Herb gave us some insight to this:

> We leave what happens over there [at the plant] out when we go to board meetings. I have seen representatives of management and unions meet on hospital boards of the United Way and the Good Neighbor Club on which I served. The best part of it is that both parties [labor and management] work together.

His sense of the harmonious working together was also expressed by a number of the directors of organizations including the Chamber of Commerce. The retiring director of the United Way spoke enthusiastically about the contributions made by General Electric, Berkshire Life Insurance, the banks, Sheaffer Eaton and other companies which each year gave a large donation. This enabled them to "market our services more effectively," the director told us. Representatives of corporations and unions vie with each other to get on the board of community organizations. While we were interviewing him, he answered a call from the president of the Berkshire Council of the AFL-CIO. They were, he told us later, deciding when they would play golf. "The links I have tried to establish with unions are important in building a framework for meeting the real needs of working people," he told us. United Way is expanding its services beyond the traditional outlets of hospitals, the YMCA, the Boys Club, and the Girls Club to include programs in alcoholism, child abuse, and the kinds of social problems dealt with by the Women's Center.

A mix of public and private enterprise is typical of new community agencies such as Berkshire Home Care which is helped by United Way, recruits volunteers, and gets matching funds from Massachusetts state agencies. Starting with a budget of $48,000 in 1974, they now work with $2.5 million, providing home care which allows the elderly to remain in their own homes. The director of this program, like the director of United Way, used the language of business to talk about programs ranging from visiting nurses to clinics to hot meal programs. He said, "I waited until we had a product to get a sustaining grant...and once you get them in you educate them on their rights."

Sports events sponsored by a variety of organizations provide the matrix for cultural integration of class-, sex-, and age-segmented social groups in Pittsfield. This was not always so. A half century ago, baseball was the mark of blue collar male worker identity, and teams were ethnically divided. In those days, men played hard ball, girls played softball, and management played golf. It is not coincidental that the former shop steward I quoted above saw Philip Murray's decline as starting on the golf links, nor that the director of United Way connected his success in integrating trade unions to his golf date.

In the 1920s, GE workers had organized their own baseball team. GE began to sponsor the team, even giving preferential hiring to good ball players. Sam told me he quit when GE began to underwrite the team's expenses, and when I asked him why, he said that it was because they did not give compensation for injuries that occurred when playing. Ball playing came to be seen in terms of the job. Other industries had their own teams. The woolen mills down in the Polish section of Pittsfield had one of the best teams. I was told that the reason for their superiority was that they were second-generation Americans and "they are always very aggressive, you know." There was an Italian team called the Wine Athletic Club which reputedly was less interested in winning since its social events were so highly esteemed.

As ethnic subdivisions lost their significance after World War II, teams were organized on other bases. Today sports events are organized by the Boys Club, YMCA, Catholic Youth Club and the Girls Club in addition to high school teams. The programs do not compete for membership, but, rather, provide a segmented division of the population that makes competition community-wide. The YMCA director compared his program to that of the Boys Club: "They shoot with a shotgun at their clientele; a shotgun makes a broad range. The YMCA is more of a rifle approach. We're after a concern, a task, and we aim for that group and we deal with it." In their sports training, they try to instill values of sportsmanship, fair play and competitive toughness. "We try to balance the most complete fitness center with the fact that you have to make a complete person. And that's our goal, to put the spirit, mind and body in one person and take him to the top."

The General Electric Athletic Association (GEAA) continues to provide facilities for sports in the rolling hills beyond the plant. Both the company and the union sponsor field days using these facilities for the Quarter Century Club and Kiddies Day. These events underwrite the importance of familism and its connections with sportsmanship. The Quarter Century Club holds annual events segregated by sex. Men like to rough it with a barbeque and field day at the GEAA and women get dressed up and go for a banquet at the Italian American Lodge at Pontoosuc Lake. Both events are paid for by the General Electric Company.

Participation in sports, whether as a spectator or player, provides the idiom for being integrated into the culture. People of all social classes and ages wear sneakers and warm-up suits or running shorts in many social settings that do not involve active sports. At the same time that it signifies identification with a sporting outlook, it negates association with occupational or ideological movements that are not part of the mainstream. In a peace demonstration in June of 1982 a group of Buddhist cult activists from out of town stood in front of the GE Ordnance plant with signs announcing their support of peace. A teenager observing the event commented that she supported their cause but did not want to be identified with them because of the way they dressed. The women wore long hair and long full skirts like the hippies of the 1960s she said. In contrast to this event, a successful mobilization of people against intervention in Central America was characterized by the *Berkshire Sampler* as organized by activists who played tennis, went jogging, and were concerned with problems of baby- sitting as well as military buildup. The identification through cultural symbolism supercedes ideological conformity with the young generation. They talk about lifestyles more than career preferences, and many have taken less prestigious, lower-paying jobs to stay in the area.

The complex network of service organizations and recreational institutions that underwrite these cultural expressions is a complementary part of an anarchic mode of production in which workers and their families bear the brunt of shifts in the business cycle. The failure of a working-class party to develop in the U.S. can be traced to these quasi-political, quasi-economic associations where workers and managers meet in collaborative action for community-wide concerns or for their own pleasures. The agencies such as Berkshire Home Care, the Women's Center, and even the Boys Club (that played a custodial function for boys whose mothers work) contrast with the state welfare agencies in local ideology. In order to be accepted as a client in a welfare agency, you become excluded from the hard-working, sports-loving, privatized, familiy-oriented persons believed to characterize the citizens of this city. Except for the hard core of welfare recipients, most members of the community would rather eat cat food than check out a grocery cart using food stamps. This final commitment to self-sufficiency and independence is the bottom line which ensures the hegemonic position of corporate capitalism. The question I shall now raise is how viable is the hegemony in a period of recession, unemployment, and loss of population.

DEINDUSTRIALIZATION AND HEGEMONIC CONTROL

A decline in employment in Pittsfield, combined with a loss of many younger people more involved in the productive wage force are putting stress on the hegemonic control that has evolved in the past century. When I first started working on the project in 1978 there were 8,000 workers in the GE plant, with about 3,500 in the Power Transformer Department. This was about half of the number who had worked in Power Transformers before the 1969 strike. By 1984 employment had dropped to 7,000 with 2,000 in Power Transformer. Women were harder hit than men, in part because their broken work histories meant that they had fewer years of service and less seniority. The response to these changes by the leadership of management, trade unions and city government were varied, yet complementary. I shall summarize what we learned in interviews with leaders in these sectors.

General Electric Management

Just as General Electric had institutionalized the role of labor relations at the time when organized labor had begun to press its claims, so they had institutionalized the role of community relations as company public relations became more demanding. My requests for information were turned over to this department. In the 6-year period of my study, I perceived a change in the character and approach of the three community relations managers that I interviewed. In 1978 the manager of community relations to whom I spoke was an affable, well-informed man who had come to the area in 1962 and had decided to make it his home rather than moving upward and outward. He occupied a 2-room suite overlooking the Power Transformer Department and the slogan on the overpass, "GE first in safety". His secretary offered me a cup of coffee and we spent two hours talking about the industry's prospects. He spoke quite frankly about the uncertain survival of the power transformer division given the lack of an energy program in the Carter administration and the continuing recession caused by the oil embargo. The city had already lost 7,000 people, down from the 60,000 who lived there when he first came to the plant. He rejected my use of the term "flight" to refer to the transfer of transformer production to the South, preferring to call it a "spinoff" responding to "the better business climate" in Shreveport, Louisiana and Rome, Georgia. This was not, he asserted, a result of lower wages--that tended to even up over time. Rather, it was a combination of factors including lower electric rates, fewer state regulations, and a more "hospitable" state administration. He waxed eloquent about the beauties of the Berkshires, the nature reserve near his home, and the Halloween parade in which he served as grand marshall. Started in the 1950s to avoid Halloween vandalism, the parade had become in the 1970s the symbol for the presence of General Electric in the community. Workers devoted weeks of overtime making a dragon emblazoned with electric lights that stretched for more than a block.

During the summer of 1981 when Power Transformer was being written off as an unprofitable venture, headhunters were invited into the GE plant during the July break. The director of community relations along with his boss had gone to the highest corporate bidder, Westinghouse. The next time I visited the public relations office, his successor was installed in a small side office. The new manager had been at his job only a month when I visited him and had to refer most questions to his secretary, who had 25 years of service in the company. He advised us that the firm had decided to "limit their entry" into the transformer market since the three major producers, GE, Westinghouse and McGraw Edison, split a market which had declined from an annual growth rate of 7-8% to 1.9%. The company strategy was to "scale down the business to take the fat out" so that a situation of "three big guns fighting for the market" would not result.

Unfortunately, he added, that meant reducing the number of employees. The plant then employed 7,700 people overall with 3,000 in Power Transformer. He expected that 90-100 workers would leave in the next 6-month period, and others would be bumped to other departments. While salaried people would be found employment, he said, there was not much "we" could do about union eligibles, adding that "if we were to try to move them and settle them in other plants, it would be exorbitant, but we have been successful in placing a few in the transformer department of McGraw Edison." Ordnance was expected to pick up some of the workers laid off, but that would take at least three years, he said, before Reagan's emphasis on defense would show up in the industry. The aging work force was a sure sign of the attrition. In 1979 the people of age 55 and over were 29% of the work force, whereas in 1981 they were 35.8%.

In the course of our conversation, it was clear that the crisis for the community posed by layoffs and loss of jobs did not threaten his position nor did it enter into the concerns of upper management. When I questioned whether there had been a great deal of anxiety stirred up by the talk of shrinking the division of Power Transformer, he replied:

> Oh sure, this is a most canny bunch of workers. At an employees' meeting we laid out the whole situation. We had three meetings with questions. No one asked about management bungling. They seemed to accept the fact that when a market goes down you can't create a market when it is not there. You can't sell overseas nowadays or you're competing with other companies with lower costs of production. We

have been losing a share of the market to outsiders who have come in. Our competitors have affiliated with Siemens and others who have gained a foothold in the United States.

Basically he implied GE no longer benefitted from the monopoly of the labor market that it had once held. This reasoning left out of the equation one of the factors that I had learned from union leaders. Power Transformer was, in fact, making some profit, but not nearly as much as other divisions, particularly ordnance and other high-tech products favored by the chairman of the board of directors. Asked what plans GE had to ease the transition, he replied:

> I don't think the business is going out--just cutting down to a break-even point.... You will hear Mayor Smith say that GE owes the city. We think the city owes GE. We had a payroll of $190 million.... It was felt that it was more humane to place as many people as it could and to try to trim the business to make it. Everyone describes the love-hate relationship with the community. Sometimes GE is described as a villain, but with the Good Neighbor Fund, GE gave $470,000; 47% of the million dollar drive.

A year later, after he was sent to an overseas plant, I returned to visit his replacement. Power Transformer was now down to 2,200 employees. The laid-off workers we had interviewed were mostly young men and a few women with short service. The new public relations manager raised the issue we had heard discussed at the union about threats of withdrawal if productivity did not increase. He was very emphatic in denying this.

> To my way of thinking, that would be unfair labor practices to say that if we can't get what we want, we will not operate the plant. It is not, however, illegal to state business realities. It is a fact that transformers are not doing well and that we have been losing money on them. But we are not Chrysler.... GE would not be in that position.

The issue of plant closing had been negotiated in the 1982 contract, and the union had won a clause requiring at least six months advance notice of any such plans. The new public relations director showed his mastery of coopting his adversaries' position by asserting that the stipulation was "a positive gain made in open communication about the corporation's plans." In fact, the corporation had fought that clause, according to the business agent of the local union. He elaborated his point:

> GE is not unwilling to communicate. Corporations are not human entities, but they are entities none-the-less and do have moral responsibilities. GE has a high moral caliber; we would not simply close down over the weekend. [This was an allusion to a comment I had made to a small electronic shop in the neighboring town that had left a sign on their door for the employees coming to work on Monday morning reading, "Gone to Jamaica".] GE can't go to Jamaica and hide.

He summed up his view of community relations as follows:

> Well, I'm looking at this through a 1-year window, but I see the relations with the community as superb, especially with the political leadership and the human social sector leadership.... I have heard stories of the 50s when GE lobbied against the other industries coming in to the community. I can tell you that now we spend money trying to get other industry in. We can no longer afford to be Daddy Warbucks. There is a need for other industry--tourism will not do it. The technology center will bring with it small plastic molders to the Berkshires.... The Berkshires stand a chance of being the Silicon Valley of plastics.

His 1-year window was already a window on the past, since over a dozen plastics firms headed by GE-trained technicians had sprung up when the local plant stopped producing plastics fixtures and casings for their products two decades before. Mostly non-union, these firms pay half the wage that GE offers. Subcontracting work from GE as well as other firms, they may well represent the future industrialization in the U.S.: high-tech research and development centers surrounded by small unorganized production shops.

My final interview took place a month after the announcement that General Electric would close Power Transformer. The community relations department was extremely busy with all the calls related to the proposed "phasing out" of Power Transformer. The manager spoke frankly about the market issues that convinced the corporation to shut down the department. The limited demand for power transformers, he told me, did not justify two major companies competing for the same market, and they could not go into partnership in the United States because of anti-trust laws.

For that reason GE intended to open a combined plant in Canada with Westinghouse. He felt that it was unfortunate that both the announcements to close the Pittsfield plant and to open the Canadian plant came simultaneously since it gave the impression of capital flight. In fact, he said, the company was very concerned about the impact on the local economy and were doing all they could to ease the transition. Just that week he had spent hours working out plans for the employment center where there would be counseling for laid off workers. The company had made space and office machinery available. The company would like to see a high quality plastic production company come to town so that the Plastics Research and Development Center in Pittsfield could test out some of their new materials, but they had no plans to go into production themselves. Ordnance would pick up whatever laid off workers they could accomodate, but they did not anticipate any increases there.

Trade Union Leadership

Union leaders were not nearly as sanguine as management about future prospects for employment. The productivity drive launched by the company in 1982, in the interest of saving the Power Transformer Division, resulted in even greater attrition of the work force. The district council leadership of the AFL-CIO recognized the problem in its 1982 Labor Day breakfast. The keynote speaker summed it up as follows:

> Part of our problem has been, and will continue to be, the fact that this prosperous nation, the people that are the movers and shakers of our society, are trying to ship our work overseas. They are taking all our technology and giving it away to other nations. If you start saying that we've got to do something about the imports, you're called a protectionist. Well, if that's what they're calling them, start calling me one now. Because we've got to start moving.

He went on to ask for support of a bill in Congress calling for an increase in the percentage of parts that are built by Americans in any products sold in the U.S.

In summing up past victories of the labor movement, he mentioned Medicare, public education, OSHA (Occupational Safety and Health Administration), and Social Security. Significantly he did not mention AFDC (Aid to Families with Dependent

Children), foodstamps or Medicaid, programs that are not based on the fiction of reciprocity toward employed workers but instead recognize and address the structural inequalities of the system. He concluded his speech calling for the same social contract with business:

> As we all know, the ultimate goals of labor, the American Labor Movement, is and always has been, to help bring about the healthiest, best educated, productive society that is possible for humans to achieve. I don't see anything wrong with those goals, and I say for shame on any of our elected officials who do not rally behind us.

The greatest attrition in employment at the local plant has been in the ranks of union eligible blue collar workers, now only one-third as numerous as they were 15 years ago. The contract negotiated in July, 1985, limited security coverage to dues-paying members and failed to address the growing numbers of unemployed youths. The union won a clause related to plant closing that would give workers advance warning of the move and extend unemployment benefits and medical coverage for a year after the shut-down.

The announcement of the closing down of Power Transformer Division, already down to 1,700 workers in November, 1986, coincided with a meeting of the District Council of the IUE. The officers of the local carried the news to the council and a press conference was called. As the business agent reflected on the depletion of production in the local plant, he summed up the loss of industry throughout the country:

> This is fine, all the things we're negotiating, all the benefits in case of a shutdown. But we're just shoveling crap into the tide if we keep allowing these companies to go overseas. We ought to get together with all our legislators and tell 'em what we think, get it in one round. Textiles is off-shore; shipbuilding is off-shore; shoemaking is off-shore; the nylon gear to put in the Bradley Fighting Vehicle is being made in Korea. What have we got left in this country? Now power delivery is going abroad. So no matter what we do, if they keep off-shoring 'em, we're not going to have any more jobs. If we had to go to war, we would be begging people to sell us these things.

His dismay was picked up by the delegates as they recounted production losses in other General Electric plants in the region. A Lynn, Mass., representative exclaimed, "They're climbing into bed with the competition and leaving us bare-assed out here in the cold!" Even in their resentment, the workers expressed their commitment to capitalist logic of a competitive market, and their objections to the company were its failure to hold up its part of the bargain in a free enterprise system.

In the weeks that followed, state representatives, union officials and the General Electric Company began to put together the employment center, amassing state funds to assist the community in the difficult transition ahead. The fact that the shutdown of Power Transformer could not be considered a plant closing because of the continuing presence of Plastics and Ordnance meant that the hard-won contract clause was invalid. The union appealed to Article 22 of the contract, losing their jobs to foreign competition, to make a claim on the company for extended benefits. They succeeded in negotiating an extra 26 weeks of unemployment benefits as well as assistance in the employment center where the laid off workers would get help making out resumes and counselling for training. When I interviewed the business agent in January, 1987, he granted that the company had been cooperative in these projects, but asserted:

> They're trying to paint their picture as a good image, but that had already been mandated by the contract.... We're the ones that filed for the Title 3 money, and now that that money has been approved, they're trying to take control of it. The union is saying, "No, you're not going to have control of it. We'll have an equal part in it or we'll be the prime contractor." But GE sees this thing now as really polishing their image. They're the bad guys in this region. They've laid off all the guys and now they want to be the good guys. And they're not really doing a heck of a lot.

In the following weeks, the union busied itself working out the bumping rights and retirement benefits of those who chose the option of early retirement. Having gained that option, they were able to hold on to some younger workers as hundreds began to be withdrawn from the plant. They felt that this was a historic move in combining union principles of seniority with alternative retirement made attractive by the company's concessions to older workers.

Along with this, the union appealed to corporate head-quarters to try to regain some of the work farmed out to General Electric plants in Shreveport, Louisiana, and Rome, Georgia, but they realized it was a tactic that pitted them against union brothers. They were joined by U.S. representatives in trying to confirm defense contracts and gain production of the Bradley tank. For the first time I heard criticism of the corporation's overseas investment, and though they did not mount a campaign directly, it is having an echo with legislators who are beginning to think of the need for a national industrial policy.

City Officials

The proliferation of development commissions and private consulting firms in and around Pittsfield is a sure sign of the economic deterioration that the county is experiencing. Development agents within the county and city administration, as well as private organizations such as the Chamber of Commerce, are working with union and company representatives trying to bring in new industries. They have developed several "industrial parks" with state and local funds, and their target is the high-tech industry pioneered by small-scale entrepreneurs. The stated goals were those of internal growth, disbursement of state bonds for existing manufacturing establishments and promotion of a diversified industrial base. Left unstated is the expectation that these industries will be small-scale unorganized shops. The owner of a small greeting card company that took up residence in a renovated public school complained to the City Council when his workers threatened to unionize, that he could not stay in business if this happened. As for the unions, survival rather than growth dominated the outlook. There is no movement toward worker take-overs in divisions threatened with shutdowns. Only one voice was raised in the City Council calling for employee operation of the GE Gynal plastics department when that was closed down in December, 1982, and no one picked up the suggestion when 300 workers were laid off.

Because of Pittsfield's relatively high wage levels, the presence of what is considered a strong union and an anti-business climate, the only growth at GE will be in the Ordnance department based on government defense contracts. The mayor denied that reputation in his speech to the assembled trade union leaders on Labor Day:

One thing we have in Pittsfield is a stigma that we are anti-business. We have a great deal of difficulty bringing in new industry and expansion of business in Pittsfield.

When General Electric decided to build its new plastics technology research and development center in the city, he became more optimistic, anticipating that:

> People will be coming from all over the United States, working with General Electric. They'll be spending their dollars here, they'll be staying here, they'll get news of our city out when they find out what a great place this is, and it may induce some other manufacturing concerns to decide to come up here too.

The mayor called for approval of an ordinance giving General Electric the right to build the plastics center, and there were few restrictions placed on their use of the site. He also succeeded in gaining a tax abatement for the corporation, reducing their bill from $1.69 million to $874 thousand. This caused home owners to bear 62.5% of the total bill as compared to 60% formerly (*The Berkshire Eagle* March 14, 1983). These actions follow national trends as corporations pay less and less of the tax bill while individuals pick up the balance. The tax reductions came in a year when GE's international profits were at an all-time high of $438 million after taxes, up 10% in 1982 over the previous year (*Fortune* January 19, 1983). That same year, the chairman of the board of General Electric received $1,018,330, an 18% salary increase over the past year.

In the months that followed the announcement of the closing of Power Transformer, local development agencies, the Chamber of Commerce, and state and federal representatives cooperated in the efforts to implement the employment services center for laid off workers. Much of their activity was still directed toward winning a contract for a shopping mall for which they were competing with a neighboring town. But there was a new initiative, possibly sparked by their cooperation with the union, in gaining new industries. The Chamber of Commerce director announced in January, 1987, that a high quality plastics parts producer that manufactured parts for computers would take one of the sites in the industrial park.

CONCLUSIONS

Corporate hegemony is still a reference point for planning and development for the future. Workers are not as yet completely disillusioned with corporate control nor do they entertain any illusions that they can take over control of decision-making. Nonetheless there is a growing awareness that, as Seymour Melman, professor of industrial engineering at Columbia University put it, "In the last 25 years, management's social contract with workers and the community has been broken as managers have turned from making goods to making money by means other than production." (*New York Times* December, 1983). The new model for corporations in the old industrial centers of the U.S. is a high-tech research and development division with production done in distant plants in the US and overseas or subcontracted to independent firms without union contracts in the area. This may well represent the future industrial presence in the U.S.: high-tech research and development centers surrounded by small, unorganized production shops and tied in with off-shore sites throughout the world.

The awareness of this transformation is only slowly penetrating the society. Community leaders are still trying to appeal to the moral consciousness of a corporation in terms of a broken social contract. The hegemony constructed out of the workers' own efforts to find themselves a place in industrial society requires, minimally, on the part of corporations a commitment to a place and to people who will work in production. With more lucrative investments overseas, and with the prospect of fully automated plants in the U.S., the corporation does not think they need consider any claims made on them. A 1982 Supreme Court ruling, permitting corporations to ignore union contracts when they close down any one of their plants, will accelerate their withdrawal from old industrial centers.

Workers cling to these past commitments not out of false consciousness, but out of a sense of their own construction of that social contract. The gap between the rich and poor is growing: the emergency meal and shelter centers in Pittsfield have increased their services in 1985 from 3-600% over their 1983 activities. For the working people of the county, two wage earners are needed to maintain accustomed living standards. It is the single heads of families, usually women in the secondary labor force, who are the most militant labor activists since they are unable to raise a family on their wages.

The unions lost the initiative demonstrated in the early post-war strikes as they became committed to a social contract in which the workers in large corporations enjoyed high wages and benefits but did not extend their organizations to peripheral industrial sites within the United States and overseas. In the present decline of industrial production in the country, there is little opposition to decisions made by corporate managers whose unique concerns are with maximizing profits. With little opposition from the labor movement, management is destroying the basis for their own hegemonic control, a control fashioned from the struggles of workers.

NOTES

1   Research was supported by the National Science Foundation and the National Endowment for the Humanities. I am grateful to these funding sources and to the many friends and supporters of this project in Pittsfield. I have benefitted greatly from the assistance of Max Kirsch in the interviews of some of the informants. I am also thankful to him and to Judith-Maria Buechler, Hans Buechler, Hanna Lessinger and Herbert Menzel for suggestions that improved the clarity and strengthened the argument.

2   Among those responsible for the cultural emphasis in Marxist theory are Raymond Williams, Jurgen Habermas, Herbert Marcuse and others of the Frankfort School. Social historians such as Herbert Gutman, David Montgomery and E.P. Thompson stress the cultural factors conditioning consciousness and behavior of economic classes. A review of these positions is contained in Weiner (1981).

3   PCBs, or polychlorinated biphenyls, were used as an insulating material in power transformers until 1977 when the growing awareness of their potentially harmful effects caused them to be banned by the Environmental Protection Agency. Japanese electrical machinery manufacturers had discontinued the use of PCBs several years earlier after people who had eaten rice contaminated with an accidental spill of oil containing PCBs suffered various forms of illness (Nash and Kirsch 1986).

BIBLIOGRAPHY

Gramsci, Antonio
  1973   Selections from the Prison Notebooks of Antonio Gramsci. Quintin Hoare and Geoffrey Nowel Smith, editors and translators. New York: International Publishers.
Gutman, Herbert
  1976   Work, Culture and Society in Industrializing America. New York: Knopf.
Matles, J.J. and J. Higgins
  1974   Them and Us: Struggles of a Rank and File Union. Englewood Cliffs, N.J.: Prentice Hall.
Montgomery, David
  1979   Workers' Control in America. Cambridge: Cambridge University Press.
Nash, June
  1984   Segmentation of the Work Process in the International Division of Labor. *In* The Americas in the New International Division of Labor. Steven E. Sanderson, ed. New York: Holmes and Meier.
Nash, June and Max Kirsch
  1986   Polychlorinated Biphenyls in the Electrical Machinery Industry; An Ethnological Study of Community Action and Corporate Responsibility. Social Science and Medicine, An International Journal. Special Issue: Toward a Critical Medical Anthropology. P.J.M. McEwan ed. Pp.131-138.
Schatz, Ronald
  1975   The End of Corporate Liberalism, Class Struggle in the Electrical Manufacturing Industry, 1933-1950. Radical America 9(4-5):187-205.
Weiner, Richard
  1981   Cultural Marxism and Political Sociology. Beverly Hills, CA: Sage Publications.

CONTRIBUTORS

FLORENCE BABB is assistant professor of anthropology and former chair of women's studies at the University of Iowa. She is currently completing a book on marketwomen and underdevelopment, based on research in Peru over the past 10 years. Her articles have appeared in *The Review of Radical Political Economics, Ethnology, Cultural Survival*, and in anthologies. Involved in feminist issues and in Latin American solidarity work, her latest feminist project is raising her 2-year-old son Daniel.

HANS A. BAER is associate professor of anthropology at the University of Arkansas, Little Rock. He has worked on religious movements, medical anthropology and the political eocnomy of health. He has written *The Black Spiritual Movement: A Religious Response to Racism* (1984) and *Recreating Utopia in the Desert: A Sectarian Challenge to Modern Mormonism* (1987). He edited *Case Studies in Medical Anthropology* (1987) and co-edited *Towards a Critical Medical Anthropology* (1986) with Merrill Singer and John Johnsen.

DAVID HAKKEN is associate professor of anthropology at the State University of New York College of Technology in Utica. His research has been in worker education, work culture and the impact of new information technology. He has just finished a major research project on the cultural correlates of computerization in Sheffield, England, and Utica, NY. He has worked in the peace movement and was, from 1979 to 1985, chair of the Council for Marxist Anthropology.

FAYE V. HARRISON, assistant professor of anthropology at the University of Louisville, Kentucky, has worked on the sociopolitical consequences of West Indian migration, with field work in England and Jamaica. Her interests are social outlawry, the sexual division of labor and grassroots activism. She is on the executive council of the Association of Black Anthropologists and is active in community-based education around issues of Southern Africa and the Caribbean basin.

PHILIP L. KOHL, associate professor of anthropology at Wellesley College, is an archeologist who studies cultural evolution and the beginnings of complex society. His most recent major work is *Central Asia: Paleolithic Beginnings to the Iron Age* (1984) and the translation of V.G. Lukonin and M. A. Dandamaev's *The Culture and Social Institutions of Ancient Iran*, in press. Currently he is project direct for the translation of the 3-volume Soviet study, *History of the Ancient World*.

DONNA J. KEREN did field work in Mexico on the creation and control of a new industrial labor force. She has worked on both sides of the desk, as secretary and professional, in several business environments in New York including video production. Her research is on work and women in historical perspective. She is currently working on the local level impact of external debt and economic crises in Mexico. She teaches anthropology in Spanish to recent immigrants at Lehman College/CUNY.

HANNA LESSINGER works in the editorial department of *The Guardian*, a Marxist weekly paper in New York. Previously she was visiting assistant professor in anthropology and women's studies at Barnard College. She has done fieldwork among petty traders in India and has written both about the special problems of women traders and about the political mobilization of marketers. Her most recent research has focused on the political economy of Indian migration to New York City.

JUNE NASH is professor of anthropology at the City College of the City University of New York. She is interested in the process of industrialization and its impact on family and community. She has done her fieldwork among the Maya of Guatemala and Mexico and among Bolivian tin miners. Her most recent research has been a 5-year project at an electrical machinery company in the Massachusetts industrial town of Pittsfield. In 1983 she led discussion at a course for shop stewards organized by the Oil, Chemical and Atomic Workers Union.

EUGENE E. RUYLE earned his Ph.D. from Columbia University and is currently professor of anthropology at California State University, Long Beach. He has done field work on outcaste-ism in Japanese culture. His current interests lie in the development of a Marxist sociobiology and in liberation theology. He is active in the faculty union at CSULB and is a member of the central committee of California's Peace and Freedom Party.

NINA GLICK SCHILLER, an anthropologist and an activist, has worked among and written about welfare mothers, hospital workers, office workers, convicted arsonists, the homeless mentally ill, and Haitian immigrants. She is currently a research associate at the Center for Social Sciences at Columbia University.

BARBARA SCHRODER is a former New York City school teacher who got her degree in anthropology from Rutgers University, where she studied under Helen Safa. She has worked on women's issues with the New York Women's Anthropology Conference. With the Educators' Committee on Central America she has prepared progressive high school curricula on the region. She now works as a research analyst in the office of Educational Policy Studies at Rutgers.

THE COUNCIL FOR MARXIST ANTHROPOLOGY (CMA) was organized in 1978 at the American Anthropological Association (AAA) meetings. CMA members felt that their task was both to promote a broadly-defined Marxist scholarship within the discipline and to maintain a progressive political presence in U.S. anthropology, as well as to establish contact with anthropologists in other parts of the world who are interested in Marxist perspectives. Since its inception CMA has organized scholarly sessions with Marxist content at professional meetings. Most recently the CMA helped to form a network of progressive groups within the AAA to oppose restrictive changes being proposed for the association's "Principles of Professional Responsibility." These principles make it clear that anthropologists have a broad responsibility to take an active role in social issues, beyond narrowly-defined scholarly concerns.

INDEX